THE STORY OF FIGARO

THE STORY OF MY REAL BLACK STALLION

Laura Luszczek

iUniverse

THE STORY OF FIGARO
THE STORY OF MY REAL BLACK STALLION

iUniverse books may be ordered through booksellers or by contacting:

iUniverse
1663 Liberty Drive
Bloomington, IN 47403
www.iuniverse.com
1-800-Authors (1-800-288-4677)

ISBN: 978-1-4917-7578-3 (sc)
ISBN: 978-1-4917-7580-6 (hc)
ISBN: 978-1-4917-7579-0 (e)

Print information available on the last page.

iUniverse rev. date: 09/17/2015

Contents

Dedicated to my family and true friends,
My mother Daina,
My grandmother, Liisa,
Omer, my two BFF's
And Mr. Figaro

I would like to add a special thank you and acknowledgement to Lawrence Scanlan for his patience, guidance and mentorship. I learned a lot from this seasoned author of many books, including *Little Horse of Iron, Wild About Horses, The Man Who Listens to Horses, and The Horse God Built.* Lawrence's love of horses, especially Canadian horses, helped me as I told my story of Figaro, a special and unique horse.

Introduction

Just a horse, some would say. Or, this is just another horse tale. Some of us, the lucky ones anyway, have had that one horse or animal in our lives that holds us and makes such an impact on our lives. So much so that the words *just an animal* enrages us. We know what it is like, at some time, to have loved an animal and been unconditionally loved by that animal.

I can say I have been fortunate to have had that -- not only a love but also to have had the greatest teacher, confidant, character builder and, most of all, a great friend. One so great I will forever compare any friendship to this, whether the friends are four-legged or two legged. You could almost say it was dream like. Who has not grown up with the dream of the black stallion, the beauty, loyalty, brains, character, courage and bond that cannot come through training but that come naturally? I can say I was fortunate to have that horse. I can say I owned the real life black stallion. Not just because he was big and black but because he was the package. I can see why Alexander the Great felt for Bucephalus the way he did. What we all wish for is one thing but if the Black Stallion was what he was in our day, most people would not be so in awe, I guess. Most people would back away from that. Black Stallion books make us fall in love with the idea but when faced with reality, how many would stick it through? Through the tough times? Through the heartache and more? Could you honestly say you see the diamond in the rough? Or the kind eyes in the spirited body? When it was time, could you stand up for your horse when times are tough through the good and the bad? And most of all be there till his last breath?

I have been with horses for many years but I am no expert and will never claim to be. I strive to learn. I learn new things each day. Some things work for me while others don't. We all have preferences, but I am still keen to listen. In this telling of Figaro's life, you will see I have dealt with many horses in many disciplines -- from foals to breeding stallions, from $1horses to million-dollar horses, from good to rogue horses. I can say, without exaggeration, I have handled well over 800 horses, some on farms, most of them on the racetrack. Being a swing groom, you deal with at least forty five horses per week and then some because some will ship in and out during the season. A swing groom takes over another groom's five or six horses so they can have a day off. This may not seem like anything significant but you learn to adapt to many different horses and their quirks. None have been a greater teacher than Mister Fig.

I am writing his story because I promised him. I believe that no matter what you get after you read this story -- whether you find this a heart-warming tale or educational in some way—you will find something in you or at least comfort. Most of the entire book will show the bond, the true bond, we had and not just that I loved my horse. Not only did he have an impact on me, he also managed to touch many people through the years as well, whether it was just a stranger or an accomplished horseman. Some knew Figaro and some only knew him through pictures, but he always had that something that drew people to him. He may have not had as many fans as some horses out there but the numbers he did have were genuine followers. Thanks to him I have met so many new and wonderful people from all over the world and was taken to levels I never thought I would achieve.

I hope I can show you so you will see what I did and why I went through what I did with Figaro from our up to our down days. All in all, we all wish for the dream horse. As the saying goes *be careful what you wish for and when it does come, the journey is not all paved in gold*. When you do hit that road you will no longer be walking on gold, but clouds, sometimes if only for a moment. I can say I had the privilege of having the real Black Stallion and am grateful to have lived the dream.

My favourite saying goes, "A dream is just a dream but a goal is a dream with a plan."

A friend of mine summed up Figaro by saying, "Figaro was a one of a kind. He is often imitated but never duplicated. "I doubt I will ever find another like him.

So here is the tale of my real life Black Stallion...

"Somewhere in time's own space
There must be a some sweet pastured place
Where creeks sing on and tall trees grow,
Some paradise where horses go.
For by the love that guides my pen,
I know great horses live again"
~Stanley Harrison Poem, Stanley Harrison

The Dream Becomes the Reality

I guess this story truly starts about four years before I got Figaro. I had just got into riding like every horse crazed child. In 1988, I was barely four years old when my interest began and it wasn't until I was close to age six before I really became immersed into the horse world. I had watched every horse movie imaginable; the one that always stood out was the Black Stallion. I remember always finding ways to make money so I could save up for a horse or convincing my parents to let me get a horse. My poor dog Sarah at the time was my outlet for not having a horse. I released my need to train so I trick trained Sarah our family dog. Mind you she was smart as a whip and loved to jump. She was obliging to learn the Spanish walk, crawl, beg, hug, and sit pretty and so much more.

When it came down to it, if it was horse related I probably had it. I used to collect every horse magazine out there. Two magazines I kept and still have: one contained an article about an Andalusian trainer (Frank would later become a tutor of mine) and the other had an article about the Canadian horse. I never kept these magazines for any particular reason. Sometimes fate guides you unknowingly. What I truly remember was drawing, at the age of seven, a small picture of a girl riding a black stallion on a beach. It was a simple sketch on a yellow sticky paper that I remember my mom hanging up on a filing cabinet at work. I was always practical as a kid and realistic on what I wanted. I wanted a nice all-around horse, good looking and sensible. Deep down if I could have it, I wanted the bond, and one like Alec had with the Black, the loyalty, but also the strength and beauty as well. I know in reality I could not have a stallion because most barns don't want stallions. *I thought how cool would it be to have the package, but reality is reality.*

I guess fate had things in store for me. Fate was going to grant me my wish. Just in a different way. Looking back, you should be careful what you wish for and be very detailed in what you wish. Regardless, if I could have done it all over again I don't think I would have it any other way. My sister once said it best: Déjà vu is the window into our future.

This is where my story really begins. I had a dream four years prior to getting Figaro, of a Dairy Queen with some townhouses across the street, then a faint image of a black horse. Could this be real? I have a very good memory, a somewhat photographic memory. I can so clearly remember things such as the weather on certain days. This is sometimes a gift and sometimes a curse. This dream just stood out. It was definitely one of those dreams that were vivid and memorable. Unknowingly it was tucked away in the back of my mind.

Four years into the future, after finally working and earning a real paycheque, my mom saw and felt my commitment and that riding was not just a faze. She finally gave me the green light to get a horse. What better 16th birthday gift could a girl ask for and get? It was then that I buckled down to decide what I truly wanted in a horse and what I intended to achieve. At this point, I was introduced to various disciplines. I had handled and ridden various horses so I had a pretty good idea of what I wanted. I wanted a horse that could do multiple disciplines, but mainly I wanted a dressage prospect, average height 15.2-16 hands high or a bit bigger. My horse had to be a gelding since I got along better with the boys than the fillies. For breeds, I was always attracted to Andalusians. I knew they were way out of my price range. Deep down I always wanted to do classical dressage and perform the high school movements like the *passage*, but I put that on the back burner for the moment. Then I considered the Quarter Horse or Appendix (a Quarter Horse-Thoroughbred cross) since I have ridden enough of them and loved them. I was most attracted to an older style Morgan. I used to ride one at a barn I was taking lessons at, a horse named Jubilee. A nice solidly built horse with a great attitude.

There was only one thing holding me back at the time. Some physical problems were starting to arise. At the age of 14 I was starting to develop hip issues, which I later found out was trochanter bursitis -- inflammation of the sacs around the hip. At the time it caused much pain. I developed a limp. Then other problems surfaced, such as pain in my lower back, bad circulation, and loss of feeling in my arms and legs. I even got to the point I had to walk with a cane since I had difficulties walking upright. My limp (which I still have even though it is minor now) used to cause me to stray when I walked. My friends had to walk on either side of me so that I did not veer out too far when walking. Aside from the pain, I always seem to strive though it and especially when it comes to animals. No matter how sore or sick I am, I will do anything for the sake of an animal. This contributed to my decision to look at a gaited breed (a breed of horse that always keeps one foot on the ground and known for being a smooth ride).

I had looked into Paso Fino and Icelandic horses. Pasos were a bit scarce at the time and Icelandics were very much out of my price range. It was at the Royal Winter Fair that a certain breed caught my eye, the Canadian horse. When I first laid my eyes on this horse, what came to mind was

Jubilee, the old style Morgan. The Morgan was related to the Canadian horse. This was discovered after DNA testing.

This Canadian horse just jumped out at me. I stayed a bit longer to watch him go into the ring. I listened to the announcer talk about the breed. It was at that moment, then and there, that I made my decision what breed of horse I wanted. I forgot about my pain. I knew in my gut this is what I truly wanted. It was a horse that was multi-disciplined. After the demonstration, I collected as much information as possible, even stopping to speak with the booth representative. Armed with all my new found information, I talked with my mother. We then began our search for even more knowledge on the breed. We gathered our facts. We both wanted to start searching for a Canadian horse.

We first contacted a breeder, Pat, a Canadian breeder. She was very obliging and very informative. She even sent us a video that was a promo for the breed. I think I watched that video so many times my mom was going to buy me another copy. After much deliberation and consideration, I contacted Pat to see if she had any Canadian horses for sale. I wanted a fairly young horse that was broke or at least had the basics like walk, trot covered, but not too young. She had one candidate but unfortunately he was a bit out of my price range.

My mother did some research, and that led us to another breeder – Brianne. We talked with her but she only had young stock at the time. Brianne referred us to another breeder and broker for the Canadian horse. He was a very kind man and very informative. We corresponded back and forth with each other almost daily by email. We even spoke to each other on the phone a few times. Once he had an idea what I wanted, he focused on finding me my horse. In the meanwhile, I was searching as well.

I found an ad for a 17-hand-high Canadian horse named Moose. I had to go see him. Mom made the arrangements and on the following weekend we took the drive out to meet Moose in the flesh. A nice horse but due to a stifle issue, I had to think about making the commitment. I found him a bit too big. I decided to turn him down. At almost 16 years old, I was long legged. A bigger horse would suit me best, but I wanted a horse I could mount comfortably from the ground.

Ryan was determined to find me as perfect a match as he could. He brought to my attention many prospects. To my disappointment, many were not started or green broke. Reality kicked: my trained horse idea would have to be put aside. At the time I was accomplished enough and I felt confident enough to start a green horse. I wasn't a pro but also after working at the racetrack I was confident enough to teach or handle a younger horse. Susan, then my mentor, was also involved in the search for a trained animal. That is what I wanted. Susan did find one quarter horse that met the criteria. Unfortunately, this horse and I had absolutely no connection. We just did not like each other. Our relationship was like his name, Toast. Nothing bad happened between us. We just did not click.

I was the type of kid my dad would say was like a sponge. The more knowledge I could gather in the better, no matter what it was but when it came to animals I could not learn and absorb enough. If I didn't know, I would find out. That was just how I was. I was opened minded and knew that there is never one way to do things. The only person who truly knows what you want is yourself. At least I knew my capabilities. I did not lie to myself. I was not going into this like a kid wanting just a horse to grow up with. This was my project. I would do whatever I needed to do to make it work. I would do so regardless of what anyone thought. No one was going to stand in my way. I didn't mean this in a selfish way or with any disrespect to anyone. I needed to make this decision for me, regardless of what anyone person said. I knew what I wanted.

Most first-time buyers buy with their hearts. I was always the type to step back and truly decide--with my head--what I wanted. In this case, I had to make some exceptions. This was because the Canadian was quite unknown and rare and there were not too many local breeders. This made it harder to find a trained Canadian. When there was one for sale it was a bit pricey for me. So I had to bite the bullet and make my decision for a younger Canadian, a two year old and up.

After much searching and then a change of mind, Ryan then presented me with some younger prospects. There were three colts at the time. Honda, Hillman and a horse whose name I can't recall. Out of the three, Hillman caught my eye if I had to pick one. After some conversing with Ryan, he mentioned that there were another two 4 year olds coming up for sale soon. Both should be maximum height 16 hands high. He said that one would probably be a good prospect for dressage. Until he could get their pictures and information, I continued looking.

After I did a bit more research, the two year old prospects were becoming a bit more of a no. I would have to wait a bit longer for them to mature and they were still colts. The number one thing was no colts, even though we would have them gelded. Most boarding places just don't want to, or can't handle, colts. Plus any extra fees I could avoid, the better. I had to budget for some training, trailering and other expenses. My top price was about $3000 but my mom and grandmother were going to assist if I needed a bit more.

The three colts were going for about $3500-$4000 each, so either one of them would have maxed out my budget. After many discussions between my mom and me, it was decided that if I could not find any other prospect then we could see if we could negotiate for Hillman.

I checked every day to see if there was a message from Ryan. The next day I got an email from Ryan saying that the two horses he mentioned were up on the web site. Ryan only had a picture of one of the horses but both had a detailed description. I decided to take a look. The one that Ryan thought would be a good dressage prospect was a 15-hand-high gelding. Originally Ryan said he was black but he was more of a dark bay. I took a look at him. The horse was green broke, well put together, but he did not jump at me.

In the meantime, Ryan posted a picture of the other horse. I scrolled down and there was this black proud standing boy. There was something about the photo that just said yes! Yes! Yes! The price was just right as well; he was going for $2800 and apparently he was green broke to drive. To me this meant that at least he had been in a bridle and had some handling.

We emailed Ryan and told him I want this horse, and I asked to whom should I make the cheque payable? The deposit cheque would be in the mail in the morning. In the meantime, I wanted a vet check done by an outside veterinarian. Consider him sold, I wrote. Ryan confirmed this transaction with mom.

Ryan contacted me back within the day. He said I have good news; the owner agrees. Then there was the "but." Ryan continued trying to steer my decision towards the other horse. Ryan had reservations about selling this horse to a young girl. Apparently, this horse was known to be very stud-like even though he had been gelded. A part of me sank. I was used to handling some tough colts at the track. I was not too worried. Looking back, I could see that it wasn't myself I had to worry about. It was others handling him. It is different if you have your own farm. I spent awhile on the phone with Ryan, almost pleading, "Please consider selling Figaro to me. My mom will tell you that I can handle him. He is meant for me. You showed him to me for a reason. I was destined for Figaro to be my horse." It took a lot of convincing but after reassuring Ryan that this was the right horse for me, he agreed to go ahead with the sale.

In our conversations with Ryan we discovered he knew Brianne. We were moving the horse to her farm. We told Ryan that we would be boarding him at Brianne's farm for a few months for training. In talking with Brianne and her trainer, we determined that the young horse would be broke there and would get some handling, then hopefully he would be alright by the time we moved him. Either way after much back and forth discussions and more displays of my stubbornness, Ryan said the horse was mine and the vet check report came back with no problems.

It was then we arranged for Figaro, for that was his name, to come down from his current and only farm in the next province to Ryan's farm where he would later be transported down to Brianne's farm for some training with her trainer, Cindy.

We arranged with Ryan to come to his farm to meet my horse. A road trip out to Ryan's farm was planned. My uncle offered to drive us. My favourite cousin came along, my mom and my grandmother, even her dog Pilkku came along. The road trip was fantastic. I got to see a lot of sites and we stayed in a nice hotel. This was my first trip to this part of the province. Though there was so much to see and many places to visit, my focus was totally on meeting my new horse.

Before we got to our destination, we happened to stop for a rest stop -- a Dairy Queen just off the main highway. We ended up sitting outside on the stone bench once we got our ice cream orders. It was very hot but it was also refreshing to be out of the van. The cool sweet taste of the ice cream was enjoyable but it melted so quickly in the hot sun. Mid-way through a conversation with my cousin, I realized that the dream I had four years earlier involved this very same Dairy Queen. Déjà vu. It took me back for a moment, however, if this was my fate all I had to do was wait and see what was in store. Either way the next day I was going to finally meet my boy regardless what fate had in store...

So long and hard I worked for this. The dream was becoming a reality.

The Beginning

It was an early summer morning, warm but comfortable, when we left that morning to make the long drive to Ryan's farm. It was a beautiful country drive on a winding dirt road along a river. We were all excited but no one more than me. This was my dream come true.

When we finally arrived, we pulled up alongside a white country home and off to the right was a bank barn – a barn built into a hillside and accessible at two different levels. As we piled out of the van Ryan came out to meet us. He told us to hold on for a moment while he moved the barn dog into a stall. Apparently it was a good guard dog. So much so that even when Ryan's brother tried to go into to barn at night and came through a different door the dog chased him up to the hay loft and he was stuck there all night. We had no problem waiting. Once all was clear, Ryan invited us into the barn, an older barn with dim lighting. The aisle way was big enough to lead one horse and a handler down the aisle. No more than that. The stalls were wooden. We followed Ryan down long aisle to a stall that was all the way toward the back of the barn. That is where we then made a left turn and in the first stall he was there. Due to the dim lighting at first I swear there was no horse in the stall. While we waited for Ryan to get a lead rope to bring him out I kept searching for him in the dark stall. While everybody else waited by the stall door I moved a bit farther down to where the opening was to put in feed. It was then a big black shadow emerged. Then all of a sudden a big black nose pressed up against the bars. I reached out to touch his nose. At that moment, maybe because I was excited, the moment I touched his nose it felt like a spark. Like an instant connection pulsating though my body. It was then that my first words to him I asked, "What do you think about your name being Daredevil or Sir Rupert?"

Ryan left us by the stall to get acquainted with the horse. After a moment or two Ryan came back with the lead rope and went into the stall to get Figaro. It was then Ryan muttered under his breath to Figaro, "Where is your halter? You got it off again." Turning in my direction, Ryan said, " Oh yeah, you may want to know he likes taking his halter off."

After leading him out of the dark barn, all I can say was wow! Even in the dark he was big and beautiful. Once we went outside he looked even more impressive. Ryan proceeded to jog him on a long shank. While watching Figaro I could not help notice Ryan watching him all the while and giving him the odd yank on the shank to keep his attention. After that he stood Figaro still to let me take my time to look him over. He was beautiful and almost looked like a black Andalusian. There was just something more. He just stood proud. He had what track people call "an eagle eye," a knowing, confident look. At the same time he had the softest eyes, alert but soft.

Ryan then said that if he knew Figaro was this good looking he would have kept him for himself. He would have made a good team mate with Ryan's other carriage horse. To see this horse in the flesh was more than I could have ever imagined. It was like getting an Andalusian or as I would say later, the poor man's Andalusian. It sounds horrible but not in any way offensive to the Canadian breed. They are a beautiful breed in every sense but at least they are more economic or affordable for the average person.

It was a done deal. We went into Ryan's house to sign over the ownership, pay the balance, and complete all the paper work, registration papers and other such nuisances as I would call it. When that was done Ryan said the owner also wanted him to give me this envelope. When I opened it up it was a letter mentioning Figaro's stud-like qualities.

Figaro was gelded. Because of some uncertainty that he had been fully gelded, the note also said that if further surgery was required, they were willing to pay up to $500 towards the cost. At that moment I thought it weird. If he was gelded, what could possibly be left? If it was a nerve there is nothing you can do about it. Either way, all I can say is I was just content at that moment regardless.

Later that evening we took Ryan out to dinner at a restaurant on the river to thank him for all his work. He brought his lovely wife too. We had a merry time and about midway through dinner he brought up concerns again about Figaro's studdiness. Ryan brought up some valid points indicating hesitation about how he was not sure if he wanted to let Figaro go to me. He voiced his reservations. Ryan didn't think a sixteen year old girl could handle the likes of Figaro. It was only after my mom explained my goals in great detail that he relented. Also, me telling him about my experience at the racetrack and how I've been around horses since I was six years old. I should say, not just around horses but working with horses, working on horse farms with experienced and knowledgeable people. Mom talked to Ryan about what my visions were for Figaro down the road and what I planned to achieve with him. This was mainly about dressage at that point. I was hoping I could possibly teach Figaro to bow and do some showing.

Ryan seemed at bit more at peace knowing that I was speaking genuinely with realistic goals. He could already see that we were a match.

The next day we said goodbye to Ryan and Fig. We headed home and in a few days Figaro would be arriving at Brianne's place.

Let the Training Begin

When Ryan and Figaro finally arrived at Brianne's, we were waiting. I remember the stock trailer pulling up. He parked where Brianne showed him would be best. Ryan opened the back door. Figaro hollered for a moment or two as if to announce he was there and say I don't want to be in this trailer anymore. Figaro then stopped and tried to turn around ready to get off after all those hours in a trailer. It was a long trip. Five hours in a trailer on a hot summer day was definitely a trip that Figaro probably thought would never end. Once he was out, Brianne took us over to a paddock between the house and barn. It had a run-out shed and this is where he would be staying during his training.

In the next coming days, Cindy-- Brianne's friend and resident trainer began to do some work with Figaro. In our first correspondence, she did mention he was studdy. She reassured us that with some work he would get better. Cindy was used to handling stallions since she had worked with Brianne's stallion at the time and was competing in endurance. However, after a few more correspondences the studdiness seemed to be a constant and prominent topic. Figaro also liked carrying what we like to say his fifth leg out all the time. After talking to Brianne she mentioned that sometimes during castrating they may leave a nerve, which can cause the horse to appear studdy. She then mentioned to be sure to get a blood test done that will see if Figaro was producing testosterone. This would involve one normal sample then another with a shot of testosterone to see if the levels increase after the shot. It cost us about $150 but at least this would rule out at least one thing -- any question about whether Figaro was fully gelded. It was a relief to know that if we had to take Figaro for surgery we could since we had the letter from the previous owners about paying $500 for any required surgery.

After a few weeks we received the results from the vet. They were negative. So we accepted the test results -- though with some reservation. The matter was put on the back burner. We just figured that was Figaro. He was studdy. In time though and through training we started to think he was the way he was due to a lack of handling. He was four years old. He was extremely pushy and his answer to most things was just plain no. He was only 15.2 at the time but he was strong. He never did anything malicious like strike out or anything but if he could use his size against you he would. Even Cindy said he is not mean, but he was a thinker and you always needed to be one step ahead of him. Looking back, I think he was pretty much left in a pasture with very little handling and probably due to his studdiness his previous owners did not do too much with him. I recall Ryan mentioning that Figaro belonged to the owner's wife. She wanted to sell Figaro because she couldn't handle him.

That is why on our weekly visits I tried to bond with him out in the paddocks. During this time I came up and visited with him. I would brush him in his paddock. However, when he came to greet me I had to admit he was a bit intimidating since he would gallop right up to you and stop a foot or two right in front of you. This later became his trademark when coming in. Once you got used to it and realized he was going to stop then it wasn't so intimidating. The most rewarding of these early days was when Figaro started to recognize me and when he came on his own accord to me. When I called him, he came running over to me. At least we had an understanding and a bond that was becoming stronger each day. During my visits we had mini conversations about my goals as I brushed him, just normal chit-chat. Figaro was a good listener. Generally before I left I would give him an apple. I couldn't believe that at that point he had no clue what a carrot was and showed no interest. This is funny because in later years to come Figaro was a carrot fanatic. Most people never believed me about this but it was true. He only liked apples at this point.

Regardless Cindy was determined. She would tell me that with him you need to be in control. Aside from that he did seem to be a quick learner. The first day she put a saddle on him he bucked once and that was it. Even when Cindy introduced Figaro to leg yielding along the wall, she said it took a couple moments but once he did those couple steps he was just so proud of himself. Surprisingly to Cindy, when she turned Figaro loose in the arena she had witnessed him leg yielding along the wall himself.

After a good work out and training session, Cindy took Figaro outside for a hose down. When she first introduced him to the hose for a bath, she said he looked at it then, that was it, no problem. He would move around but that was about it. It was more about just being impatient. The diamond was trying to appear from the rough. The only problem we could all see was that we were still looking at the rough not knowing that these small things were going to help totally reveal a diamond underneath.

In time when he settled a bit more he seemed to realize working was amusing and seemed to enjoy starting a job. Figaro was also quite content to test whoever was handling him at the time, as much as possible. I still had to figure out whether he was doing it just to be stubborn. Some people will say this is the breed. But that is no different than saying all thoroughbreds like to run. Each horse is an individual. And with all the horses I had handled from good to bad, this boy you can say was dominant. Cindy mentioned it too.

15

In later sessions we started to notice he was not spooky at all and his reaction to the lunge whip was minor. If anything, he was not reactive at all. Mind you sometimes that is not a bad thing. When Cindy took him out on the road for the first time he showed no concern. This was reassuring to me. Cindy mentioned how Figaro would look forward to going out. When Cindy came and was riding the resident stallion, Figaro was at the fence line. Things started to look up.

Figaro was improving. Cindy made arrangements with me to be at one of Figaro's training sessions. She thought it would be a good idea to let me work with Figaro under her guidance. Figaro and I worked well together. Cindy could see Figaro's basic training coming to an end for her and a new beginning for me and my horse. Cindy was sure he should be alright to move to the farm where I previously worked. I was just happy to bring my boy there so my friends could see him. I was looking forward to working with him and eventually ride with my friends again.

Once we got the okay from Cindy and after working with her in a few sessions together, we felt confident that Figaro was ready to move him to his new home, the barn where I used to work in Milton. Before we parted for the last time, Cindy said that if for whatever reason, if I was ever going to sell him she wanted to have him. She really liked him and she liked a challenge. In the short time I had owned Figaro; she was the second person to mention buying him.

To the Farm We Go

When Figaro arrived at his new home, my fellow co-workers and friends were waiting to see my new boy. We had always dreamed and talked about owning a horse. I was the first of our group to get a horse of my own so this was an exciting event. Figaro announced his arrival. When we got him off the trailer we let him take a look around. The main barn was an old bank barn with an arena attached. In the middle of the parking lot off to the side was a large green drive-in storage shed for farm equipment. Beside the indoor arena was a large outdoor arena with small paddocks on the other side and beside that was a smaller green barn with only seven stalls. The smaller barn had once been used for breeding stallions and broodmares. On the other side of the driveway about 100 metres back, close to the tree line stood a two-storey old brick home that was quaint but showed years of wear on the exterior. The home was picturesque against the backdrop of the hay fields and cows from the neighbouring farm.

From early on Figaro always seemed to have this air about him -- just the way he stood. Just proud and observing whatever area or domain he considered his. I guess this is what made me most in awe of him. Once he had looked around, we decided to let him stretch out after his trailer ride and let him explore one of the surrounding paddocks across from the smaller barn. After a good roll and a buck or two, he grazed for a bit. Afterwards, I joined Susan, Brianne and the others. We were discussing Figaro and how to handle him. Brianne said her goodbyes and was then on her way. In my own mind, watching him, all I could think was that this was truly the beginning. It was now him and me. Our work together was truly about to begin. Unbeknownst to me, it was just the beginning of our bumpy road ahead.

I wanted something that was a bit of a challenge. I didn't want a horse that was a "Tony the Pony." The horse I chose would be my project. I would train him. I wanted to grow and bond with him, become one mind and spirit with my horse. That was one dilemma. The other was Fig. It would take me a few years to realize this. Though he was a handful, I cannot fully blame him. There was an unknown chapter in his life, an experience that made him who he was and how he was toward people. However, in years to come, I would soon learn that he had a reason for giving certain people a hard time. If he liked you, he might test you. If he was with a child he wouldn't but with an adult, he might. If you tried to manhandle him, were overconfident or he didn't like you, he made things difficult. If I didn't know at that moment why, I would find out later. His judge of character was pretty much dead on.

After his first few days we decided to try Figaro out with the boy herd. You opened up the back door of the barn and the boys went out to their paddock. We thought since he was young we would put him out in the herd with two big draft geldings, a chestnut 17.3-hand warm blood with a miserable attitude and a quarter horse cross gelding named Buddy. The problem in time was that Fig basically became the boss. The big boys stayed at the other end of the field and became shy of him. Fig was not big at the time (15.3 hands high and about 1200 pounds) but he was the boss. There were mares next to him that he wanted to try to breed through the fence. Good thing for electric fencing, but the decision was made to move him into a single paddock.

Cathy, the girlfriend of Jim who owned the farm, and who was also a blacksmith, said she observed him many times. She said, "I don't think he is mean. Just a young man in a big man's body trying to figure out where he needs to be." This was a bit unnerving. Figaro at the time seemed to have issues with smaller people. I figured it was, "I am bigger than you. You can't make me do anything." In years to come, he would meet someone who had as much determination as him.

This one day, I think there was more to the story than I knew. Susan said she was trying to get his halter on and he smacked her in the head. She had quite the black eye. At this point, I had no difficulty getting a halter on him. But then she said, changing her story to she went to take him to his new paddock, he knocked her down and she let him loose running up and down the fence. Susan had no intention of catching him. One thing I know for sure about Susan was that she wouldn't go down that easy. We did always remind her to take Figaro out with a chain shank over his nose. Cindy did say that Figaro learned to respect that shank in some of their sessions and if it's used properly you can get the horse's attention easily enough. For those who say it is cruel, it is only cruel if used inappropriately. If it is used and done right, a horse learns respect. With unruly horses or colts, the shank is a good preventative measure. Some will say a shank is evil. When "natural horsemanship" was starting to make an appearance a decade ago, my thought was this: natural horsemanship has been around for years. It was just not labelled as so. As one renowned trainer said, "Once you put a halter on a horse's head, it is no longer natural." Regardless, many would say why not use a rope halter. Yes it could work due to pressure points, but a chain in Fig's case was a bit better, since he was not as thin-skinned as most. Later we would call it rhino hide. Mind you, at the same time, a rope halter can be just as misused as a chain due to it pressure points and because of it being labelled "natural." Some people think they can use more pressure. This is not the case. If a horse needs discipline, within reason, then set him straight. If a horse is a bit studdy or needs discipline, then correct it. Fig needed to be reminded when he was going to be led. He was not the greatest at being led. That is why we used a chain shank over his nose. In any case, he got out of Susan's hands and started running up and down the fence line.

Luckily Cathy came and caught him. Thankfully the driveway was long and she had seen Figaro running back and forth along the fence line trying to get to the other horses. She said she caught him no problem and brought him back.

Even on days like this when you wanted to pull out your hair, funny how something so small helps you stay strong even if for a moment. Cathy was that one thing at that moment. She said she never had any problems in dealing with Figaro. He has a moment where he will think. When he realizes he does not have the upper hand, he is fine. What's that saying, "Every horse seeks a worthy leader?" It was at that time that Cathy said that Figaro is just like a young man in a grown man's body. He has the size and is not too sure what to do with it. It was hard to understand why then, but in looking back a true horseman seemed to see something in him. A real horseman sees that diamond in the rough.

Animals usually react for a reason. Sometimes it takes some Sherlock Holmes detective work but sometimes the small things explain a lot. There is nothing better than a mother and a child relationship. Once you learn your horse or child or whatever deep relationship you have, you will know when something is up without them ever saying a word.

Either way our search had to start for a new farm. The status quo was not going to work.

A time like this can be stressful. Fig was not an easy boy to deal with; at the same time he just needed the right person to handle and understand him. Most people would have given up on him, as my father almost did. You have to understand: not every horse started out a saint. It was great that Figaro had bonded with me but if others could not handle him, that was going to make things difficult. In the movie *Black Stallion*, you never see what it would be like to have him in reality. Most people don't know how to handle a horse like that and would get rid of him. If the Black was real, he probably wouldn't be in the average boarding facility. We had to find someone. Frank was going to be our rescuer -- though we didn't know that yet.

Fig was a handful but also there was the odd time that made me stop to think that maybe there was something I didn't know yet.

Consider, for example, this story -- when I was just starting to back Fig.

He was still very green and stubborn as a bull. He was constantly trying to test me. They say the Canadian breed is like that but that is like saying all thoroughbreds want to race. He was pig-headed, stubborn and head strong, with a rhino's hide. One thing about him, though: once he learned something, he knew it.

Figaro's tenacity to discover new things, to learn from his environment and from me was something that kept me challenged and inspired, surprised, proud and in awe of him. One thing I learned from Figaro: the mutual trust we had for each other had to be *earned*. In hindsight, that made him one good teacher even as I was teaching him. Many would ask: Why I did not take him to this trainer or that trainer, or why not use natural horsemanship? I had no problem with possibly considering that but I don't believe it is for every horse. However, when we were deciding what to do with this boy and other farms that could handle him, we contacted various trainers, including a few natural trainers. That kind of training was not as big or popular as it is now. When the subject of a stallion or stallion behaviour was discussed with probable facilities, many replied, "We don't deal with stallions," or they did not reply at all. To me, if you are a trainer and claim to deal with young or troubled horses you should be well rounded with all genders. How do you fully understand the behaviour of a horse if you do not understand the language of the horse? Even a gelding can portray stallion characteristics. Horses speak one language. A stallion might just be a bit more expressive or have more meaning behind his actions. It just takes a moment for us to step back to understand what they are saying, for us to help them understand what we are saying and for them to show respect for us. This was fate's way of saying, "I have something in store for you." If there was a problem I was going to try and solve it. If I didn't know, I would try to learn or find out. And this was going to be the best education I would ever receive in horsemanship. We all have that one horse that teaches us and Figaro was going to be that one horse for me.

Even in the arena with other horses, he was a bit studdy, but not bad. Unfortunately, one day while still at the Milton farm one of the horses he used to paddock with came in. It was the miserable 17.3-hand high horse. They didn't care for each other. I told his owner just to give Fig and I some space and to not pass too closely. This was just a courtesy since her horse was a bit of a kicker as well. She said alright and was riding for a while. At one point she was too absorbed into her riding and cut cross the arena to change direction. The proper rule of the arena is that you pass left to left or right shoulder to right shoulder. She came way too close. Before she could move her horse pinned his ears at Fig. Fig saw the challenge and seized the opportunity and went after her horse. If I had not been on the rail I could have moved, but I had nowhere to go. I got Fig away from both her and her horse. They were both fine and, of course; she blamed me even though she came too close. Another rule of thumb is that if you know your horse is a kicker, the rider should give others more space as well. She knew not to get too close. I see this a lot in arenas and people get too carried away with their own riding and forget the rules of the arena. Just like driving on the road, you are supposed to be aware of your surroundings at all times. That split-second mistake could have been avoided. Thankfully there were no injuries to any party.

A few days later, this same rider told me Fig had managed to turn her horse evil. Never have I heard that in my life. Secondly, her horse had a nasty disposition long before Fig did this. He was a bitter and a kicker. He even used to bully the field horses. I know because once while putting on his winter blanket he got me good.

About seven years later I bumped into her. She asked about Fig and I told her how he was doing, that I had trick trained him and that he had mellowed out. This was the best part. When I asked her about her horse, she said that she had to get rid of him because he had broken a fence and bullied other horses.

During those early days, my young four year old Fig began to show his true side. He used to love picking up branches and carrying them around the paddock. Unfortunately, he used to take them off the tree and any branch in his reach was taken. I remember trying to go out to get him one day and there he was happily carrying a four foot branch in his mouth trotting around the pasture like a playful puppy. I can say he could keep himself very amused. The down fall no tree was safe from him as long as there were branches within his reach.

In time, this playfulness also revealed a sense of humour as well. Eventually because another horse needed the one paddock as well, Figaro moved to the lower half of the outdoor arena – a space that was at least forty feet by forty feet. It had a gap big enough to allow three round bales on the other side to be packed side by side. There was also a small arena with a small gap to the large outdoor arena -- big enough to allow barrel racing or roping or other competitive events. One day a group of us decided to sit on the round bales to have some lunch. The gate was left open so Fig could munch on the bales. As we sat and chatted Fig, decided to come over for a visit and we all petted him. Then he was content to just munch away as we talked. One of the girls, nicknamed Kat, had rested her juice box just behind her. Figaro seized the opportunity and grabbed it. Poor Kat. Once she realized it, she was off that bale in a hurry and right behind Fig. He seemed to enjoy being chased and was joyfully swinging the juice box in the air while at the same time squeezing it and drinking it. It was almost like an older brother taunting a younger sister. By the time he dropped it, she was exhausted. At that moment she said, "He just drank my juice." It was hard not to laugh.

As much as I was butting heads with Susan and how studdy Fig was, I really enjoyed being in his stall while he ate his hay and I just sat with

him. It was nice to be with him and I never felt I was in danger. We spent
many afternoons chatting or sitting together. Many times I sat on his hay,
and when he wanted more he would nuzzle me to move over. A lot of the
time nobody even knew I was in there with him. Not only did I want to
spend time with him, but in these moments I would just ponder. How was
it that this horse that can cause such terror but when I was with him in
the stall it was nothing. Just total calm. I even would ask him some days,
"Why do you have to be like this? Why can't you just understand?" How
could my dream be such a nightmare at the same time? But just when you
think you have hit rock bottom, a glimmer of light comes -- maybe not as
bright as you may want, but it is there.

That glimmer of light came in an unexpected form. One day when I
was in the stall with Fig brushing him, Jim, the owner of the farm, an
accomplished reiner and roper, came in on his mare, Rosaline. She was
one of his recent purchases. Rosaline was a really nice quarter horse mare.
He had been working on her recently to get her ready for some upcoming
competitions. I generally never saw him too much when I was at the farm.
He was around after I went home. I was lucky to get a "hi" and a wave of
his hand or a tip of his hat the very few times I met him. He was a man of
very few words. So to see him ride into the barn was a bit surprising. He
stopped halfway from the stall. I was in a bit of shock and I looked like a
deer in the head lights. Before I could even think why he was there he said,
"Nice animal. Is that a stallion?" I told him no (I didn't know he was at the
time). After a short pause he said, "Oh that is a pity. He is a nice animal.
"And he rode out the barn. I will never forget that. Made me wonder:
was there something he saw that I didn't or know of? A professional and
horseman had seen something in Figaro. I was simply hoping that what
drew me to this horse was actually there.

Figaro and I had to buckle down and start training. Like any young horse
he was started off with a snaffle bit. I always started our session with a
light lunge or, better said, an attempt. Since he was green I took him to
the lower half of the arena that was sectioned off and later became his
paddock. Generally I would loop the lunge line through the one side of the
bit then over his head to attach to the other side. This generally gives you

enough control. However, Fig always liked being the exception to the rule. He would walk in a circle alright. It generally took quite a few snaps of the lunge whip to convince him to walk on. This was my first clue that he was more of a fight than flight type of personality. A few minutes on is when the fun started. When it came to the trot, he would be nice and oblige the first few circles. Without even a twitch of the ear he would take off to the gap in the arena -- and he was strong. Most young horses have a sensitive mouth and would generally stop. Not Fig. He would take a hold of the bit and drag you. No matter what I did. Making smaller circles at the lower half or even putting a chain over his nose did not work. He would just defeat me. After a few sessions and even with my persistence, he seemed to be getting the better of me. That is when finally I said – enough! That is when I would just get on him instead. For a green horse he was pretty good; he never ran off. That was not his style. Some would say I had taught him nothing and he got away with something. Generally I would work with this and reward good behaviour. Figaro, you see, was not fitting into the norm. Therefore, we had to approach our training differently. Right now he needed to just work with me. At the time I was no more than 130 pounds so he could pick me up like nothing. At least this was one hurdle that seemed to have been overcome.

I recall our first ride was not too bad. We were only doing the basics and occasionally would do a little canter. His gaits felt so different from what I was used to. He seemed to flow more. His canter was different. He didn't seem to know how to canter (as weird as it may seem) -- especially with a rider on his back. When he seemed to get the rhythm more, his canter felt like a rocking horse going back and forth and you never moved. It was so smooth. Eventually he would get more hind end power and it was still smooth but it was more normal to the feel. The thing I enjoyed the most was that he would naturally carry his head nice and rounded. Many horses need to be taught this by making them move forward and to go into the bit. Figaro just did it. This is perhaps why many thought he was a Friesian. All I can say is that he had presence from day one. I just wish he was a more sensitive horse. Everybody is different; the same is for a horse. I had been working on our aids and would give him a nudge with my heel and then get him to move off the leg. With much persistence, eventually it became clear

I needed an extra aid. So I started carrying a dressage whip. With a gentle tap he was more agreeable than with just my heel. Some days he would treat me as if I was a fly. He was very well aware of what he was doing. It was like watching an old school horse standing in the middle of the arena while a small child with all her might was kicking the horse's sides only to have the old school master just stand there and go to sleep. That was Fig.

Because Fig was the new guy, generally we would have some onlookers. Jess, one of Susan's long time workers, was watching us. She was short and the same size as Susan. She had great balance and was a good all-around rider. After she watched me and Fig just sauntering around the arena she gave me some pointers. After a moment or two I said, "Would you like to get on him?" When she got on him, she went to ask him to move on. He just stood there. He knew full well what he was doing. She gave him a harder kick in the sides. Still nothing. Then she gave him a tap with the whip. This time he moved but only a few steps and stopped. It probably took five minutes before he decided to oblige. One part of me was thinking "what a mule," but another part had to smile. Figaro was saying, "I don't care what your experience is. Make me." What I came to understand was this: Fig had no mule streak; this was just how he dealt with cocky people or people who manhandled him. This only proved to me that you couldn't dominate him. You had to earn his respect. The key was to get others to see what I saw so they could work with him and get into his head.

It was a short time after this that we moved Figaro to another farm. We hoped this would help. Figaro would be turned out all day and hopefully give us some mental rest as well. We wouldn't have to worry about Figaro's care and treatment.

Crossing Fingers

When Figaro got the upper hand, he took advantage of it. It amazed me how many boarding facilities claimed they could handle stallions and difficult horses when all they could really handle was calm, trained horses. Best to see what they have in their barn and ask for references. My advice from hard experience: visit the farm you are considering. See how full a barn is and how many of those horses are the owner's horses. Because most of the time that will give you a general idea. We decide to move Figaro to a farm that accommodated stallions and could handle them. It was a nice farm. The husband, wife and son were nice. The wife was a bit eccentric but bubbly and knowledgeable. She was about average height, blonde short hair and a constant smile. This was good and generally it was nice to have such an upbeat instructor. The son was down to earth and not scared of horses. The husband was at least 6 foot tall and a standard build. You could tell he was an outdoors man. He had a very calm demeanour about him with his short brown hair and moustache. He just had that very straight forward, straight from the hip personality. He told it like it was. No sugar coating. I hoped this would help Figaro out and maybe with this man's disposition Figaro would settle in a lot better. We felt he was accomplished enough. He told us he would be the one to handle Fig. He said they had handled a stallion in the past-- once and for a short period. This should have been our first clue. They tried to reassure us by telling us about some of the problem horses they had in the past. Figaro was going to stay in the smaller barn next to some geldings. His paddock was just outside the door. The main barn was about 50 feet away with a large arena and a nice viewing lounge upstairs. The stable was a long row of stalls on one side with two large doors at each end. The atmosphere was nice. The son and

I had some nice long chats and he was very down to earth. He was about the same height as I was but had confidence behind his words.

Fig did alright the first day or two. They had put a horse near his paddock. They had noticed he didn't like being alone. I had noticed this myself. I don't ever feel like it was because he was herd bound. He was not panicked at all. It was as if he had been secluded from others in the past and did not like having horses not in his sights at least. If he could see horses, he was fine. He couldn't have cared less if he was in a paddock with another horse. With every passing day with Fig, I found I had to become Sherlock Holmes. The answer to the questions his training posed were never obvious or on the surface. And I continued to wonder about his past history.

This new farm was working out. One day they had him in the arena loose. The wife had to tell us what she saw when she went to take a peek at him. What he was doing in the arena, she noticed, was some dressage by himself and leg yielding (without a rider). He was also doing diagonals, serpentines and figure eights on his own. She asked how long I had been working with him. I said not too long. She even commented that Figaro seems to enjoy what you are working on. She said he was quite beautiful and he seemed to have a natural talent for it. Talking to the owner's wife at least put my mind at ease. I don't like pushing an animal into doing something that animal doesn't care to do. No sense making a horse that loves to jump, do roping. A horse likes to please their owner regardless. When both can enjoy the same thing it makes things that much easier and enjoyable.

So things were looking up. At this point in the game I really did not mind what discipline we did but it was nice that my main interest -- dressage -- was something Figaro seemed to enjoy. There was a ray of hope. The sun was managing to break through the dark clouds.

Then that little storm cloud had to drift in. The husband handled him every day and was the main person to turn him in and out. This one night he fell asleep watching TV. So his wife decided to bring him in. I think she was well accomplished with horses, but she lacked confidence and that bit of authority. Figaro knew it. You gave him an inch; he could take a mile in a heartbeat. When she brought him in, he basically couldn't care less that she was the one on the other end of the lead. Worse part: Mr. Man's eyes caught a filly in heat at the other end of the barn. So he decided to drag her to that filly. When she tried to pull him back he knocked her down, not maliciously but at the time he was small but solid and if you did not weigh much he did not have to really use any force to make you move. Judging by what the husband told us later, she lost her footing and Fig dragged her the length of the aisle on her belly. She was a bit sore and bruised but luckily nothing broke. The rule of thumb is that when you are down, you let the horse go. Worry about it when you get back on your feet. As an accomplished horse person, she should have known better. She could have just opened the arena door and chased him in, then worried about getting him later.

When we came up that Saturday, Fig was in his stall with chains wrapped around the door and doorframes from top to bottom. I don't think I ever saw a jail with as many chains as this stall. Worst part: she was just throwing the hay over top and filling up his water bucket by putting a hose through the bars. The son and husband were not scared of him and both admitted it was just an accident. The son and husband would still go into the stall. Then she went on to say he was climbing the stall walls. The stall had no evidence of any hoof marks or scrapes on the wall. Dad took it with a grain of salt. If you were locked up in a stall for a week, I would not blame you for getting cabin fever. If he was curious about another horse he would raise his nose to sniff.

She could handle difficult horses but Figaro was different. Figaro was stallion like. He told her she was supposed to wake him up. He did, however, say Figaro was pushy, but he not mean. On the other hand, he declared that "of all the horses I handled, I just cannot get into his head". So we thanked him for his honesty and yet again we were on a search for a new farm ASAP.

As much as you try to feel optimistic at times like this, you just feel hopeless. Mom was my greatest supporter and she was determined not to let my dreams down. My dad, however, was not so optimistic. His negativity came through in this situation. He mentioned at one point if he is that much of a hand full just get rid of him. You should not have a horse till you're at least thirty in any case. Mom was determined and called Brianne to see if she could take Figaro or if she knew of anywhere that we could take him. Brianne would have taken him, but had foals on the way and she needed the stalls for her own horses. After some thought she said, "I do know somebody. He deals with stallions and problem horses all the time." His name was Frank.

Mom said she knew of him. We had met him several years before at the fall fair. Mom still had his business card. After a quick call to Frank, we went to meet with him. We discussed our situation and he said, "Bring him over." Frank was not concerned even after mom told him what we had gone through. My mom felt reassured and relieved but she felt some trepidation too. Frank could sense our desperation to get Figaro out of a bad situation. Regardless this man was our last hope. If most of the big name trainers wanted nothing to do with Figaro and not many other places could deal with this thinker. What next?

So we made some calls to horse transporters. We found one that would move Figaro that very day. It was arranged and Fig was taken to yet another new farm.

Frank, Our Last Hope

It was a cool early winter afternoon with some sun gleaming through the drifting clouds. It was one of those years where when there was a dusting of snow, the roads would get a bit slick. At that moment I was just concerned for Figaro. He seemed to feel that something was in the air that day and his head was up. While my parents were outside tying up the loose ends, I went to Figaro's stall and just stayed with him. The stall had a faint light coming through the window. He was alert and would take the occasional peek out the window. Once reassured there was nothing, he came back over to me. I just sat there for some time brushing him.

I remember telling him "Please let this new place be the one and Figaro I can't take this stress anymore. Please just behave. I worked so long and hard to get you. Please don't let this end badly. I think you and I can go far together."

Then after a moment he just came over and nuzzled my chest. He just seemed to get this look in his eyes that said, "Don't worry mom. I love you no matter what." Then he resumed eating his hay and I finished polishing up his beautiful black coat. I wanted his first impression to be a good one no matter what. I still have a pride in my horse looking super clean, as if he was going to a show. Then I put on his shipping boots just in case he wanted to be rowdy.

After some time had passed our shipper, Louie, came in. He had reassured us he could handle colts and when he found out where we were going he said, "I know Frank. Don't worry. This trailer is Andalusian proof."

When I went to get Figaro, he was trying to get his shipping boots off and had his leg up in the air pulling off the Velcro. I said, "What are you doing?" He kept the Velcro in his mouth and just turned to look at me as if to say, "What? I am not doing anything." It was then that Louie came in. He took Fig and loaded him up with no problem. You could see in just the way he handled Fig that he had dealt with stallions and bad boys. Later I would meet him again at the racetrack, which explained why he was used to handling high strung horses.

It was a good hour and a half drive to Frank's farm. As we turned to the farm you could see trees on either side of the driveway, with a sign at the entrance welcoming you in to the world of classical dressage. As we went up the small dirt road we passed Frank's house on the right then proceeded down a small but fairly steep hill that then turned into a small round-about encircling a small red barn. As we parked we then took a look at the white brick barn that was built in the style of Portuguese barns, with a small white sand paddock in front.

We made sure to get there before Fig. Dad was concerned about him coming down the hill given the icy conditions. With Figaro being the way he was, my dad thought Louie might need a hand.

Louie had decided to park at the entrance to the farm where he unloaded Figaro and walked him down to the barn. Louie did fine.

Frank had opened up the big brown sliding doors to the barn. Frank was an older gentleman with silver hair, medium in height, but you could tell he was a veteran rider by his bowed legs. He welcomed us in and showed Louie which stall to put Figaro in. When you first entered the barn there was a small hay room, then you either went left or right to go to one of the two aisles of stalls. Many of the stalls were simple wood stalls, some with swinging doors and some with gates or sliders. Figaro had the first stall on the left when we came in. It was a fair size and Figaro would be able to hang his head over his wooden stall door. Across from him was another stallion and next to him a gelding named Amanti. Most of the horses hung their heads out trying to see the newcomer and the odd stallion called out to let him know who was boss. Frank took a hold of Figaro and said, "Go ahead. Take off his shipping boots. "Frank took the end of the dressage whip and gave him a tap on the bridge of his nose and said, "Stand up young man." Fig was somewhat taken aback. However, he stood still while I took off the boots. It was then that we properly introduced each other and the first time I got a Frank handshake. This man had a *strong* handshake. You could tell that this man did physical labor and had handled tough horses. The nice part? The handshake was confident, like his smile.

Eventually he gave us a tour of the barn and showed us his stallions. Even though I was a teenager, I was drooling inside to be in a barn with all these Lusitanos. At the time he was the only trainer who trained them in classical dressage. He demonstrated the *piaffe* in the aisle way with one of his stallions. I was in heaven. When I was just starting to take riding lessons, I had taken one with Frank years ago. I had always liked Andalusians and loved classical training. Fate had brought me here again. After a short tour he invited us up to his house for some lunch.

When we sat down in the kitchen, Frank's lovely wife Claire came in to join us. Frank said, "Tell me about the big boy." We told him everything with all honesty, from the herd to his dilemmas with people handling him. Frank showed no sign of concern. He said we would even try him out in the herd after we told him about the anxiety. Frank said, "We will try him out there and they will fix him or worst case we put him out with the brood mares and they will settle him."

After talking some more, Frank had an idea of what I wanted to accomplish. I felt more relaxed, just not fully. However, this was my last hope. After meeting Rose, his youngest daughter, she reassured us she would email us with Figaro's progress. She was upbeat. She was of medium height and looked a lot like her mother. She had long black hair and was currently at university.

Rose did e-mail us almost every day and would let us know his progress and how her father was dealing with Figaro and his antics. The most reassuring thing was when Rose told us not to worry because her dad loves a challenge. He doesn't like the easy ones. Well at least he got his wish. Fig was to be a challenge for a while. After that I was more at ease. Despite his antics, no one at this farm ever seemed concerned.

I would soon come to learn Frank famous line about Figaro for the next few years: "Don't let him think."

Fig and the Herd

We talked to Frank about Figaro's herd issues and whether he was a gelding or a stallion and in the end we decided to put him out with the other horses. At least he would be given a chance to work into the herd. If he was too studdy, then he would be given single turnout.

After the first day, we heard from Rose. Figaro's first day was apparently okay. He was acting like Mr. Man and he was challenging whoever was in charge of their little herds. Thankfully it was a big field, a good 8-acre paddock. Frank said horses all figure out their places, which was true. Most horses do find their place in the herd. Figaro never seemed to want to fit into the norm. That is why he taught me so much.

Fig challenged the mini herd leaders, including one of the main leaders, Raphy, an older bay Arabian gelding who acted a bit studdish at times. He was 15 hands at most and probably a 1000 lbs max. Figaro was 16 hands and about 1200 lbs at this point. With his size, Fig was not going to be an easy competitor. Figaro was determined to be king of the herd. The idea of just fitting in didn't seem to be an option for him. The vagabond wanted to be a ruler. He was earning himself a herd at this point. He managed to get a few into his herd. He had Tico, an older white Lusitano gelding, Sly, a Lipizzaner cross, and a few other geldings and mares.

Due to these battles, quite few horses had scrape marks on them and Fig tried to breed most of the mares, with not much success. Some could not be bothered. Most were older mares and some mares, I noticed, like to tease him. That was true of a younger Arabian filly named Calamity.

Figaro's studdiness did not seem to be dying down, as we had thought. Sometimes after castration, a nerve is left and the gelded horse will appear studdy but only during certain times of the year. Figaro, on the other hand, was Mister Man every day. Due to his maturing and more exercise, he was developing more muscle mass and a thicker neck. A thick neck is part of the Canadian horse breed and for his size, his neck seemed about right. Or was he simply taking on the look of a stallion?

Poor Raphy -- as valiant and stubborn as he was -- was no match for Figaro. It was like watching a lightweight fighter go after a heavyweight. After some correspondence with Rose, I decided I wanted to see the big boy in action for myself. I stood in the outdoor arena overlooking the paddock and watched as Raphy made a rather impressive challenge. As they approached each other, they sniffed and that was when Raphy went to Figaro's side and delivered a swift double-barrel kick to his side. You could hear the kick from on the hill. You would think with that force he would have broken one of Fig's ribs. Luckily Raphy had no hind shoes; I thank the Lord for that. To my amazement, Fig stood there as if the kick was nothing more than a fly bothering him. He had a cool and calm approach to fighting. He took a moment and as Raphy continued his dance around him, Figaro made his move and was on Raphy heels. Once he had him in the right position, Fig turned and gave a swift kick in return and then turned for a bite to the neck. Then as quickly as it started, the skirmish ended and they both went back to grazing. At some point in his battles Figaro received a permanent mark on his front right leg – not a scar because the skin was never broken. The hair just never really grew back. Fig was left with an upside down partial horse shoe mark on that leg – his very own lucky horseshoe.

As the days went by, Fig eventually became top dog. The girls at the farm Trish, Laura and a couple others told me constantly about the adventures or horrors of Fig. I would rather know the bad stuff than have it hidden and thank God they were honest. Laura told me of one day when Fig was the last of the herd to come in. Frank had an easy system for bringing in the herd of about twenty five horses. He would open the gate that was placed at the top of the hill on the far side of the outdoor arena. Before the gate was a long chute that had a bit of a slope. On a dry day, the hill was fine. On a winter day, it could be slippery. Once the horses reached the gate, they would then turn to the left and enter the large side arena door leading to the two aisles of stalls. The horses were pretty good and knew their stalls. On occasion the odd rebel decided they wanted to live in a different stall. After a few words from Frank, they would go back to their proper stalls.

On this one particular day, it was a bit icy. The horses coming in after a day of turnout did their usual thing and they were almost in the barn. Mister Fig, though, had gotten in a habit of making them chase him into the barn or leaping over the snow bank in the outdoor arena. He was indeed the black sheep of the group. Going into the barn like every other horse was too easy and not dramatic enough. Figaro decided that galloping at full speed to catch up with the others was a great idea. The downfall was that even though there was a layer of snow on the ground, it was still slippery. The others would sometimes gallop but they knew how to negotiate the ice and would slow down as well. Figaro's approach was full tilt. He slipped and he was almost sitting like a dog as he skidded across the ice for about ten or more feet. He then collected himself and went into the barn. It was hard not to laugh when I heard all this. All I could picture was Bambi on ice.

When the warmer weather came, Fig wanted to extend his herd and he was in the mood for love. He did get his herd and he did have more battles with

Raphy. Now there were more horses in his herd. Fig also liked living the life as a king and he wanted to be outside all the time. One day the king had to come off his throne. Rose emailed us this story of that happening on the very same day.

For the most part Figaro was enjoying his kingly duties and he took them quite seriously at this point, like the king he was. He took good care of his herd. When owners came to collect their horses he would generally herd the owner away from the horse or out of the field.

Fig also liked the highest point of land on the farm -- a pretty big hill that was great for developing the hind muscles of a horse if needed. Once at the top you could look over the farm and even the house that they were slowly developing behind the farm. This hill is where Figaro decided to rule. He loved hills. If there was one in his paddock he preferred to stand on the hill and he made it his spot. Figaro liked his spot and when it came time for the horses to come in, all the others went in. A few from Fig's herd went in, but most stayed back with him.

Frank wasn't going to put up with this. He proceeded outside with a lunge whip and Zorro, the farm's large German shepherd dog. As they walked toward the hill, Frank was yelling in Portuguese. He generally did this when he was not pleased. The other horses knew Frank was not happy and went in; Fig was not going in too easily. That is when Zorro went after Figaro and was hanging off his tail. Figaro eventually started to gallop with Zorro still hanging on. Meanwhile Frank kept yelling at him and snapping the lunge whip. Eventually Figaro gave up -- or so we thought. Once he was in the outdoor arena, the gate was closed in hopes that Figaro would go back into the barn. Fig decided that he still did not want to go into the barn and he turned around and headed toward the gate at full tilt.

Most horses would have stopped since it was not a low gate but a good four foot high wooden gate. Fig decided to jump the gate but instead of clearing it like a jumper he managed to get stuck in mid jump. His determination was strong and he wiggled off the gate and galloped back up to his hill. Again Frank headed back out with Zorro in tow. This time, however, the yelling became more like a screech. Only those who speak Portuguese would know what he was saying. I don't think it would take a rocket scientist to figure out what he was saying. Eventually Figaro was back in the barn. It was at this moment that a unanimous decision was made: the king needed single turnout.

Now that he had no herd to think about, Fig would have to conjure some new adventures.

Down to business

In the first few years, other than Fig's handling dilemmas and pasture fun, we also started more work under saddle.

Fig was obliging and not bad for the most part. I still tried to ride him in a snaffle bit, which is always good for a young horse just learning the ropes. For Fig it was just not enough. Most horses starting with a bit have what is called a soft mouth and can be sensitive before they get used to the sensation of the bit. Figaro did not fall into that norm. Figaro was rhino hide -- inside and out. He was aware that your leg was there, but if he chose to ignore you, there was not much you could do. You would end up looking like a young child trying to get a horse to move. As Frank said, he needed artillery, which really meant either a whip or spurs. Most will say this is cruel. A tool is only as malicious as the person using it. Any training tool, whether a carrot stick (used in natural horsemanship) or a whip, are just extensions of your hand and used as a guiding tool. A spur is no different. A spur just amplifies your cue.

Since Figaro had a rhino hide, if you didn't use spurs you would have needed something like an iron leg. Up to this point he was dominant and not so sensitive. He was aware of you but he chose whether he would respond or not. I tried many different ways to make him more sensitive to cues, such as gently poking his sides and waiting for a reaction, then rewarding him. But the battle of the minds – mine against Figaro's – continued.

Frank, meanwhile, opted for the double bridle (which deploys two bits). This can be used many ways. You can use just the snaffle for most training.

The curb bit assisted with more response and helped to keep the horse's head in a correct frame. In addition the extra bit gives the horse something else to think about. The double bridle worked but in time I would go back to the single bit.

In any case, things were not too bad. Figaro did like to challenge me in many ways – sometimes by dragging my legs against the arena wall or bucking. His bucks were not rodeo-style nasty. Rose described them as a bum-it-tee, bum-it-tee. They had power alright. They were generally pretty smooth to ride to if you know how to sit a buck. To get Figaro out of the bucking habit, Frank would have us gallop at full tilt in a circle. The faster the horse goes the harder it is to buck since the horse is leaning as he circles. This may sound extreme, but in time most horses will figure this out. They give up bucking because they know they won't win. All animals want to preserve their energy. Similarly, with a horse that likes to go fast all the time, take him out on a trail ride for a couple hours. Eventually the horse learns that contentment comes from going at an even pace.

In time, the circle exercise worked. Fig was always game to figure a way out of things. Eventually he humbly backed down. On occasion he would let out the odd buck, but most times it was a happy moment and would end as quickly as it started. For me at this time, some days were alright but most days it was hard to sit in the saddle due to a hip problem that had started in my lower back. It was like pins and needles in my hands and feet too. I could be fine one moment but then next it was like a shock of electricity had gone up my back. Frank had gone to an osteopath named August and found great results. Frank recommended him, gave me his name and contact information. August was my saviour. I would eventually be able to walk straighter and have a bit more balance. Some days, though, I would have to get off Figaro due to the pain. Even when Figaro was having his moments, he seemed to know when he needed to stand and would let me off with no problem. I still live with pain but have learned not to push it. Eventually it does get the better of me and every so often I still limp. Apparently I carry twenty pounds more on one leg.

Like any green horse, Figaro still had some youngster moments. He still did not care to stand still while I was mounting. I think this is a reason I can mount a horse easily from the ground even when my hips are sore. He would tease some days and pretend he was going to stand then move when I was halfway up, and then walk away. Most days there wasn't anybody around to hold his head so I had to improvise. If one thing doesn't work, I will find another way. I am for the most part a self-learner. Hence this is why I observe as much as I do. Either way I was not going to let Figaro get the best of me on this. He knew the word stand. We went back to standing in a corner to prevent him from moving. He figured out how to bend his body. Then I tried tempting him with a treat. He was not that interested. I thought of clipping a lead to his bridle. I would give him a reminder mid-way up. It worked for a bit but then he got wise and that no longer worked. What ended up working was pure distraction. By the arena stairs there were hooks that held various leads, lunge ropes and other horse equipment. When he stood by the door while I was getting myself organized before mounting, I noticed him playing with the ropes with his nose. A voice inside my head said get on and forget about doing our mini-lunging session. So I got up. To my surprise, nothing. Once I got his attention, I moved him from the stairs and made him stand again and rewarded him. In time, he got better and we no longer needed the distraction. Later on he would become so good. I would just stand on the mounting block and he would move up himself and park himself. It got to the point I no longer even needed to hang onto the reins. Sometimes you need to think outside the box.

There were some days were mounting from the ground was difficult. There was one day I was particularly sore and Frank had noticed. He came over to the stairs and said, "Use the stairs." He gave Fig a tap with the whip to make him line up with the stairs. After a moment or two, Fig lined up. It took me a while to notice but Figaro did not seem keen on people holding his reins when someone was on his back. In this case he was just feeling fresh this day. Once lined up, I was about to mount when Figaro decided he wanted to go forward. Frank pushed him back. Where Figaro thought he was going I will never know, since he was blocked by a very large sliding door. Figaro did not like being pushed around. Once again he made his move forward, this time pushing this large metal door out as if it was nothing. He then proceeded to back up and I got on without incident and we went on with our ride.

This was an early indication: if Figaro could get the upper hand he would take it. This is why when it came to ground work in the early days, Figaro was a challenge. On one occasion Frank wanted to show us how he was progressing with leg yielding. I watched Frank work Figaro on this occasion. He was working Figaro, trying to get him to leg yield along the wall. One thing was certain: Fig was more cooperative in the saddle than on the ground. Frank was doing well till Fig had had enough. Fig used his head to lift Frank about a foot off the ground and just held him on the wall. Fig didn't do anything else but just held him there for a second or two. There was no striking. Nothing. Fig just held him there. Frank was the true professional and kept his calm. Most people would have panicked. I have experienced this myself with a horse panicking in the stall due to a commotion. As hard as it is, when the horse ran circles around me and was bucking I stood still and when the opportunity presented itself, I got out. Most horses do not want to harm you. Injury generally ends up happening when someone moves at the wrong moment.

After Fig let him down at the wall, Frank intended to take him to the middle of the arena to make him do some leg yielding. Fig was going to resist and did what almost looked like a *levade*, but Frank had a firm hold of him and they went back to work. Figaro was the type of horse Frank liked. He liked the challenge and I was grateful that he did. I, too, liked a challenge. A well trained horse teaches so much and builds our confidence when we first learn to ride. It is the difficult horses that truly do teach us about horsemanship, calmness and determination. They are the ones who make us problem solvers and teachers. Up to this point you may only see an ill-mannered rogue; I see a great teacher in the making.

I loved the few sessions Frank had with Figaro. Frank was mainly teaching Fig basic ground work. Unfortunately, reality was a factor. I was paying for board and only working on the weekends, so my funds were limited. I couldn't take too many lessons or afford the training I wanted. Still, it was clear to me that with each session Figaro was getting better. I thought he would be okay for others to ride. The riders in the barn were pretty accomplished and many – young and old -- had ridden a stallion at least once. My second thought was if Fig was used in lessons and ridden by experienced riders, he would learn more and get more exercise. Plus he would get used to working with other horses in large groups. I managed to still get up to the farm at least 2-3 times a week. Meanwhile I was trying to juggle high school, college at night, work and Fig. It was hard at times. My energy was down. So the idea of other riders on Fig, I thought, would be the perfect solution.

It did not work as I had hoped. Figaro was being used in lessons when I came up -- but not with experienced riders. I noticed younger, beginner students on him. I wanted to question Frank about his judgment. I didn't want Fig being used with children. My final decision to stop this was the one day I came up and Fig was in a lesson with some younger students. As I watched, Fig was taking this one kid wherever he wanted and Frank was instructing the little girl, "Don't let him think, don't let him think." It was at this point I decided I needed to take charge. That little voice in my head said, "You wanted a project. You should be the one working with him -- whether you're hurting or not. "I removed Fig from lesson classes before he could start reverting to his old habits or learn any new ones, maybe even bad ones. From there on it was going to be him and me. No matter what.

To truly meet your dreams you need to be the one to work at it. Like my favourite saying goes *"a dream is just a dream but a goal is a dream with a plan."* I had dream but eventually an unexpected goal would come and take me to a whole new level.

A Knight Emerges

Even with all our minor ups and downs, and even when I was in pain or wanted to pull my hair out due to his antics some days and even threaten him with the glue factory, I still would not have gotten rid of him for the world. I loved Figaro and for every time he did something bad he would do something else to earn my respect. What made me truly do a 360 was one particular act. From then on I knew, 100%, we had a bond.

It was about mid-week, during March break. I was lucky because I could get a ride up to the farm. I was a bit sore and while I was dealing with Fig generally my dad would take a nap and mom would sweep out the barn or read a book. I proceeded into the barn as usual and was brushing Fig in the stall. The barn was fairly quiet and the arena was generally empty since almost all of the barn staff and clients had gone home or to Frank place for lunch. I would generally take these opportunities to work with Fig on a more one on one basis.

Once I tacked Fig up, I began heading to the arena. I had in my hand my whip, which was generally there for riding. Figaro had come to learn to respect a whip. I had it while leading him and I would use it to make him put away his fifth leg or just to get his attention. All was well when I called "door." There was another rider in the arena, so once I got the ok from her I entered the arena. Just as I turned to close the arena door, I looked over my shoulder. Figaro had been waiting patiently while I closed the sliding door but I could hear a commotion behind me. Relicario, one of the resident stallions, was giving his rider in the arena a hard time. Relic was a mature, dapple grey Lusitano stallion. Just as every person is an individual, this horse had his preferences – and one was that he did not like black horses of any kind.

His owner was an alright rider but it was the look of panic on her face and her raised voice toward Relic that caught my attention. That put me on edge. She had him working on some circles to calm him down but Relic had other things in mind. He started to do some mini rear ups and was trying to get closer to Fig. With my sore hip, I was not moving too fast. Thankfully Fig was much better about being led so I used his body to try to get ourselves to a safe position. Just as we came in past the door Relic, stopped rearing and began half passing to get closer to us. His rider's look of panic increased. He was getting closer and fast now.

"Oh crap!" was my first thought. Because I was on the ground I was also able to watch Figaro watching the whole scene. I could see Fig's posture. He stood upright and was getting puffed up. His ears were not back but his muscles became rock hard. You could have bounced a quarter off them. With a limp and really nowhere to go, I put myself in front of Fig with the whip in hand just in case. Not the safest thing but at least if I had to I could try to keep the boys away from each other. Fig had other ideas. He put himself between Relic and me, keeping me shielded like a mare protects her foal from other horses. He continued doing that no matter what position Relic took. Fig was always keeping his eye on Relic. It was nerve-racking but I felt so safe at the same time.

Luckily the rider regained control over Relic and she was able to get his mind back on work. Once all was calm again Figaro started to relax and I got up on him and I got his mind into work.

My eyes were really opened up and it all made sense. When Fig was in stud mode, he was more worried about protecting me than attacking another horse.

Fig never did knock another horse down after that first time. I came to realize that when he was on guard, he didn't want to hurt anybody. He was like a young man in a big man's body. He was trying to say something but no one could understand what he was saying. After this episode, I saw that he was maturing. I think that time out in the field let him figure things out and if anything learn his place. I am glad he realized that I meant something to him and that I had at least earned his friendship. This is another reason I started to trust his judgment more.

The one thing I most admire about horses is that sometimes even the toughest can be as gentle as a lamb, especially to the disabled or to a child. I eventually realized that the big tough boy show he put on was what it was -- a show. He would stand up when the need arose. Instead of letting his true side come out, he felt he had to be defensive. I had to step back and realize that this rebel was just not sure of himself. He needed to be guided. He was not dumb by any means; the key was not, as Frank had suggested, to get him thinking less – but to get him thinking *more*. A child who misbehaves at school sometimes just needs to be redirected. I was now listening. I knew this much: Figaro was truly a good soul.

Always an Adventure

When I boarded my horse I wanted honesty. No matter how good or bad, I wanted to know. I have boarded my horse at various facilities and worked at various facilities and there is nothing worse than people hiding things. In relationships among horse owners, facility owners and workers and horse themselves, we all deserve the courtesy of the truth. As much as we all like hearing praise, it is good to know when something is not working. To better understand my equine partner, I have to know: what was his day like? Maybe he had an off day. Humans do. Animals do too.

At the barn I got my wish. No one held back in telling me anything about Figaro. Some days I admit I would cringe when I heard the words, "You know what your horse did today? "On the other hand, I was pretty used to it at this point and the stories were interesting most of the time. By the end, it was hard not to chuckle a bit. Fig was always a source of entertainment.

Most tales involved Figaro's escapes -- whether it was opening the arena door to go to the mare's barn or opening his own stall door. He had a brain and he used it.

On two occasions Figaro managed to escape from his stall. Because he was able to hang his head out of his stall it gave him a bit more opportunity. How he managed to manipulate the lock open amazed me since it was hidden by a piece of wood. He would have had to really bow his head and stretch out his lips to get underneath. With those strong lips he managed. After his first escape, he was found in the hay stall standing on top of the bales munching away. Luckily he was cornered so he was caught and put back in his stall.

For his second escape, he managed to get out and visit some of his old herd mates. Figaro was quite intrigued by one of the older mares, one named Chestnut. She was well beyond her breeding years but Fig was quite taken by her and was trying to woo her. Meanwhile, this was irking the other stallions in the stalls adjacent to Chestnut, along with some other mares and a gelding. This time Figaro thought being caught was not as much fun and he had to be herded around the H shaped barn till he went back into his stall. Eventually Chuck, a resident boarder and maintenance man, put a chain on Fig's stall so he could no longer undo the latch. In Figaro's eyes one door closes and another one opens.

Due to the number of stallions at this barn, turnout was short and they would be rotated among the six paddocks and the arena. Figaro would generally play and roll during the first few minutes. People were quite amused to watch him, especially when he rolled, because he made such groaning sounds as he rolled from side to side. However, once he was done rolling, Fig would look to find stuff to amuse himself. Sometimes he would take whips out of the whip container or pull a shank off the rack near the stairs or basically anything he could find to play with and pass the time. When he had too much time to think, the arena's small side door to the mare's barn was the next step. The latch was a finicky, older style latch and had to be pressed down then out. Most times I would have issues with it. It didn't line up properly when it latched or it just plain stuck. How Fig got it open I'll never be sure.

Ciara, one of Frank's more experienced students, would handle Figaro more than some of the others. Frank generally did not let his younger students handle him. At the beginning only Frank himself or Joseph, his right-hand man, handled Fig since he constantly tested people. With each passing day Fig was mellowing out.

One time when Ciara went to get him, she noticed the side door open. That particular day the mares were in. She could hear some nickering squeals and Figaro's grumbling. As she walked in Figaro was making moves on one of the mares because she had just come into heat. When Ciara went to approach him, Figaro changed his mind and decided it was time to bail away from the scene. The aisle way was no bigger than 10 feet across. With his size and his brains working overtime, he dodged the chasers. There was no escape because the end door was closed. Fig had decided that catch me if you can was a better idea. Luckily Ciara had closed the door. Fig could not get out. Still, being caught was not one of his ideas. He turned around and galloped full tilt. Ciara jumped out of the way. I can't blame her in the least. A horse will generally stop if you wave your hands. Obviously this wasn't working. Fig was not that easily intimidated unless he was well out numbered. After a few attempts it was clear that Fig just did not want to be caught. A few more recruits came in and they finally caught him.

In some barns there is always that one horse that most people do not want to take out. Fig was that one at this time. Laura told me once that they almost drew straws to see who would take him out. I couldn't blame them. I was used to this and generally at this point he never gave me the same trouble as he did with others.

Figaro was crafty and he managed to get out of the arena many times. Chuck had to put a new latch on the door, one that required a push and a turn. Figaro was foiled once again. Even his paddock gates needed to be tied shut or chained. The outdoor paddock latches deployed a piece of wood that slid into the next gate. Most horses don't bother. Figaro managed to figure it out. This mainly happened when he thought the grass looked better on the other side or he ran out of hay. Idle hands do the devil's work. I would later see this for myself. When I was riding near the mares paddock (luckily the mares were in), he demonstrated how to unlatch their gate and this is where I learned that he could push the gate open himself and close it with his nose. I still had to latch it. I was fortunate that Figaro would let me hang half way off his side to close it.

I was grateful that about 98% of the farm was locked up. There was only one paddock, however, that was not enclosed (with gates and perimeter fencing) like the others. This one was at the bottom of the driveway and it was no bigger than 30' x 30'. It was big enough. It overlooked the mares paddock and the little red barn. Eventually this would be Figaro's paddock most of the time. He earned this privilege after he got better about being led.

In spite of all his escapes he was improving more and more. Eventually the teenage girls started handling him. Fig was pretty good as long as he had a chain over his nose. Probably Frank's best advice when it came to stallions was that you never let your guard down. Stallions are like sleeping lions; you never know when they will wake up.

The Great Escape

We had been at Frank's farm a few years and Figaro was getting better under saddle.

In fact, he had gotten better about most things. Frank was away on a trip and Rose was running the farm till her dad got back. All seemed fine.

It was a nice warm summer day and we had come up to see Fig. I had gone through my general routine with him and I noticed he was tired. Figaro was not a fan of the heat. This particular day, I also noticed he was wet and he seemed dirtier than normal too. I didn't think too much about it since Joe, Frank's right hand man, would sometimes take the stallions out and hose them down on the hotter days.

When I rode Fig he was very sluggish, not himself. Part way through the ride, Tracy came into the arena and after a moment or two told us that Figaro had escaped earlier. Rose came down and filled us in on the details.

Fig was in a small sand paddock at the base of the hill when you came in. You had to leave the barn to go through the small gate then you were in an open area.

Fig had done this for a while and had been doing well. One of the girls became more confident with Fig and instead of putting the shank over his nose they decided to just clip it to the underside of his halter. For safety reasons, one other girl went with her. Fig walked out but when they went to pass the small red barn and the bit of grass, Fig went for the grass and dragged young Helen. He then went to go around the apple tree in the front. This caused Helen to lose the shank. There would have been no chance to stop Figaro at this point, even if she hung on. He saw his opportunity and he ran with it.

Figaro realized he was free. He trotted up the drive way, up to the house. At the time poor Rose was in the house. She had just woken up. Rose thought she something run past her window. She looked. Nothing was there. Again, there was that feeling of something lingering outside, in the shadows, amongst the trees, big or small? Rose drew back her curtains to take a better look. As she turned to leave her room there was rustling outside her window. Now she was hearing hooves. At this point she was having breakfast and was still in her pyjamas. It wasn't till the girls called for her and told her Fig was loose that she knew what was going on. Fig ran around the play set a few times, went around the house then headed for the road.

What he did on this journey was a mystery. By now Rose had thrown on some clothes and headed down the road. Before she left, Rose made a few calls then made a few house visits, stopping anyone along the way for information. She finally managed to track where he was. He was at a neighbour's property – 5 kilometres away. Figaro had managed to scare a guy cooking breakfast on his raised deck, chased somebody's dog, and then he rolled and became a brown horse.

Luckily Fig had crossed fields, backyards and forested areas instead of staying on the road on his cross-country journey. His last stop was a neighbouring farm that belonged to Doug, a friend of the Frank's family. Rose and others had undertaken a frantic search and were at the point of saddling up horses to search that way when the call came. "We have your Friesian here," Doug said.

Doug said they had to give chase to wrangle Fig into the round pen. He wasn't an easy catch.

We later saw Doug to thank him and give him a gift. I felt we couldn't apologize enough for all the hassle Fig had put them through. I was just grateful at this point that my horse was alright.

Doug described being in the barn and hearing a squealing noise. When they went outside they saw a dirty brown horse making the moves on one of their mares. Doug didn't want this rogue horse from who knows where breeding his horses. Luckily he was on the other side of the fence. During the roundup one of their horses, a gelding, went galloping and he just took a tumble.

Doug quickly analyzed the situation and was on top of it. A worker on the farm ran down the long driveway and closed the front gates of the property. This prevented Fig from going onto the road and into the next property; it also allowed them to trap Fig in one of the aisles between the paddocks. As Doug grabbed the shank, Fig took off in a gallop with poor Doug hanging on with all his might. From what his wife said he was basically leaping alongside. She said it was quite a sight.

After their battling, they got Fig into the round pen and called Rose. Frank's farm was the first place they called because Doug knew they had stallions. Rose confirmed it was Figaro and said she would come right over. But Doug insisted on bringing him back. I remember my mom and me measuring the 5-kilometre distance between the two farms. Fig had covered the distance in short order. Not bad for a horse not bred for speed. Doug walked him over to the farm. Rose said Doug came over the hill with Figaro; Doug looked like a knight in shining armour. Rose met Doug at the path at the edge of their property. When he arrived Rose said there were lots of chains around him over the nose, in the mouth and over the head. At least he was not going to escape again. Then Rose took poor Doug back to his farm. He must have been tired.

The girls attempted to call my mom and me and couldn't get a hold of us.

I did feel bad that I rode the poor guy after the day he just had. In the end I was happy that no harm or injuries had befallen anyone involved in the Great Escape. After giving him a good bath, I told Fig that if he ever scared me like that again, it was the glue factory for him – and I meant it. He seemed to heed my words and from that day on he never escaped his paddock or went cross-country trekking again.

First Trail Ride

These were the adventures in the early years when Fig was still pretty green. I still had him in a snaffle bit.

I remember it was a nice day and Natalie, Laura, Tracy and I were heading out on a trail ride around the fields. They asked if I wanted to join. With some persuasion from Laura, I went along. I remember saying to them whatever you do don't gallop up the hill. I knew Figaro would get excited when other horses galloped. I remember Laura saying, "Don't worry. We won't."

We walked for a bit and all was fine. As we went into the mare's field, there was a dip, and then you crossed a ditch with a small stream before ascending a steep hill.

The girls had gone over. Laura was the last of the trio. I was still on the other side. As Laura went over, they all took off at a gallop. Not two seconds later, Fig leaped the ditch, I lost one stirrup and he galloped plus bucked up the hill. I managed to keep my seat and made it up the hill. When we reached the top, Figaro stopped and stood there like nothing had happened. I remember turning to Laura and the rest of the gang and saying, "What happened to 'we are not going to gallop up the hill'?"

We had a good laugh. If I did not have a seat in the saddle, I was getting one now.

From Houdini to Comedian

Fig was not only an escape artist but was a comedian. His days of escaping were over. Now his sense of humour came to the surface.

One thing he loved to do was play. Over the years, I always felt like Alec playing on the beach in the *Black Stallion* movie. Fig would chase me around the arena and he would buck, leap and perform other playful antics. Because he was studdy, I made sure to have a whip in hand just in case. I never really had any problems; it was just that he came too close. However, there was something so mesmerizing about this big black horse and the way he moved and how he did come so close. Sometimes I would jog beside him. It's hard to explain the feeling. You just felt in awe when you were so close. In a way we started to move as one and we knew how to read each other. There is no greater feeling than having a horse just enjoying life, including yourself as well. This was not something taught. This is what a bond is all about.

Sometimes Fig forgot that there is a time and a place for play. He did not understand that not everybody could understand him. Laura was one of Frank's pupils and she learned this when she wanted to bring him in one day. He had upgraded to one of two paddocks now: the one by the mares field or another single paddock that was close to the house amid a bunch of trees on a hillside. There was a small gap between the paddocks so the horses could not reach each other, then a small sand paddock in front. Fig generally got the back paddock since many of the stallions were being used and it was just easier. I liked it since he got some shade. When it came time to bring Fig in, he would at least come to the gate. That made things easier. He would stand there and wait for the shank to be put on. He was even getting to the point where he would move his head to make putting the chain on easier.

This day he was at the top of the paddock, but he didn't when she called him come so she went to get him. He decided to have a game of tag before going in. So poor Laura ended up running around the trees for a good 15 minutes, dodging the trees while running up and down the hill, trying not to trip on rocks and fallen branches or slips and fall on the hill. Finally he got bored and decided to come in. Laura told me later that she was intimidated during this game of tag but knew she wasn't in any immediate danger. Part way through she started to play with him. He would toss his head and hop a bit in his joy. Laura was daunted because he was a big boy; that was a good 1300 lbs of horse running behind you. As someone would later say, the day he realizes his strength and brains and uses them against you, you have no shot.

I should have turned him into a cutting horse. Regardless, Fig just liked a good game of tag. A few years down the road, one of the boarders and the girls were having fun running around the arena. Fig was good at this point and they decided they wanted him to chase them. Still cautious, I said it wasn't a good idea. Despite my warning, Kristen insisted. Luckily the side arena door was there, slightly open, just in case. When she ran, Fig was cutting her like a cutting horse would a cow. I had the reins, held loose in the Western style, so there was no danger.

At Frank's we had fun. Where most people worried about doing things this way and that way, we did do things outside the box -- but in a good way. This, in turn, made for confident riders and bold horses. Eventually your eyes are opened to what horses are capable of doing. There was the time, for example, the herd came into the arena through the back door when their horses and riders in there. We did not get off the horses. Frank just said, "Go to the corner," and the horses went to their stalls. In such cases the odd horse would want wander over and visit but you just made a move and they went on their merry way. Where most people would panic when someone was hosing down the dust in the arena and most horses would spook, we would just ride through it. It was the best bombproof training ever.

In her game of tag with Fig, Kristen realized she was not going to get past him. As she backed up, she was looking for the door handle and escaped. We both laughed. I told her she wouldn't win. It was not threatening but just play. For a horse his size, Fig had some pretty good moves. A bee is not anatomically built for flight, yet it flies. Figaro was large he never seemed to let his size dictate what he was able to do. He would prove many nay sayers wrong, many times.

Other than playing tag Fig also liked to grab lead shanks or halters off the door and toss them across the aisle. On occasion he would grab the odd bale of hay that came into reach when they threw down hay. He would then pick it up and put it in his stall. He had the strength and his neck was getting thicker each year. His crest was solid.

When I groomed Fig, I just brushed him in his stall. It was easier since there was always traffic in the aisles. There were horses going back and forth in the aisles as well as riders and even dogs. I liked to and always did take my time on my visits to the farm. They were never short. The least amount of time would be a minimum of four hours. An hour of it was just brushing. I used about ten different brushes, a shedding blade if it was shedding season or to scratch his armpits, which he loved. I used a massaging curry first, then a black normal rubber curry comb, then a rubber mitt for the not as easy to reach sections. From there I would use a hard brush, then a softer brush. Up next was a soft, long-bristled brush. Then a finishing brush to polish. A small brush was used for Fig's face, then a rag. I used a nice mane and tail brush for the finishing touches. I liked my buddy to gleam. I never once had him clipped and I just good old fashioned elbow grease. People always asked what product I used to get him so shiny and clean. The best product, I would reply, was me, myself and I. Brushing your horse is when you not only clean your horse but develop a bond. You can see if there are cuts and blemishes or what is out of the norm. This is how I discovered a weird mark on the side of his sheath. You could tell where there had been an incision made about three inches long and where there was a scar that indicated about fourteen stitches. I thought this very odd since most castrations are done underneath for better drainage. Here was evidence of a side castration, suggesting that the surgeon had gone in searching for the other testicle. The scar also suggested that Fig's studdiness had a history, and that a previous owner had tried to fix it with surgery. All of this would eventually mean a lot more to me later on.

Fig was always full of surprises.

I remember when he just arrived at this farm and he was in the first stall on the left. I would brush Fig in his stall without tying him up. He got the idea and enjoyed being brushed as he as ate a flake of hay. It was quiet in the barn since everybody had gone up to the house for lunch.

All was well. Anyone who has ever brushed a horse will know that a brush can spontaneously jump out of your hand. That happened. I bent down to get the brush and before I could blink he had my belt and the back of my pants in his teeth and he picked me off the ground.

The weirdest thing was that he just held me there. It was only a moment but it felt a lot longer when your toes are a couple inches off the ground (the whole 130 pounds of me at the time). I wasn't frightened. After working at the track for some time, I learned not to panic, because truly deep down I was not scared. Then he just put me down and went back to eating hay. I remember just looking at him and from that day I really had a respect for Fig's strength.

I realized afterward that I generally had carrots in my back pocket and he thought he would seize the moment. Instead of a carrot, he got my belt. It wasn't an attack. What I gained from the incident was trust. He didn't want to hurt me but with his strength, he could.

When it came to saddling him, thank goodness for Wintec synthetic saddles. He was good about me hanging the saddle on the chain on his door. On occasion he liked to pick the saddle up and toss it across the aisle if I was taking too long to saddle him up. Another thing he liked to do was to take his halter or lead off the door if he was trying to get some one's attention, mainly mine. I still have that Wintec saddle and it is in the best shape ever even after 12 years of constant use.

Figaro's penchant for picking up items should have been my clue to his future as a trick horse. The first true indicator was when he used to pick up my whip when I dropped it. Getting it out of his mouth was another story. He would eventually let it go. He grew out of that habit, but he still liked to grab the whip when I was leading him or getting on. He would just hold it.

On a ground work day, Figaro liked to grab the lunge whip the odd time and make the snapping noise with it. He was showing me what he eventually was going to tell me. I was just not quite sure in those days. I just thought that Fig was too human.

Figaro had gotten much better about standing still and most of the time I mounted off the ground. This is a vital thing for a rider to learn. There will not always be a rock, stool or log to use to get up. If it is done right, you will not be reaming on a horse's back while mounting. This requires staying fit and getting the right momentum to take the pressure off. What about aches and pains? I have trochanteric bursitis in both hips. I could not walk straight if my life depended on it. My greatest accomplishment is mounting a 19-hand high Percheron from the ground, unassisted.

There was one particular winter day that this was no exception. In the cold I was a bit stiffer than usual and I was not as limber as usual. I had taken an Extra Strength Advil to help me out. I had taken Figaro to the center of the arena where we did our small lunging circles with just the reins. I had just finished pulling my stirrups down and was standing by his side ready to get my foot in the stirrup. Once I got my foot in place, it generally took a couple of tries to be up and over.

In the beginning he used to walk away when I was mounting. After many sessions, he no longer did that – but this didn't mean he stopped thinking. Mounting was somewhat of a chore sometimes. For the most part I mounted from the ground, even when my hip was sore. I was not going to give in and use a mounting block. I believe in strengthening the muscles within reason. This time, when I was going into my second bounce to get up on Fig's back, I just did not seem to get more than two feet off the ground. I was tired but this was pathetic. So I tried again. This time I got a bit higher and could feel a tug on my jacket. I thought I was hung up on something. When I turned around to see what I was stuck on, I realized what it was. I was attached to Fig's mouth. Mr. Comedian had grabbed the bottom of my jacket as I was trying to get on. How he grabbed it without me feeling it took talent. At that moment all I could say to him is, "Smart ass." He then pulled me gently back and I eventually got him to let my jacket go. That day I used the stairs to mount my horse.

Some days it was just too hard not to love him.

An Arena Is an Empty Canvas

As much as Fig and I had our adventures, many of our rides were non-eventful and rather enjoyable. I always like to tell others an arena is like an empty canvas. It is up to you to make it into a work of art. Many people will say dressage is boring. Yet I find many people seem to fall in to the same rut, and most do not ever notice this. Sometimes I think it because we spend so many years getting lessons and training for us and our horses. Some people have hard time thinking outside of the box even when they know things they can work on. Such riders fall into what I call circle-itosis: they never go out or beyond the circle, and some only work at one end of the arena. Circles are great strength builders. They can calm an excited horse or help a horse learn to bend and balance. However you need to do more. Some riders will only work one end of the arena because the horse spooks at the other end. If anything, I will work a spooky horse more in that area. The number one problem for most horses is boredom. Think about it. Wouldn't you get bored working on circles all the time? So do they.

When you have a horse that thinks like Fig, doing the same old thing just gave him the opportunity to think more. And when he thought, mischief resulted. There was one time he protested. He backed up to the end wall and sat down on the edge of the kick board wall and refused to move. Another reason I never taught him to sit (I also just find it too hard on a horse's hocks).

That is why even in those early days when we were still working on the basics -- transitions and leg yielding -- I liked to put him to the test. We generally worked on figure eights, serpentines and more. To make things more interesting, instead of a normal three-loop serpentine I would make it a six-loop. Our transitions were from walk to trot, trot to canter or halt to canter. The key was changing it up. In time I would make a clover leaf pattern to make things different. Once he had gotten the concept of leg yielding, instead of just leg yielding along the wall or walking up the center then leg yielding to a corner of the arena, I got inventive and would make him leg yield a diamond shape. I would start at "C" or "A" (each end of the arena), then leg yield to the center of the long side then back to the center mark. Once I reached the end, I would make him pivot on his hind end and then continue. It was challenging stuff like this that made him think. Once he got the concept, he got the turn on the forehand (pivoting with the front end) and turn on the haunches (pivoting with the hind end). This was all meant to make his mind work and stimulate both mind and body.

Most arenas do not have pillars. These are two fairly large poles that stand in the middle of the arena, typically no wider than ten feet apart with a tie on each pole. This is generally used to teach the horse pillar work such as the *piaffe* and *levade*. A rider wanting to perform this next exercise with his or her horse could always use two pylons or two jump standards. Sometimes I would use a person to pivot around. This requires lots of trust on all parties, however, and it's certainly not for everyone.

You may ask how much can you could do with these poles. I say plenty -- if you think outside the box. Sometimes I would get Fig to leg yield sideways through the poles or do small figure eights. As I discovered later, it would help him achieve tight turns for barrel racing. I even would get him to do small circles facing the pole and have his head facing the pole then pivot on his front end or hind end around the pole. To make things more interesting, I would pivot on the front, then get him to leg yield through the poles sideways, followed by a pivot on his hind end. To change it up, occasionally I would do this with his back end touching the pole the whole time. You can even spice up a standard diagonal by adding a small figure eight around the pole then continuing on.

Even the spookiest horse can manoeuvre like this. The challenge gives them less time to think. I have had people tell me their horses are scared of the doors at the end of the arena. Generally it comes down to the rider having to stop thinking about it. Horses feel more than you would ever know. Occasionally I would have a rider sing a stupid song while riding and actually make them sing the words, not just hum or dum-dee-dum through it. Sing the same song over and over as you are riding around the arena. Depending on the horse, within minutes, the horse will pass that corner he is afraid of with no problem. The problem is that issues become a crutch and then they remain a crutch. You just need to push the boundary. Most of all just have confidence.

This is how I discovered so much about Fig. I had seen an article in a magazine about cavalry training. Many people reading this piece would conclude that the exercises are too dangerous. They don't understand why that type of work was done. In those days and for that soldier, his horse was his life line. He needed to rely on that horse to get him through the war.

A photo in the magazine article shows a cavalry officer standing on his horse's back while firing a gun. Does this feat have a military purpose? No. It is mainly a demonstration of trust. The key was where you stood on the horse's back. Riders who get bucked off while standing on a horse's back are often on the wrong spot. First and foremost, don't use shoes that can dig into the horse's back. Secondly, don't stand over the horse's kidneys. Some will stand on the saddle. My spot of choice was the plumpest part over the hind end on top of the croup, just ahead of the horse's tail. My first inclination to do this was that something inside my head just said, do it. Many will say it is dangerous. If you don't use your head, most things are dangerous. You just need to use common sense. Next to that it is important to have faith.

I remember my first attempt. While in a sitting position, I got my feet behind the saddle. Once he was still and relaxed, I then put my hands on the pommel and pushed myself up a bit. If he moved, I thought, I can get back into the saddle quickly. Again he did not move and his ears were relaxed as well as his muscles. In a flowing motion, I moved my feet back so they were placed on his croup and then I slid my body back. I was crouched on his hind end and still I got no reaction from Fig. My knees were generally stiff so I had no choice other than to stand up in one motion. I kept the reins in my hand, just in case. Still nothing. If anything, he was so relaxed that he had tipped up one leg as if he was going to sleep. Then with full faith, I put the reins over the pommel of my saddle. He turned and looked at me. That was it.

There was always something to test our friendship. He always accepted in some way each olive branch I handed out to him.

That made Fig priceless – to me at least. I told people all the time that you could offer me a million dollars but Fig was never going to be sold. This I say from the bottom of my heart.

After one of our great sessions one summer, I gave him a bath and put him back in his stall. Almost every time I was there the barn was full of life, this day was quieter than usual. Frank was not around and his daughters were in charge at this point. Another reason the barn was quiet could have been due to reduced lessons while he was not around. Regardless, because Frank taught classical dressage and had Lusitanos, it was never surprising to see someone come into the barn looking for lessons or inquiring about horses.

I was starting to clean my bridle when an older gentleman walked in. He had silver hair and dark shades on. He was clean cut and by the way he approached and spoke, you could tell he was been well off. He came around the corner and then said, "Good afternoon." He mentioned that he was in the market for a dressage horses and asked if there were any such horses up for sale. He also inquired about lessons. I told him that Frank or his daughters were more likely the best people to speak with because I was just a boarder. He muttered something under his breath about coming back later to inquire again. He was going to check out a couple other farms. He was looking for a dressage horse. When he strolled down the aisle of the barn I kept my eye on him. After a moment or two, he stood in front of Fig and asked if he was for sale. I told him no because he was my horse. He said he liked his look and liked black horses personally. I think he must have thought Figaro was an Andalusian or a Friesian. I said, "Thank you. He is not for sale." After a moment he just looked at Fig then looked at the other horses in the aisle. He came back again and asked me if I was sure he was not for sale. The gentleman asked if I would you take $10,000 for him.

I said, "No." At this point I was thinking that this guy must be pulling my leg. That is when he pulled out a book of business cheques.

I said it again, "Sorry, he is not for sale." I was getting more perturbed that this guy did not get it. *Figaro was not for sale.*

It was then he said, "What about $50,000? I really like the look of him."

The man had his pen out and had already started to write out the cheque. To show me he was serious, he said, "You can authorize this at a bank first if you like."

I stood by my conviction and once again said firmly, "Sorry, he is not for sale."

He said, "What a shame." He said he would come back.

Later when I saw one of Frank's daughters I told them about this guy. They would keep a look out. I never know if he came back or not. In the horse world you never know who is up to no good. He could have been an honest guy looking for a horse. Maybe he found something he liked somewhere else. In any case, I never saw him again. I just remember looking at Fig when I took him out to the field to graze, which was always our routine in nice weather. It was just our time to be together. All I could think of that day was wow. There is something people see in you, bud. That was some pretty good money to be offered. I am glad I never accepted any offers for Figaro over the years, because he gave me more than money could ever buy.

All Work and No Play...?

It was important to me to treasure our moments together. Not long after the offer to buy Figaro I knew and appreciated the time we spent in each other's company –working or playing.

After the incident with Relic in the arena, I found I was better able to put more trust in him and riding became easier. I knew he wasn't out to hurt me, so I had to change my approach. It is hard to explain. In simple terms, what I would do with one horse didn't work with Fig. Too much repetition and he would get bored. And if he got bored that is when the fight would begin again. So we had to look for an alternative.

We didn't always concentrate on riding. We liked to play. Because of the problems I had with my hip or if Fig had a stone bruise, our riding would get put on hold. I began to work him loose in the arena. This is where I learned he just likes to play. For a big boy, he would buck, leap and run. It was during our playtime I realized I could get him to come with a whistle. When you teach a horse they come when whistled. You have them on a lead and when you whistle give a gentle pull and when they move toward them praise them. In time you increase the distance. Figaro did this on his own accord.

Horses, like humans, can't be working all the time. Fig needed breaks to avoid becoming ring sour. I probably wouldn't recommend playing in the way that I'm about to describe unless you can fully trust your horse.

Playing with Fig was not for the faint of heart. He would gallop within inches of your side and without knocking you over, or he would buck a safe distance away. He never struck at you. He would always stay at least ten feet away. Regardless, it required lots of trust.

As time went on, we learned each other's moves. He would cut like a cutting horse and follow me like a puppy. I always had a whip in hand to be safe but I never had to use it – primarily because he did not spook easily. I would try to chase him around for a bit of exercise. The result was myself getting more exercise than him. I could get so close and have the lunge whip snapping almost as loud as a gunshot and he just stared at me. I would test him some more and eventually I found I could crack the whip behind him or snap it in the air above his head. Figaro would not twitch a muscle.

Up in the saddle, I learned too that many things didn't spook him easily -- whether it is someone tossing a whip or dogs running by or loud noises. This was a blessing especially when it came to winter riding and half the snow on the arena roof would come crashing down because of the sun melting it. Most horses panic at the roar of snow sliding off a roof. If I could hear the snow moving overhead, I would stop and then he would direct his ears forward and listen. Fig would be alert but when the snow came down he just stood there. I tell other riders it is just like driving a vehicle; you always need to be looking ahead and be aware. Remember, though, that sitting on top of a horse is different. Unlike the vehicle, the horse can think and feel. If you're on a horse and you see a dog running across a field, acknowledge it. When the moment comes and the dog comes out of nowhere you will not be surprised, and therefore if your horse spooks his reaction will not be as extreme, because you know it is coming. The key for the rider is to stay calm and not tense up. Just breathe. Even though the horse spooks if you are calm you will find the horse relaxing much quicker because you are not tensing up. They can sense it. This is the key to most successful trainers: calmness. How do you think they get results? They do because the horse senses the calm and learns to trust that handler or rider. That is all any horse wants is for you to guide them. My bond with Figaro grew because he knew he could trust me.

Because of lessons and human and horse traffic at the barn, I started riding outside more. The mare's paddocks were right beside the arena. This was also a good way to teach Figaro to keep under control. Frank did this with his stallions many times. The mares most of the time would stand by the fence line with their foals for some entertainment or when it was time to come in. Fig was usually okay with them there. The odd time would he nicker or have that fifth leg out. Interestingly, the mares were good and stayed out of reach.

This is where I learned that Fig liked foals.

It was spring time and Frank was having a lesson so I went outside. The new foals had arrived and were content playing around. I was hesitant when they came up to the fence since "mom" would generally intervene. One colt, a little bay named Loki was by the fence. Every time I trotted by with Figaro, Loki would gallop alongside the fence. He did this quite a few times. Eventually I stopped but kept Fig a little distance away just to see his reaction. He was very relaxed. Loki was trying to reach for him and luckily mom was by the pond so I brought Fig closer, slowly, to the point they were touching noses. Mister big and tough was a suck for babies. People say stallions wouldn't do that or the rider should not allow it. People also forget that in herds, stallions do deal with foals. They are not dumb either. I think this little guy knew that Fig posed no threat and both were fine. Sometimes your intuition just tells you and so far it was not wrong. Fig was a big old teddy bear. Eventually when we moved along and went back to work, Loki would wait for us to go by and he would buck and gallop. This natural behaviour could spook some horses. Fig seemed to just enjoy it and would give an ever so slight buck back. Later I would learn that Fig had a similar affection for children as well.

Each day I came to see Figaro I was learning more about him. On the occasional evening I would ride in the outdoor arena, which thankfully had a few lights. The lights were not really bright and produced lots of shadow. At the same time Fig felt more invigorated in the cooler evening and he liked the night riding. Some of our best rides were at that time. The shadows and noises never bothered him. Sometimes I felt like we should

69

play and pretend to re-enact the ride of the headless horseman from the story, *The Legend of Sleepy Hollow.* Fig would have been game for that. Riding out at that time was just wonderful. I remember us casting shadows across the ground or into the trees as we cantered by. It was mesmerizing to see. Things were getting better.

The quietest moments were just as special.

The afternoons were reserved for siesta time. Not for Figaro. Most times it was difficult to catch Figaro lying down. He was a pretty proud horse and I think in his eyes he needed to be on guard all the time. On a warm summer day I noticed his head was not up, like it usually was. Nor did I hear his low grumble nicker. So I took my time taking each step, as quiet as a child trying to sneak past a parent. As I approached and peered over the stall wall, there he was, a small glimmer of light shining down upon his back. He was not lying on his side; he was half way up with his muzzle nestled into the shavings. I slid underneath his gate and sat down softly on his hay by his head. For a moment, he raised his head without even opening his eyes. He must have realized it was me and within seconds his big muzzle was back nestled in the shavings. I just sat there and looked at him. This big mighty boy just looked so peaceful. He was in such a deep sleep, and within seconds he was dreaming. You could hear him making soft nickering noises in his sleep. He would do this around mares or if he was happy. All I could think was, "*What little filly are you wooing in your dreams?*" After another few moments, he finally decided to lie on his side. If this is not trust I don't know what is. Horse will not leave themselves exposed if they do not feel comfortable. I sat there and let him sleep. He was just so peaceful. I did not have all the time in the world to stay up there but it if it meant sacrificing some riding time it was fine by me. I enjoyed his presence and looking at him as the little light rippled over his great heaving chest while he breathed. It was these small moments that I needed and wanted to enjoy. There is more to having any animal than just one purpose or even a relationship. If you can't enjoy the small things, then you will never appreciate the big things.

Let's try Croupa

Both Figaro and I were always up to trying something new. He was growing in more ways than one. By this point Fig had really matured and was quite fun to be around.

One day Laura was sitting on the stairs talking to me while I rode. I know Frank wanted to use Figaro to do what is called Croupa. This is when there is a male rider on a horse with a female behind the rider sitting sideways and wearing what looks like a flamenco dress. The croupa can be seen in most Portuguese parades. Laura thought we should try it out. Since Fig had a broad backend he would have been perfect for riding croupa.

I wasn't too sure, but Laura was game. She was going to ride side saddle, I was glad I said, "Ride astride directly behind me." Just to play safe, I took Fig to the stairs and she got on. All was fine for the most part until about twenty feet from the stairs. I guess he did not like the extra weight, who knows. Figaro decided to show his detest and started to buck. I told Laura to hang on tight; I could feel her grip a bit harder to keep her balance. We went for a good round around the arena. It's a good thing Laura had a good seat. Figaro's bucks were not violent, more of a slow motion type of buck. The bonus he had a nice broad back end which gave her a better seat. With his hind power he could have some oomph behind the bucks. I finally got Fig to settle and Laura jumped off.

I think it startled her. It took her a moment and I said, "You want to try again?" and she said, "I don't think he cares for it." So we basically scratched that idea for now till we had a new test dummy and a future dummy was about to come on the scene. He did not mind it later down the road but just at a walk.

Time to Put These Brains to Work

With many days of Fig and me on our own, my mind would just turn. Sometimes the most interesting things can be learned by observing. I was brushing Figaro in his stall when I say a fly land on his neck. I then watched him shake his head. It was then and there that I realized he was such a clever cookie. I have always liked watching the higher level dressage so another of my goals was to teach Fig to bow, if nothing else. It was this moment that I got the idea of imitating a fly. I took out my hoof pick and touched his neck further back, imitating a fly. Figaro responded by shaking his head. I rewarded him and again touched his neck with the hoof pick.

Within seconds he had figured it out and I could just point to his neck and he would say, "No."

From there I started figuring out things and Fig seemed to be on the same page as me. He seemed to be into this. I toyed with a couple things and within a first session we had almost completed a bow. The next session he got it. I figured out a cue so that in future it would not conflict with another cue. It was amazing to see him really shine. This was something he seemed to like to do. I don't believe in pushing a horse to do anything they don't like. A horse generally wants to please. Some will do it regardless because they are taught. Figaro, though, really seemed to enjoy it. The fact he started to pick up on it so fast was a bonus.

Any horse can learn a trick. In my eyes, he picked up on it so quick. Most tricks are things some horses already do. There are so many things you could teach a horse; I vowed that I wanted him to be dignified. I always like to consider the horse. There are limits and physical issues. Figaro was fit. He was a big boy and keeping his dignity in mind, I vowed not to teach him to sit or lie down. Because of his size and weight I did not want to perform the sit. Yes a horse will sit while getting up. This is something horses do not do on their own because it isn't something natural to them. Most things we teach even tricks are not natural. When it comes to things that require more strength or puts strain on their body. I weigh the options and decide is it really worth it or necessary for what I need them to know. Then I consider the individual horse as well and their capabilities.

Now the bow. A horse does this to get up and down or to get that one blade of grass under a fence. I wanted Fig to learn the circus bow, which is kneeling on one knee. This is harder on a horse and can be hard on the knees. That is why I would generally only ask him to do the bow on soft surfaces. My thinking was that that tricks would make him shine a bit more. People will judge a smart horse by all the things they know. I know a couple horses that know many tricks. One problem; they don't have an off button. This is something I wanted to keep in mind when working with Fig. I didn't want any of these tricks to become a nuisance or to be cued by accident. Luckily Figaro seemed to have a good concept about doing tricks. Some people don't understand that it is not a good practice to have your horse cue to everyday natural behaviour. Just because your horse paws the ground it does not mean you put a cue to it and encourage it. You must train the horse first to not do it and to respect you. From there you can teach your horse what you want him to do and when. You must be in control. Figaro taught me this and never once did I have any of his tricks become a nuisance. This is where his brain really made him stand out.

I have seen many smart horses just do things for the sake of doing things or to please. As I see it, a smart horse not only wants to work with you but also thinks and uses logic.

I will give Figaro full credit here. If you ask a smart horse to bow on rocky ground, he will bow and put his knee on the ground because he is asked to and because he wants to please. Did that horse feel obliged to please or because he *wanted* to do it for his owner? Asked to bow on rocky ground, Figaro would bow but keep his knee somewhat raised off the ground in order to avoid hurting his own knee. It is these small things that most people don't see. Tricks are always neat to watch and I constantly got requests. Many people just saw Figaro doing a trick. Only those observing closely could see that he was working in partnership with me. Frank was right. People, he said, always want to learn the cool stuff and don't necessarily want to take the time to learn it properly. I have had people ask me to teach their horse to bow. I don't just teach one thing. I take time to talk to people learn about them and their horses. Most times I will have to decline because of an issue. Some may like me for it, others will dislike me. However in time this is what has earned me respect. I could teach and take someone's money. In the end though I'm doing it for the welfare of the horse as well as the rider. If the person and horse are alright I may help guide them. If there is a red flag in my mind I will explain my reasons. In time I found I earned more respect from people for this. Money is not everything.

I have also been asked about teaching a horse to lie down so they can get on. In some cases, this involved an old horse with back issues and because the rider had limitations. I always like to explain myself and offer another choice. In one case, the person had a fused ankle. You can mount a horse from a lie down but you have to be aware that in time this can be hard on your horse. This is where you need to be able to assist the horse as well. If you watch any acts where a rider gets on and off a horse, make mental note. You will see most of these riders are able to mount the horse with ease, without a stool or stirrup. They rely on their strength and momentum to get on. They are not always fully relying on the horse and assist in their own way.

Figaro would learn many tricks and most of them were not too hard on him. In working with him, I always thought about how cool it would be if he ever became a movie horse. From there my dreams were born and I had a goal. I did want to show him and eventually I would perform in some of Frank's shows. This was my motivation. I had watched so many horse movies as a child, and now I started to watch them again. With my newfound interest I observed more. I knew the story but now I focused on the little nuances of each scene and how it worked overall. That is why most of my tricks with Fig were more practical. Next I wanted him to do tricks that did not require or include a bunch of pedestals or objects to perform. Sometimes one item can do so much. A tarp, for example. You can use a tarp to bombproof a horse but you can also teach the horse to pick it up, drag it or unroll it.

I have seen trick horse trainers lying on a horse's back. It demonstrates great trust. It can be hard on the horse's back. In learning anything; it seems to me, it's best not to look at one aspect. You need to look at the whole picture. This is that makes for a true horseman. It is not just about teaching things to your horse. It's about the bond. And that means taking into account the welfare of the horse. Let's say your horse can perform a bow. If done too much it can be hard on his knee and if your horse is not fit bowing can create back problems. Positively the bow can help stretch the muscle, just as yoga works for humans, but it needs to be done gradually. What worked to my benefit was that Figaro was fit. I worked with him 3 - 4 times a week. No matter the animal, once you make that commitment, you need to realize you have to be there for them. Our lives can become filled with commitments. We tend to forget and start making excuses. At one point, I was in high school, did night courses at college a couple times a week and still worked with Fig at least 3 evenings a week while working on the weekend. I was tired. Dedication, determination and drive pushed me.

We can always push the limits -- in every way and in all disciplines. Tricks were not going to be an excuse to not strive in riding as well. I find ground work is a great bonding process but some riders use it as an excuse to not get in the saddle. You can end up with a 20-year-old green broke horse. I tell people to put fundamentals under saddle first. Then go from there. This way you don't confuse the horse. It is alright to teach youngsters one thing: teaching the horse to stand on a stool will help them with trailering. When the horse's minds impressionable, you have to think about a trick becoming a nuisance and to factor in his growing body. I can work with a young horse and know when to stop.

This is what helped created such a strong bond with Fig. He had his blah days, days when giving him his liberty was a good idea. The next time we worked on dressage. If mentally we were not in that state, maybe just a trail ride. You need to change things up. Routine is good but sometimes we get nervous to go beyond that. Our work was progressing. Fig learned to bow, say no, nod yes and pick up an item. One time a girl at the barn was playing with his lip, so I worked a bit more with him and he smiled. That was the only trick he would perform when asked by others.

At least those tricks required not too much energy. I want to repeat: I wanted him, always, to be allowed to maintain his dignity. I was not going to treat him like a dog and make him a joke. At home my dog Sarah was trick trained. So what I would not train a horse could be easily performed with another animal. Each type of animal is unique they can learn the same trick as another. Just some have better capabilities to perform other forms of tricks. Figaro was a classy boy and regal in his ways. I was not going to degrade him in any way. I was going to see how far I could go with him -- in different ways.

Working with Figaro more and more. People always dream, but I found myself more driven toward a goal. In time I thought I would love to have Figaro excel at liberty as well as under saddle. My goal was to get my own farm and host charity events and more. To get some other horses and train them as well. The first step was to get him trained first.

Doe, a Deer...

I had my goals and dreams but every now and then we put it all aside for pleasure.

It was one of those days when the field horses were in and the back field was empty. I took full advantage of it since it was rare to be able to ride back there.

I am not the type to want to be always in the arena or do anything too repetitive. Then working with horses begins to feel like a chore. Besides, the back field offered Fig good exercise going up and down the hills.

We were half way through our ride when we passed the woods at the far west corner of the field. Fig heard something in the woods. I could hear rustling. I have pretty good eyesight and I could not make out a thing. I thought it was coyotes on the move. I still could not see anything. I thought it best to continue on. We did a second lap and we were about to go up this long sloping hill along the back half of the property near the fence line when a deer popped its head up and without hesitation took off up the hill on the opposite side of the fence. The deer had been hidden in the long dry faded coloured grass.

Fig for a moment stopped but then took off -- like a thoroughbred out of a starting gate -- after the deer. One thing is certain: this horse had one really powerful back end. He went with one big leap and was ready to race. The force sometimes was so great that if he caught you off guard I could have ended up with my legs propelled to his neck and me almost lying flat. My Aussie saddle saved me more than once. It would have not been too bad if Fig had not decided to leap at the same time going up the hill. The deer has long flowing strides and moved gracefully with ease through the tall grass. As the deer reached the top, it went to the right and Fig turned left. He then turned around to watch it bound off into the woods. That was exciting. How many people can say they got to gallop with a deer? At least Fig gave me that opportunity and I won't forget it. However, I told him next time to take it a bit easier on me.

The Judge and Jury

Figaro and I would have many memorable times. For almost three and a half years it was just him and me.

I had been working at the track for some time and now I was working in a new barn. I met Pierre, who would become my significant other and in later years he would be only a chapter in my life, just there. We had much in common or so I thought but that is another story unto itself. With both of us working at the track, it made things much easier. When you work at the track, it is hard to meet people who understand the hours and the life.

Thankfully it worked out for us both at the time. He was an animal person. That is what probably attracted me to him and he was a nice person. His only fault that I could see at the time was that he was at times a bit full of himself and he liked attention.

Some people are so charming and so convincing that some things get overlooked. I so badly wanted to leave home, and into my life came Pierre, a new man who seemed to support me in every way. I was working at the time, attending college, doing a correspondence course and, of course, I had Figaro. I had a full plate, an overflowing plate. Life on the track, meanwhile, had its own challenges.

In any case, I fell for Pierre's charm and charisma. If you ever want an honest opinion about another human being, trust an animal you trust. Everything in life happens for a reason; whether good or bad, these things make us who we are. What truly matters is that Figaro was there for me at all times, whether I listened to his verdict or not. That is the mark of a true friend.

Pierre and I were spending more time together, and we eventually started to court each other. After talking about Fig to Pierre, for what must have seemed to him endlessly, he was curious to meet my horse. It was time, so I invited Pierre up to the farm. My mom came that day as well. There was a clinic in the arena that day.

I was not able to ride Fig in the indoor arena with the large side doors open. I groomed and saddled him up and took him to the outdoor riding paddock on the other side of the mare's barn. It was warm and Figaro was a bit headstrong. Of course, Fig would do this when you were showing him off. Pierre bragged that he could ride him no problem. "I have ridden worse," he said.

The clinic was almost over and it soon cleared out. We were able to head into the arena. I said to Pierre, "Fine. Get on him and show me then." As I stood beside my mother we both watched on in anticipation to see what would happen. Pierre got on Figaro. Fig must have sensed his over the top self-confidence and that was a big no-no in his book. I legged him up. Pierre had the upper body strength. *If you could do that with ease*, I thought, *maybe he did ride as he claimed*. In the first minute or two, Fig gave him a hard time. I knew at this point that Pierre was going to gallop him around the arena to take the edge off. After a turn or so I turned to mom and said, "Fig is up to something." Pierre was thinking he was in control, but Fig wasn't backing down easily. Within a split second Fig took advantage of the open door and turned at a gallop out the door, never once signalling with his ears or showing any intention. Good thing for Pierre's reflexes. He moved his leg in time as Fig had turned so sharply around the corner of the door a barrel racer would have been envious. With such accuracy he turned the corner of the door putting his body so close as to not harm himself but he did take the stirrup off. Pierre would have had his leg grinded against the side or worse if it were not for his quick reflexes. He came out unscathed.

He gave Fig a little reprimand for his action then led him back into the arena. He just went back to like nothing happened. Pierre got off and remarked on how he almost had his leg taken off. I just shrugged and looked at mom. Mom just gave me that look and I said, "Well, you can't manhandle him."

For these two it was just the beginning of a long few years of battles. Animals generally took to Pierre. Figaro, however, just did not seem to give in so easily. Looking back, I compare it to a daughter taking home her boyfriend for the first time. In this case the father did not like the new boyfriend and was going to do anything in his power to make his life difficult. Pierre would give Fig goodies, which Fig accepted. But not all affection can be bought. I think in time Figaro just accepted that Pierre was not going to leave.

Pierre had been around horses since he was a child and had done most jobs related to horses when it came to handling horses. He was pretty good with bad horses. On the other hand, Pierre had sustained many injuries while doing that work. I had worked with just as many rogue horses and fared better.

In the beginning, he would say it was a fight between two dominant males. I laughed at this then but almost believed it. Figaro needed no convincing: he was dominant. He always carried himself with such pride even with that soft look in his eyes. Animals either have it or they don't. Human beings, likewise, either have it or they don't. Some seem to need to constantly do things or get things in order to make the appearance of dominance. Pierre, unfortunately, always seemed to need big trucks. He said he would use them to haul horses but we only shipped a few. It seemed it was more for show.

Pierre did help with the odd thing. When Fig thought he could throw his weight around, Pierre for the most part could get his attention. Fig was getting better but Pierre helped refine his behaviour. Over time when we would take Figaro out to graze, some of Frank's students would come out. Sometimes, we would let them help bath Figaro or even hold him while he grazed. Still, most humans just could not be on the same page with him -- or they just got arrogant. However, the big boy was not dumb by any means. When a child was around, he was bombproof. He never lifted a leg at anyone. If anything, he was becoming a bit of a favourite. Most people would just call out, "It's Fig!" as either he passed them or they passed him. Chuck the maintenance guy would go in his stall with ladders and without tying him up. Chuck would be drilling, hammering, wiring or fixing things. Figaro did not care.

He was just mellow. Some of the younger students used to follow us and ask questions. Pierre liked kids and enjoyed explaining things. I found him to be a big kid himself in many ways. For the most part Pierre was light hearted and would joke around. When there was something to teach someone, Figaro became the best teacher because he would just stand there.

When I introduced Pierre to Figaro playing with me Pierre was not afraid to run up beside him, give him a quick slap and have Fig chase him. The only thing that irritated me was when Pierre told me I did not know how to play with Figaro. In time, Pierre would dominate the play time and I became the one who worked Fig. When Pierre was not around, Figaro and I played. I would still run beside him, change direction just like we used to and always did. We knew how. Sometimes you try to give someone that one thing so they can feel good. It worked to my advantage. In time when Pierre saw that Figaro was intrigued with tricks, he encouraged me to work with him more.

But with Pierre, Figaro was not going to give in that easily either. On one occasion it was hot and instead of riding I figured I would just lunge him. I didn't feel like putting on the surcingle, side reins, bit and other equipment because that was the only way you could lunge him without getting dragged. So Pierre said he would lunge him with just the lunge line. No chain, just clipped underneath his halter. I told him it was not a good idea. Pierre, however, was not going to listen to me. I knew Fig was going to take full advantage. More and more I began to understand why this man got injured so often. It is good to be fearless sometimes but you should listen as well and not think about your pride.

It was a good thing nobody was in the arena. Frank must have stealthily come in because I did not notice him. Fig was okay at the walk, but when it came to the trot he wanted to drag Pierre and drag him he did. Pierre had strong hands and got Fig's attention with a simple jiggling of the lunge line. Pierre thought he had gotten his attention. When he went to start again, Fig decided to change tactics. He proceeded to rear up. Pierre managed to keep the line from getting tangled. For about ten minutes, the battle of wits continued.

Eventually with enough cursing in French and Frank chuckling, I asked him what Pierre was saying. "You don't want to know," said Frank. Pierre finally managed to get him to trot a few circles. I told him he needed to end on a good note. Who won this battle I can't say for sure. It was entertaining regardless.

It didn't end there. Pierre was good at massaging equines. I will give him that. He had learned from an equine vet he worked under. As smug as Pierre was, he could be good at observing on occasion. He had a knack for pin-pointing nerves and muscle problems. He tried to help me with my knees, hips and back on many occasions, unfortunately it did not make much improvement for me. With horses he did a good job.

With Fig, he got to know his movement and his muscles, so one day he started to work on him. Things were looking good and Fig was moving much better. One day he must have moved funny and Pierre could see he was stiff on his back. When he went to work with him, Fig was not too keen. The massage must have bothered him so when Pierre went to work on the troubled back area Fig reacted and leaned on Pierre against the wall. He didn't push or ram him. He just started to lean. I remember hearing Pierre say, "Get off me" and cursing in French. Fig continued to lean and pretended Pierre wasn't there and looked around. Eventually Pierre got him off with no harm. Where Fig gave, he still needed to remind Pierre he was not that easily bought. It was quite hard not to laugh but Pierre finished fixing the sore muscle and Fig was fine after that.

Another time I was riding Fig and Pierre had seen he liked to play and wanted Fig to chase him. Fig restrained himself. As Pierre was running back and forth through the arena, I thought about it for a moment. I could feel the big boy tensing up in his muscles. He wanted to go after Pierre. I thought about it and the way Pierre ran back and forth like a jackrabbit, mocking Fig with his tongue I decided to let Fig go. Fig was more than happy for a good game of chase and went after Pierre. He was catching up to Pierre and it was a good thing the man was agile because he then jumped up on the side of the boards in the corner of the arena. Pierre ran across and then Fig got a bit excited. Figaro reared up, Pierre reached out and smacked him on the leg as he reared up again because he was a bit close. Pierre wasn't worried. After he got Fig's attention all was fine. It never deterred Pierre from playing with him. If anything he would test Fig more. He agreed with my views and thought this was a good change from the normal routine. And if I was ever too sore or too sick to ride, at least I knew Figaro could get some exercise.

Pierre himself broadened his knowledge of horses. He learned a different type of riding style and he would listen to Frank teaching as well. He also watched Fig and his reactions to things.

If I was in the arena he would start tossing whips, which Fig had done before with Frank. This was done in a circle with riders on horseback tossing a dressage whip back and forth. What is the purpose? It teaches the rider balance and coordination. Also trust because for a moment you need to trust your mount in order to focus on the whip. This is where Frank brought to my attention that I was ambidextrous. He asked me once which was my dominant hand. Sometimes Frank would ask random questions out of nowhere. I learned that sometimes he just said things maybe to test us or to open our eyes to something. In this case he said go around and I did -- but at a canter. I caught the whip to the right no problem, and in some cases bending in weird acrobatic ways in order to catch the whip. I did have enough faith in Figaro. Then Frank said, "Now the other direction." Same thing. We even went at full tilt. At the end he asked me the same question about which of my hands was dominant. I still said right but he said, "No, you are ambidextrous." Not fully, but he was correct.

Pierre made his own observations. After watching Fig, he noticed that this horse does not shy from much. One day when Fig was loose, he was in one of those moods where just standing felt good. Pierre tried to persuade him to play. He played, and then was content to stand. I worked on a few tricks with him. That was when Pierre went up behind him and started to snap the whip. He had a knack for making it crack and sound like gun shots. Figaro never even flinched so Pierre got closer. Nothing, nothing at all. Not a twitch or indication that his muscles were tensing. Pierre stood right behind his rump cracking the whip and still nothing. I would not recommend doing this to your horse. I have worked with different horses and even when I trust them I still don't trust any horse as much as I did Figaro. Pierre then got two lunge whips and cracked them on either side of Figaro. Some people in the barn jumped and eventually came to see what we were doing and they could not believe how laid back Figaro was during this exercise. One observer said if he can take that noise he would make an excellent movie horse. We both looked at each other. Really? This inspired Pierre to test him more. Pierre was the one to test him and not be afraid to do it.

Fig became more "Pierre proof," as I called it. Pierre said he wouldn't do this with any horse and he also said Fig handles things pretty well. Pierre eventually had enough trust that he could slap Fig on the butt any time and get no response. Even while Figaro was cantering around the arena, a slap on the butt would produce no reaction whatsoever. I really don't recommend doing this with your horse. Most horses would let out a kick. Since Pierre was Pierre, I am glad that Figaro was both Pierre-proof and bombproof beyond belief. Otherwise, Pierre would have landed in the hospital more than once.

Pierre found this out when I had Fig loose in the arena for the first time with him. Pierre loved the way he bucked and played. Me, I could never run quickly enough. Pierre jumped in. I have to admit Pierre was the perfect play person for Figaro. He would run with Fig, leap in the air, and then run up to him, slap him on the butt and run. Fig would give his little buck, and then come to him. When Pierre would crouch on the ground, Fig trotted up to him about five feet away from Pierre. Like a Jack in the Box, Pierre would leap in the air and Fig would respond by a leap then do a 360-degree spin in the air, then gallop the other way. Fig would even gallop inches away from Pierre. One time he went around Pierre as if Pierre was a barrel. Pierre had the sense to stay still. He even said, "He won't harm you, you just got to know when to move or stay still."

This rings true even when a horse panics. In the stall the worst thing you can ever do is move. As frightening as it can be, even if a horse is bucking and kicking, don't move. Odds are the horse does not want to hurt you. I have experienced this at the track when a horse gets spooked and starts bucking. Not moving has saved me quite a few times. The horse will settle down on his own.

Fig must have figured that if he had to accept Pierre at least there was this part. Fig eventually associated Pierre with play and me with work. Pierre knew that Figaro was not a dumb horse. Pierre would tell people that what he did with this horse he wouldn't do with others. However, it took many battles between the two of them, especially in the saddle, for Pierre to admit that. When it came to riding, I was top dog. It was the same with trick training. Figaro would do anything for me.

Visitors to the barn noticed. One of the boarders at Frank's farm, Darcy, once brought along a friend who was also a trainer. She watched me ride, along with a few other riders. Darcy had stood by the side, telling her about the horses and their riders. I was not doing too much, just enjoying my time with Fig. Once I was done, I rode over to the side and Darcy introduced me to her friend who commented on what a nice horse Fig was, how the two of us really have a bond and how she could she could see that we read each other.

There was something gratifying about hearing it from a perfect stranger. It rang of a purer truth. Figaro was not at the same level as the other horses, and this trainer had noticed it. This little encounter encouraged me. I was going to work harder and take Fig to whatever level we could go together.

The Nut Cracker

Pierre would typically watch one of Frank's lessons and encourage me to try with Figaro an element of that lesson. Pierre was intrigued by the croupa — where there is a rider in the saddle and usually a lady sitting sideways behind the rider. (Laura, you will recall, had tried the manoeuvre with Figaro and me three years beforehand and it had not gone well, to put it mildly.)

In general, Pierre was quite keen to learn more about classical dressage and he would apply as much as he could to Fig. Some days I was game to have Pierre as coach. Other days it was more annoying. I had come so far already with Figaro on my own. Figaro was always ready for whatever I threw at him. I did the garrocha pole -- manoeuvres around a ten-foot pole. We did alright but it was not our cup of tea. The whip toss was great for developing coordination and trusting your horse. Sometimes I would set up items on the ledge of the arena and play jousting. Figaro and I had an understanding.

Meanwhile, Frank had been working on different things with his students for different acts in an upcoming show. He mentioned again about Figaro doing croupa. I told Frank it was not Fig's thing. Of course, Pierre had to put in his two cents and said we would give it a whirl. I strongly objected to the suggestion.

Pierre then retorted, "Why not? If you ever want to show him you will have to do what they want."

I said, "Yes, but why push it?"

Laura happened to be around and she told Pierre about her experience with Fig and the croupa. "That was then," Pierre countered. "And this is now." I shrugged and agreed. There wasn't any point trying to argue the point. He wanted to be in the saddle but after what I had seen the last time he was up on Fig, I nixed that idea. I told him he could be on the back end. He was a much quicker mover and if he needed to, he could bail off. He wanted to try this? Fine. He could be the guinea pig.

At this point there were some people in the arena, including Laura, so at least, if anything we would be a source of entertainment. Pierre got on with all the confidence he could muster. He said, "Fig won't do anything to me, I am the dominant male."

Shortly after saying this, Pierre got on. He was no lightweight for his size, weighing in at about 167 lbs. Fig seemed less than amused. Before Pierre could finish adjusting himself, Fig started to buck like a bronco. The kind of buck that started from the front and sort of rolled through his body before ending in a smooth-motion buck. He went for some distance. I have to give Pierre credit. He stayed on. However, Figaro was not done. Fig got some pretty good height and he also got in some crow hops (a stiff-legged jump that sees all four feet leave the ground at once).

If a woman hits the back of the saddle, it can hurt but not the same as a man's pain. Pierre did alright, but that constant banging on the saddle was starting to hurt. Most of the onlookers were chuckling at this point.

I finally got Fig to stop. Just as Pierre was about to dismount, Figaro had to get that one last buck in to prove a point -- and this one was going to count. Pierre began to adjust himself. Fig gave one good buck. It was hard enough that Pierre hit the back of the saddle. Then Fig just stood there. As if Figaro knew what he did he let Pierre slide off. When Pierre's feet touched the ground. Figaro turned around to look at him and watched him as he slowly walked off toward the onlookers then into the barn. One of the ladies watching asked Pierre if he was alright.

"My poor nuts," was all he said

Maybe I should have felt sympathy but he brought this upon himself. I could not resist what I said next.

I said, "I guess Fig's future bronc name is the nutcracker." One girl laughed so hard she was in tears.

We never did the croupa again, well at least not with Pierre.

I Am Still Going to Test You

My bond with Figaro grew with each ride and day. Pierre was still trying to get there with Figaro, still trying to dominate Figaro, who was not going to back down.

Figaro would cut him a bit of slack but he was not quite there yet. Pierre gave him goodies and got him spoiled on salted black licorice and other treats, which was good. I think Pierre still had to prove himself. He was just not getting it. Pierre could be good with horses and he was pretty strong. He needed to put the pride aside. Figaro did just not give you something. You had to earn it. That is why I laughed when one person told me that trick training was about dominance. I said, "You have not met Figaro then. You should tell him that."

Pierre was trying to create a bond with Figaro. As a spectator it was quite amusing at times. One time after playing with him in the arena, Pierre wanted to jump on him bareback from the ground. For the most part, he could do it, but with Figaro's height and broadness it took a bit more for Pierre to get on him. He had gotten on Figaro once but it took a few attempts. Figaro got wise and learned. This time when Pierre wanted to mount him, Figaro was ready. As Pierre was getting ready to jump up from a spot alongside Fig, Figaro tried to grab his pant leg so he did not quite make it. Pierre tried again. Figaro was just as quick. This seemed to be his new thing. I could get on him no problem but with Pierre it was another story. Pierre even tried to be nonchalant about it and Figaro still was ahead of him. He was loose the whole time and could have walked away. Figaro generally won these battles -- until I grabbed Fig's head and gave Pierre a leg up.

It was like watching the Road Runner and Wil E. Coyote episodes from Bugs Bunny. It was a constant battle where Pierre was determined he was going to win the war. This was going nowhere. As the viewer why not watch?

Pierre, you will recall, had tried to lunge Fig the first time with the lunge line under the horse's halter. You would think Pierre would have learned from that experience, but no. Figaro had gotten a bit more laid back with Pierre but not to the point that Pierre thought he was. I was not in the mood to ride this particular day so Pierre said he would lunge him. I saw him put the lunge line on the halter again. I said, "You know what happened last time."

He said, "We have an understanding."

Why argue? Figaro was obliging and went a couple turns no problem and did a bit of a trot. Then Pierre changed directions with him. It was then he asked the same thing but this time when he went into the trot, Pierre wanted him to go faster. Figaro said fine. This time when he almost got to the wall he went the other direction. He just bowed his head and went. Figaro was a good 1300 lbs and he had one really strong neck. Pierre tried to dig in to the ground. He had a good hold of the lunge line. Both were not backing down. It was a battle between a 180-lb man and a 1,300-lb horse. This was entertaining. Pierre dug in but Figaro dragged him, like a power boat pulling a skier. Figaro at this point was cantering around dragging Pierre behind him like nothing was there. Pierre was still standing but instead of water shooting up behind Pierre it was sand.

The rooster tail of sand was shooting up as tall as Pierre was and you could see the marks from his shoes in the sand. It took about three laps before Pierre saw his opportunity and moved the lunge line around Fig's front leg. Figaro is not dumb. He felt it and stopped. After some words to him in French, Pierre kept Figaro going in much smaller circles and did only a few laps. You could tell Pierre was annoyed and when he was done said, "I want to end it on a good note. "The score card as I read it was Figaro 6, Pierre 0.

Times a-Changin'

The big boy was not a menace by any means. He was quite the gentleman at the barn and was becoming something of a favourite for some. With more and more frequent visits, people started to socialize with us more.

When I was annoyed or just had a plain old bad day Figaro was there. He generally would just come to me or nuzzle me the odd time when I brushed him. Generally I was a quiet person, more so sometimes when I was annoyed. People would come over and talk about Figaro and compliment him on his shine.

Sometimes we would get the odd young spectator and he eventually got a young entourage. When they were around, they would come over and visit Figaro. We included them when we bathed Figaro or played with him in the arena. Sometimes when I worked on tricks, I would let them direct Figaro. He was generally happy to perform whatever he knew. Sometimes when we grazed him after a bath, we would let one of the girls hold him. When it came to children he was considerate. We were always close at hand just in case anything went wrong.

One time someone had brought some of their friends to the farm. One had a two-year-old daughter. We were just cooling out Figaro after a ride. It was fall and we rode him with his big wool cooler. Pierre, of course, decided to use the lead rope on his halter as reins. Fig was fine with that and it was about as much as he would let Pierre do at this point. Pierre started talking to the gentleman for a few moments. Pierre had the two-year-old girl in the saddle. She was smiling ear to ear. This was the first time she had been on a horse. When it came to children he would walk slowly and take his time. A child could squeal in delight and he would not panic.

Her father said, "I think she likes riding."

It is so nice when you make an impact on a young person. Sometimes you never know what impact you make until years later. Chantel was one of Frank's accomplished riders and one of the nicest girls I have ever met. Figaro and I had an impact on her. The first time I met her she was only about 14 years old. She was pretty short, and just so bubbly. She was taking lessons and on occasion she would help out around the barn. She used to watch us and gave Figaro kisses and the odd carrot. I recall one day after one of my rides Pierre asked her if she would like to cool him out. She was unsure at first, but after a moment was up on his back. It was nice. Figaro took his time and was a good boy. I got a bit of a rest while he cooled out. After all these years, Chantel still remembers this. That was probably fifteen years ago now. She even remembered when we let her graze Figaro under the pear trees as well.

The best story I got from her was this one. Once after a half hour of grazing, Fig was stumbling a bit. Chantel called us because she was worried and a little panicked. It took me a moment or two to realize it but Fig had gotten himself a little drunk from the fermented pears that he picked out himself from the ground while he was grazing. He was fine after a little while. No worse for wear.

Once Figaro needed some meds for a minor cold and we let her give him the syringe in his mouth. Chantel said she remembered it because it was the first time she got to administer medication to a horse. It felt so good. That is why I like to try to help others. If I know how to help them I will. If I don't, I will try to find out or direct them to someone who does.

So Figaro had young fans but not every creature under the sun admired him.

Figaro and the Barn Cat

It was one of those warm summer days and everyone who was at the farm just went up to the house for lunch.

I must have been riding for about half hour when I saw Cali. The female barn cat, so named because she was a calico cat, ran across the arena to the back. At the time, she was notorious for running across the arena while you were riding. On one occasion she jumped on the back of a horse when someone was riding. Cali would also jump down from the mirrors (set up along the side of the arena so dressage riders could watch themselves and their mounts) and spook horses. Fig was never bothered by this. The only time he took notice was when she ran across the arena. He would acknowledge her but never really reacted.

I thought that maybe to deter her from her antics, I would chase her when she came in. Fig did not mind trotting after her since he liked to play chase whenever he could.

On this particular day, I was talking to someone while I was riding when Cali decided to run across the arena. Fig and I had just finished a twenty-metre circle when he spotted Cali. Fig must have had enough. He jumped forward and slid (from what we measured ten feet of skid marks). This happened so fast that all I can remember is Fig disappearing from underneath me. He was as low as a cutting horse on his knees trying to get the cat but he missed and Cali ran off faster than ever. It was so quick and fast. Luckily I had a witness.

I was told that if Cali had been a second slower or Fig a second faster, Fig would have had her. From that day on she never ran across the arena when Fig was in there. Also, there were no more complaints about her spooking the horses. So I figured if anything Figaro stopped her in her tracks. Cali would on occasion run across the arena, but she was more cautious and you could tell she was having second thoughts about doing it.

Perhaps Cali was thinking about that one day when Figaro was in the arena. She was sitting by the stairs. Fig looked in her direction, but had no desire to chase her. From the way he acted it was like he was thinking, "Now have you learned your lesson, cat, or are you going to test me again?" They must have had their own little communication just by looking at each other. Now she opted to cross the arena at a slower gallop. Most times Cali would go behind the kick boards in the arena if she saw Figaro there.

Sometimes I laugh. Figaro always seemed to be like a king in his own way. No matter what animal or person he encountered, he seemed to rule. When an animal was out of line he would get that animal's attention and get order back. It was not as noticeable at the time since there were not many stallions in the barn. In time it would become more noticeable.

Let Us Watch Together

It is always fun remembering the funny little stories like with Cali and Figaro. We had some mindful moments, shared just between him and me. It is those times that I will treasure the most.

Looking back I really can't remember the date but I know this next tale coincided with the Orchestra of Fire – a unique blend of classical music and fireworks.

I remember that life in those days – what with work and school -- was making it hard to go out. When it came to Fig, I found time regardless of the circumstances. Some people can go to the barn whenever it suits their schedules, when you work with thoroughbreds at the track you can go six days a week, sometimes seven. Also with Pierre being in construction, his hours varied. Fig was still in his earlier years and in training but every once in while I needed a break from training, horses and everyday life just to enjoy myself.

To accommodate our schedules, Pierre and I would go up to the barn later in the day or into the early evening. The nice thing about this farm was that you could go up later -- as long as you turned off all the lights when you left. Even nicer was the fact that since the farm was on a hill: you could see the city lights from the arena at night. This time it was night time. Fig was doing well and we had had a good ride. As we were cooling out and as I passed the back door, I could see fireworks in the sky. This was the same day as the Orchestra of Fire -- a competition among artists coordinating classical music and fireworks.

As we passed by the door Figaro hesitated and stood still, gazing into the darkness. I admit I looked out into the distance as well. You could see the different colours shoot up into the sky and then explode into intricate explosions of colour. It was quite amazing to watch. Figaro seemed quite intrigued with the display of fireworks. He stood still for some time. Occasionally he would even lift his head as if to get a better view. I think he was trying to figure out what it was but he didn't seem worried. It was a pity we couldn't hear the music; still it was wonderful to watch. By watching the well planned display it was if you could hear the music. It was just one of those nights that not many people experience. Watching fireworks in the country on horseback.

I can say there was no better way to end our nice ride then gazing up into the night sky together.

Challenge Accepted

Not long after that night, I remember it was a nice day and we were invited up to Frank's house for some lunch. Claire always made the best lunches. This one I remember well because she had made homemade eggrolls and a seafood dish. We were having a grand time. We started talking about the horses. Then somehow the conversation got turned to Figaro. Frank asked about the big boy and remarked on how he was improving. I told him how I would like to do shows with him and promote the Canadian horse because they were rare at the time. Their numbers were only starting to increase. I even mentioned my goal of trick training him some more. The last thing I remember was mentioning how it would be neat if he could get into the movies. I told Frank I recalled that someone had brought it up in a conversation one day.

That is when Frank said, "They need horses that can do something more, like mine do." Then he mentioned how Christopher Reeve once rode one of his stallions, Negrito, for the CBC-TV series, *Road to Avonlea*. In my mind, I knew that Figaro was no Lusitano or Andalusian. I also knew that this was a challenge I was willing to accept. I never back down from people who tell me, or insinuate that I can't do something. I am the type who will do it. A high school teacher of mine once suggested that I could not handle a college course while I was still in high school. I did it and still have my certificates and diplomas for these courses.

This movie business was going to be no different. I would not pursue this dream for financial reasons, just my own personal fulfillment. Figaro owed me nothing. This was something we were going to achieve together.

In time Figaro and I worked on more tricks. He had a knack for it. I wanted to teach him to step up on a stool. My only problem was finding something that could hold his bulk but something not too heavy to move around. We got lucky one day and someone had cut down a large tree and sectioned the trunk of it into pieces. There was one piece just perfect for at least his front hooves, if anything. It was heavy but due to its round shape I could roll it to save my back.

To try it out, I took Figaro out to the much smaller side paddock. It gave me the opportunity to work with him loose and he could not wander too far. There was an added bonus to being here: the shavings pile and the barn blocked most distractions and the east side of the barn had very little action. Nothing ever really happened there. With Figaro, on the other hand, distractions hardly mattered. When I rolled the log out to the paddock, Figaro just watched with his head in the air. Ears forward but no sign of shying. After rolling the wood piece out and placing it in the middle of the arena, I gave Fig a moment to investigate. He walked over and sniffed it thoroughly. Once he seemed alright with it, I took him by the halter and signalled him to extend his one leg out. He already knew how to count and raise his leg. He did and then tapped the stool. I asked again, and this time his hoof hit the top of the stool and he left it there. I gave him a moment and he bent down to check out his hoof on the stool. I asked him to back up and then I asked again. This time Figaro put his hoof on the wood and after a gentle tug on the halter, he proceeded to put his other foot on the stool. It was not square at first and the stool tipped. Figaro did not panic and he just backed off. So we tried again and this time he seemed to get it. In less than a half hour, he was up. Just for the sake of it, I walked away a couple steps. He seemed quite proud and just stood up there. Figaro put his head down a bit, as if to say is this what you want. When I said "good boy" he then raised his head up as if he was proud of himself. In our next session I wanted to see how much he remembered. He saw the stool and walked over and with one tap of the stool with my dressage whip he was up. People around the barn were curious about what I was doing and sometimes I had onlookers. Figaro's talents were coming out more and more. He seemed to be catching on so quickly.

Frank must have noticed as well. One day when I was on Figaro, Frank walked across the arena. Within moments he had two whips in hand and was walking in front of the big boy. I had worked on the ground with Figaro doing the *Spanish Walk* (the horse, in the walk, lifts each foreleg with a pronounced forward and upward thrust). A rider on him was the next step. Frank gave him a light touch and he would raise his leg. It is much easier for a horse to perform this with no rider. The horse needs to be balanced and in forward motion. Fig had to hesitate between switching legs; his "lazy" leg was always his right front leg. After some persuading, Frank got him to do the Spanish Walk. They went for at least ten feet. That was a big accomplishment on Figaro's part. Even though I never took formal lessons from Frank, these tidbits of information and instruction would get me thinking. Frank does not do things like this if you don't work at it. With all the work I was doing, Figaro was flourishing. Frank had noticed.

This little exercise gave me an idea, something to change things up and to make my life easier. I learned for the first little while to have two whips in my hand and with some coordination on my part I could tap Fig's legs without me having to flip my crop from one hand to the other hand all the time. I could tap his leg and get a reaction. Figaro, the smart cookie that he was, quickly picked up on this technique. It got to the point that all I had to do was tap with my heel and jiggle the rein on the same side and he would raise his foot. When he became a real pro at this, he would do the Spanish Walk with just a shimmy of my seat.

What a thrill it was to see my dream coming into effect and with a horse I could not love more.

Figaro seemed to be mastering tricks left and right. Even better, he never got too excited about doing tricks and he was not doing things out of turn – except for smiling. Rose was actually the first to get him to do it. When he thought you had something (a treat, a carrot), he would reach out with his lips, which acted like a Hoover vacuum. Rose showed me. When she put her finger near his mouth, his lips started to move. To improve on this, I would encourage him to hold his lips open with a signal -- widening my thumb and index finger. As usual, it did not take him long to figure this out. He had learned to smile. In time he would follow my fingers and with inspiration from *Mr. Ed* and *Francis the Talking Mule*, I could get him to look like he was talking. It was comical at times. Smiling was the most he would do for others, which made him safe for them to handle without the worry of accidentally cuing him for a trick.

I had a dream and the goal was becoming a reality. The next thing I thought about was the rear. This is not something I suggest all horses should learn. Even the best trainers will tell you that not every horse is suitable for this. What made me decide to do this was that to this point Figaro was safe about his tricks. He had amazing balance and was fit. I will not explain how I taught him because I don't want people to start jumping to train this without the proper steps. You need control of your horse at all times. Secondly, he was pretty well accomplished under saddle at this point. Finally, he had no injuries that could cause him any discomfort.

This trick Figaro picked up quick. This one he just had natural talent for. At first he did not go too high. I did not push him too much at first. I did not want him to get too excited. He just started to shine with this trick. When asked, he went up high keeping his front legs close together. He just had the balance for it. There was my Black Stallion -- flesh and blood. He never looked so regal as he did at that moment.

One of the boarders, Jaclyn, mentioned that Figaro would be perfect for the movies. I said that would be neat. I did not know how to go about it and I thought there were specific trainers for this task. She said that even the pros need extras. I was quite intrigued and she gave me some contact information for two wranglers. The one wrangler I managed to reach said he used his own horses. He wasn't interested in the least. "It's a tough game," he said, "but you never know." All we could do was sit and wait. At least my goal was becoming more real. Dreaming is easy but goals take work. I knew I had to work at it and I was learning how to get there myself. I am grateful that this journey was with Figaro.

Someone needs to test the Water System

There never was a dull moment with my boy. He would glow with pride at our training accomplishments. Then there was Figaro being Figaro.

It was one of those hot days in mid-summer. Pierre and I arrived at the farm to see Fig. Figaro stood out amongst the white fencing. He was out in the front sand paddock. This was unusual because the stallions are only turned out in the morning.

When we got out of the truck and looked at him more closely, we could see that he was soaking wet. So we ventured in the barn to see why he was out. Nobody there. On closer examination of his stall, we could tell it was soaked. It had small pools of water sitting on top of the already saturated dirt. It was then that Pierre took a closer look at the automatic watering system. Fig had chewed on the hose leading to the automatic watering system.

This system was relatively new to the barn. Due to the number of horses, the automatic watering system would save so much more time than dragging out a hose all the time. When Chuck was installing them, he put the waterers toward the back of the stall leaving quite a bit of hose exposed. It is common practice to put the waterer to the front of the stall nearer to a corner in order for the hose not to be exposed.

Pierre had mentioned to Chuck that a horse would chew on that exposed hose before he started installing the system. Chuck said no; this is how it is to be installed. We were not going to argue. In the back of my head all I can think was this: *please let the culprit be one of the other stallions.* I really didn't think Fig would care too much for chewing on rubber hose. At least that was my gut feeling. I was hoping that the responsible horse would be one of the newer stallions, Orguloso.

Rose finally came down to the barn and told us what had happened. Rose said that Fig must have chewed the hose an hour beforehand. They removed pretty much all the shavings and were hoping the stall could air out. Even after his stall was gutted out it took more than two weeks for it to dry. Figaro got upgraded to a larger stall on the other side of the barn, which was a bit closer to the arena and generally had less traffic. He now had two new stallions beside him. Brillhante, a younger smokey grey Lusitano, was to his right and Pimpao, an older white Lusitano, was to his left. I wondered whether Fig chewed the water hose out of boredom or if he sabotaged his stall to get the upgrade. Many would say an animal does not have that capacity to think. Fig was not normal by any means and was way too smart for his own good. I could not rule out scheming.

Before we moved him over to his new condo we had to Fig-proof the new stall. So Chuck got two long pieces of wood roughly one and a half by one inch thick. He then placed one over the top of the hose and the other under the hose. Then, as an extra deterrent, I placed pepper-spray-strength cayenne pepper on the wood so that it would deter Fig from chewing on it later. I was not going to take chances. He eyed it for the first little and figured it was not worth it. To distract him and keep him occupied I got him a Likit (a treat-dispensing toy) for his stall that he enjoyed and better yet kept his mind occupied. Refilling the Likits constantly was well worth the peace of mind. He really enjoyed the cherry, apple -- and licorice when it was available. That was his favourite flavour.

The only downfall from Figaro standing in the water so long was that his hooves must have been a bit soft when he went outside and he ended up getting small abscesses in his foot. He was off for a week recuperating, then he was back to normal.

After that there were no more hose breakages ever again.

My Pal, Pimpao

Figaro was enjoying his new condo. We had brought steel gates to the farm awhile back and Chuck had painted them up nicely then hung them on the stallions doors. At least during the day Figaro could enjoy having his head out and on rare opportunities he used it to his advantage to charm people for goodies.

One day as we came to the barn and had just finished chatting with some fellow boarders. Melissa, Frank's oldest daughter, came by and said she had to show me something. She opened Figaro's sliding door, then Pimpao's feed door. The feeder door could be opened to make it easier for feeding but it could also work to let a horse hang his head out. In a moment or two Fig brought out his big head and then Pimpao curled his head around to see Fig. I was a bit apprehensive at first since Figaro was a dominant boy and Pimpao was a stallion. At Frank's you never know what you will see.

The boys just sniffed each other. Fig proceeded to give the odd little nip. Not aggressively but playfully. Boarders came by the stalls to see the new tenant and how he was settling in. Luckily someone had her camera handy at the moment. Both boys did not disappoint. Pimpao proceeded to grab Figaro's halter from the side and gently started pulling it back and forth. Fig just sat there just moving his head to the motion. Then after a bit they would duck back a step or two into their stall and then peek around the corner trying to get each other's halters. It was so nice to see these two boys just play. You could see clearly who the man on top was. When Pimpao at one point raised his head above Fig's, he puffed up and gave a look, with his ears semi-back and then in the moment just stopped. It seemed like the boys had an understanding. This would become more apparent later, of course, in Fig's own way and thankfully that moment was also caught on film. As Pimpao backed into his stall, Fig, in true Fig fashion, stuck out his tongue.

After a good laugh, Melissa told us that when she was haying the horses she had Pimpao's feeder door open. She then heard a noise. When she came around the corner, she figured that Pimpao had played with the latch on Fig's stall door. I would not be surprised if Figaro had pushed the door open with his nose. If you recall, he was quite good with doors. Regardless, she went around the corner and thanked the lord for the gate. She said she stopped in her tracks. Melissa said she just had to watch. Throughout that week she noticed the two boys on occasion touch noses over the stall walls that divided them. Sometimes Fig would *levade* by the partition in order to play with his buddy. Regardless, he now had a neighbor and good buddy. It was funny how two studs that had never been in a paddock together could be such good friends or even have respect for each other.

Days passed. We got one of those nice spring days when there were no bugs yet. It was cool enough to be comfortable. The large arena doors were open. That day I did most of my work indoors and I intended to go outside to cool Fig out afterwards. Laura had come into the arena with Sly a grey dapple cross, was one of the resident geldings. He was a bit on the chubby side since he was not worked too often. Laura said he looked like a pregnant mare.

After Fig and I did our thing I went out the big door to cool Fig out. Linda, Pimpao's owner, had come into the arena with Pimpao. Since spring was in the air, the stallions were a bit more awake these days. When he saw poor Sly, he got excited and started nickering at Sly.

Pimpao was a quieter stallion with a lot of flare. His movement was very extravagant. He had also recently just bred some mares. So he was awake. Laura took Sly to the other end of the arena. Fig heard most of this and he raised his head, perhaps trying to figure out what was going on. You could see it in his ears as well. So I decided to let him check it out. He moved toward the door with an inquisitive and confident walk. As we walked to the door his head raised up a bit more and his steps became slower. As we approached the door I could see Pimpao. Just as Pimpao saw Fig, Pimpao stopped hollering and looked at Fig. When Sly moved again, Pimpao started up again. This time Figaro took two steps forward on his own accord and again, Pimpao stopped. As I stood there Linda got up on Pimpao, no problem. That is why when I noticed Pimpao stopped, I stood there, to keep Pimpao quiet. Once Linda was up and her horse got close to Sly, Pimpao would prance but Linda had him under control. It was more of a display at that moment. I dismounted and took Figaro in.

Again I was amazed that how two horses that had never been in a paddock together could generate that respect for one another. Figaro was a dominant horse and horses are not stupid. They know. If Fig was not a king, he was to me now.

Pat and Cherub

Figaro would work his charms in more ways than one. Not only did he make friends with another stallion, but he could also work his magic on humans or mares.

Pat had recently come to the farm with her chestnut Morgan mare, Cherub. We had met briefly a couple times. One day as I was riding she came in and sat on the stairs with Pierre. As they chatted, I rode. Sometimes I would just lose myself when riding. After I was done cooling out, Pat came over and formally introduced herself. She was an older lady with hair almost the same colour as her mare. She was always pleasant and I never saw a frown on her face.

As she came over Fig stretched out in his own way of introducing himself. Pat said she had been watching us for some time, including when I was doing liberty training with Fig or just playing with him. She said he was a nice horse. From there we got talking about the Morgan breed and why I ended up with a Canadian horse. As Fig relaxed he decided to really stretch himself out -- almost into a show stance with his feet placed perfectly together. Pat noticed this and asked if I had ever showed him in halter. I said no and I told her I don't know if he had ever been trained in halter as a young horse. Out of curiosity I took him around, Pat asked him to do some things and he more or less did them when asked. She said he must have learned this at some point. Made me wonder but it was neat.

After much chatting, we decided to start meeting up for arena rides. We had quite a few nice rides together. Not only did Pat and I have a fantastic time, Cherub liked Fig and, of course, Fig loved any lady that loved him. One time she was in heat and she backed up into him while I was on him. Luckily he was always the gentleman.

One of our most interesting rides occurred on the day the farm got a donation of several mirrors. Chuck had been working making wooden frames for the mirrors and placing the smaller ones on the corners. This helped Frank to see and us riders to see if our horses were performing certain dressage movements correctly.

Chuck had just finished the larger mirror. This one was to go at the back of the arena. It would be placed high enough to be away from the horses but low enough so that we could see. This one was handy when we would perform *quadrilles* and when all eight riders need to be in a straight line. The mirror was a great addition and it really helped. The most correct straight line is when all the riders' heads are perfectly aligned, one behind the next.

For Chuck to install the big mirror required extra-tall ladders, pulley systems, his jeep and lots of rope. Pat and I rode outside as they did their work. Fig couldn't care less about the drilling, hammering and other noises. When I was done riding I wanted to check up on what is going on. So I rode Figaro through the big arena door. I took him down to the end away from the construction and he pretty much just looked around. Chuck didn't panic about Fig being there. He knew Fig didn't care. When it came time to pull the mirror up, we stood out of the way and watched as Chuck, Frank and Pierre pulled up the mirror. The mirror plus frame must have weighed at least two hundred pounds. Chuck took the front, Frank was behind and Pierre took the back end. He was pretty strong and he took the brunt of the pull. At one point Chuck had to let go of the rope to position the mirror on the ledge. I personally think Pierre just wanted to impress the onlookers and make it look harder than it was. In the end the mirror was installed.

The whole time Fig seemed amused. Pierre said afterwards we should have just tied the rope to the saddle and let Fig do the hauling. He would have probably done it no problem. At that moment he just watched the little humans do the work. After it was up, Cherub came into the arena. Once she got to the middle of the arena, she stopped and snorted and started to walk sideways. Figaro looked at Cherub and then at the mirror then back at Cherub again. It seemed he was trying to put two and two together. Then he did a small shimmy -- as if the mirror had spooked him. I could not really call it a spook. I felt like saying, "Fig, you have just been standing here the last 20 minutes and now you spook?" Pierre called it the most delayed reaction ever.

Pat commented on how he calm he was about handling all the commotion. I said he generally does not care what is thrown at him. Then she asked how he was on trails. I said he does not seem to care for going out by himself. That is when she brought up endurance riding. It was around the same time that the movie *Hidalgo* came out in theatres in 2004. I wasn't too sure about the idea. Pat said she had done it many times and started to explain about conditioning. How in endurance riding you rode in two point, how there are vet checks and the different levels of competition. It was then she mentioned doing some mileage rides and there were two different distances perfect for beginners. There was a 12- and 20-mile trail ride. She then came up with the great idea of getting a group of us from the barn to go for one of the mileage rides.

Once we got a bunch of us together, Pat arranged for a vet to come out to the barn and educate us on taking our horses' heart rates and how to monitor their breathing and read other vital health signs. Pierre and I knew most of this information already. It was entertaining when the vet tried to take Fig's pulse because of his large neck. She had a hard time finding it. Pierre knew Fig's overall health and he would take it upon himself to monitor his heart rate and breathing once we started training. Now our next step was to get Fig fit for the endurance ride.

Alexander the Great and Bucephalus

Figaro was already pretty fit at the start of our training. The key was to get his hind end more developed and improve his cardiac fitness. Working on the track, I got a good idea about conditioning horses and all that it involves. We were not going to gallop him all day. There was no need for it. We figured out the distance to go around the back paddocks and we figured doing the outer perimeter was probably at least a little over a half mile. I went one round at a trot. Figaro handled it pretty easily with a brisk trot and little huffing and puffing. We did it in about 7 minutes. Not bad and that was going up and down hills. In time he would get faster and we incorporated some canter work on the back half of the property. I can't remember where his heart rate was. It stayed pretty consistent and not out of the normal working heart rate. By a few weeks we were able to do five rounds of the back field with no problem even with all the rain and varying weather conditions. Because of the design of the paddocks, heavy rain every year created a lake in the middle of the paddock that was affectionately called Lake Grelo. It got deep enough that a horse could go up to mid-neck in water. Many of the herd horses enjoyed a good roll in it in the warmer summer months. Once the lake was there, I had to make a detour around it. It was mid-summer and I know with the warm weather that in a few weeks it would dry up again. We still had a couple months before the endurance ride in the fall.

One particular day after we had done a couple rounds I could not help but look at this little lake. I thought it would be so nice to go in there with Fig. The sun was shining so beautifully. When there was a slight breeze, the water created small waves and the sun just sparkled off them. Finally

I decided I just wanted to do this. Was I dressed to get wet? No. But my synthetic saddle would be fine and it was warm enough that I would dry in no time. As I took Fig up to the water, he seemed fine. Once we got closer, I asked him to just take one step. He seemed to want to go forward but he would let out the odd small snort as if to say no. I had ridden this horse at night with puddles and he couldn't care less. He was not scared. I just could not figure out why this big black beast was saying no. It was then I remembered the tale of Alexander the Great and Bucephalus, Alexander's famous black steed.

The tale goes that when Alexander first came across Bucephalus he was supposed to be a mount for his Father, the king. The horse was so wild that the king ordered the horse to be destroyed. It was then Alexander, the prince, saw something and in a bet he asked his father to give him a chance. His father said fine. If you can do it, I will give you a small fortune and part of my kingdom. No one thought this young boy could do it. When he approached the big black steed, he noticed the horse was spooking from his own shadow. It was then he turned the horse toward the sun and jumped on his back. From there history was created on the back of Bucephalus.

So I rode Figaro to the other end of the lake where the sun was not reflecting too much. As we walked forward, Fig's great bulk thickened and he bowed. As we hit the mud by the edge he took a couple quick steps and made a slight shimmy from side to side. Then he was in the water. I stood him by the shore to see what he would do. In seconds he just pawed at the water and in he went. I was only going to go in no deeper than the bottom of my stirrup. Then I heard Pierre, who was on a nearby hill, say "Go in." So I went in a bit farther. Figaro was loving it. He had no problem with the water. It was just the reflection. He was wary of what he couldn't see. He had no fear.

I went back out. Pierre had come down the hill by then and asked why we did not go deeper. I felt I made a big step. I said, "If you want, go ahead." Pierre never cared if *he* got wet (though I know that if I had gotten wet he would not have let me in his truck.) Pierre got on Fig and headed out into the water. This time Figaro went in without hesitation. Pierre could not reach the stirrups but he went in this time right to the middle of the lake where there was a ridge in the middle. At that point, the water reached to just above his shoulders. Figaro just looked so fantastic. He went through the water with ease as if he were walking through air. As he went in deeper he seemed to prance through the water.

The water splashed up as he went, making his coat glisten gloriously. Pierre stopped him in the middle of the lake and Figaro pawed at the water as if he were doing the Spanish Walk -- all the while getting Pierre wet. Pierre urged him on because Fig seemed to wanted to roll but instead he moved forward. Suddenly I was a child again, watching the Black Stallion movie and especially the scene with Alec and the black on the beach. My favourite scene and here it was in the flesh, my own and quite real black stallion. I regret I never got a photo of him and me in that lake. With his balance I would have loved a rearing shot of him. Figaro going through the water was good enough for me.

Once we were back at the barn, we gave him a good bath so the sweat or the water (who knows what could be in it) did not sit on his coat. With black horses it is always good to wash the sweat away since it can bleach him. We made sure he was nice and clean, then we went for our graze afterwards.

At this point with his training, we made sure to put back into him what we took out. We made sure his diet was replenished with what he lost from training and most of all we were concerned about electrolytes. Fig was not a fan of receiving electrolyte supplements via syringes. As a substitute, Fig got Gatorade. Pierre liked to experiment with Figaro's taste buds and probably gave Figaro his acquired taste for most things. Figaro did love red Gatorade and would drink it out of the bottle. He preferred to tilt his head while you poured. He even got the taste for beer as well and got spoiled with Guinness. In moderation, this is not bad for a horse. In some European countries, horses that can't keep their weight on are given Guinness or beer because of the yeast.

I loved this war horse of mine and was more than happy to give him what he needed – and he knew exactly what he needed and told you so. He didn't want a blanket in the cold, only in extreme cold. If I rode with polos and he had no need for them, he would stop and put his nose toward the polo and keep his head there till you acknowledged it and have you take them off. He was a horse content with the basics. All he asked was to be loved and taken care of, and I was more than happy to oblige.

Let's See How High We Can Go

It is nice to condition your horse, but you need to change things up. One day Laura was playing with Sly and going over a small jump. I watched for a bit. She had another girl take pictures. I never really thought of jumping him, but now I said sure. Jumping was my passion before dressage and so I took Fig for a large circle then headed toward the jump. He gave a slight hesitation then heaved himself over it. He had a lot of power and I almost popped out of the saddle. Laura then asked if it would be alright to take photos of him as he went over. I said sure. She wanted to get a shot of the underside of a horse jumping and Figaro could not care less.

It was then that Pierre said, "I wonder how high he could go."

Again we went toward the jump slowly and over he went. When Laura was ready, she positioned herself and got some shots of him taking the jump. When it was time for her to leave Figaro was still pretty game. I don't recommend going this far with a horse jumping for the first time, but he was fit and we were not pushing him. At this point the jump was three feet high. Pierre decided to raise it to three and a half feet. I let him know I wasn't too sure about this. First off, I was in not the right saddle but I agreed to do it. This was where dressage training can make a huge difference. I collected him and counted my strides one, two three, and as we hit the third stride he went over. This one was quite smooth for the height and surprisingly he made it. It was then that Pierre said this will be the last one and he raised it to about four feet. Risky, but I took a shot. This horse had in the past jumped the wooden gate -- and that was aboutfour feet high. However he was older and was stronger than before and should have no problem.

116

Pierre said, "If he can jump that, he can jump this."

So I went around. Figaro was a bit more tired now but this horse had what we called pump – he was a horse with determination and courage. We made our rounds again but this time I got him to lengthen his stride a bit more. He obliged. Figaro gave it all he had and heaved his great body with such force that when he landed I did pop a bit out of the saddle and ended up with my legs in front of the leg guards on my saddle. My feet never left the stirrups and I was sitting sort of on his neck. Luckily he did not panic and I got him to come to a standstill as I got myself back in the saddle. I can say I have more respect for trick riders now.

Pierre was quite impressed and I have to say so was I. Afterwards we gave him a good rub down. Pierre worked on his muscles and Fig was still quite loose. We even braced down his legs with the mixture we generally use for the thoroughbreds at the track -- ¼ part Absorbine and ¾ parts rubbing alcohol. Fig got pampered. On our way home Pierre said that a jumper would like a horse like him. I thought for a moment about taking him to some small jumping classes but that thought passed. Because of his size, jumping would have been hard on him in time. It would have affected his hocks and stifle. At least I knew he could do it. I would jump him the odd time but you could tell it was not his thing. His thing was to be a showman. He liked the crowds.

It did not hurt for him to learn. Another time I taught him to go around barrels too. He was good and even though he did not really have the speed, he made up for it with his tight turns. This is where dressage helped again. I used to bend him so close that my toes dragged around the barrels without knocking them. To get him used to the sound I used to go up to the barrel and beat it with my whip to make a racket. He couldn't have cared in the least. There was nothing I did not introduce this horse to and in return he did not disappoint me. As the saying goes, a horse is only as brave as his rider. I never considered myself to be brave. Only much later did I realize – and others would agree -- that Figaro was showing me that I did possess that attribute.

Endurance Ride

Jumping was a fun thing to do with Figaro but we needed to put our attention to getting ready for the endurance event, if we were going to give it a try. Once we made the decision to do the endurance ride with Pat and others at the stable, we focussed on getting Figaro as fit as he could be.

I never would have thought I would get a chance to do endurance riding. Thanks to Pat, who had a beautiful chestnut Morgan mare named Cherub, I got the opportunity to try.

Organizers of these rides offered an introductory level called mileage, which gave riders the idea of what endurance riding was all about but without the competitiveness.

Pat and I enlisted quite a few people at the barn who were interested in joining us in this adventure and she arranged for her vet to come out and show us what they look for at the vet checks and other useful tidbits of information.

So that was when Pierre and I started getting Figaro more fit for the ride. Many times we did cardiac conditioning in the arena and once in a while we took him to the fields in the back. Then I would take Fig for rides in the field, monitoring his breathing and how he was taking the rides. The best parts were the hills and open areas where I could work him and really see how he was taking it. At vet checks they monitor the horse's heart rate, respirations and overall condition. If these measurements don't meet the standard, you do not continue. I wanted to make sure Fig was in top form before heading out.

I had to give Figaro credit. His strong will and determination made the training easy. That and he lived up to the Canadian breed standards. The Canadian horse has a reputation for not tiring easily, and Fig did fit that description.

Getting closer to the day, Fig was starting to feel his oats. He was fit and strong. When I rode him in training, I had him in a double bridle. When he took a hold of the bit, I might as well have ridden with nothing. Luckily I found ways around that, since he taught me well. I didn't have to manhandle him but I did what an exercise rider would have done and crossed (or bridged) my reins and let him pull against himself.

One day a week or maybe even two before the mileage ride, I wanted to take him for a practice ride. Pierre watched from the outdoor arena. He wanted to see how long it took us. To kill time he helped Chuck with some fencing in the outdoor arena.

The ride went well. For a bit he was a little strong. He was full of himself that day and the house behind the fields was undergoing some construction and there was a bobcat (a miniature bulldozer) running. Fig was not scared of it. He didn't care when it was close by and making noises. Fig would enjoy a playful buck and stop to watch it. Eventually my arms and back had had enough. So I brought Fig up to Pierre. After some discussion, Pierre got aboard Fig and went to finish the ride. I saw him go up the biggest hill and disappear to the other side. Chuck and I were just chatting when we heard some very loud cursing in French.

Chuck beat me to the punch and asked what all that was about.

"He went after the bobcat!" Pierre said.

I was puzzled so I asked, "He went after the machine? It's on the other side of the fence."

"No," said Pierre. "Not the machine. They were done by the time we got there. No, the fuzzy kind. A bobcat. The large cat."

I didn't think bobcats were in the area. Chuck then jumped in and told us that there was one on the property, in the woods. They released a couple a few years back to control the deer or turkeys. (A year or two later, I think that was about 2005 or 2006, I spotted one running cross the paddock into the woods). Pierre then told us he and Fig were coming down the hill with the bobcat trotting along the fence line. Fig saw it and stopped for a moment and wanted to go after it just as they were coming down the steeper part of the hill. So this was definitely not an option. Fig protested and managed to do a 90-degree rear on the hill (thank goodness Fig can really hold his balance at a rear).

Pierre said he was like that for a minute or two. I guess because of Pierre cursing at Fig in French the bobcat hightailed it out of there. Finally Pierre managed to rein Figaro in. Pierre said he is definitely fit enough. Figaro was fine after that day.

Two weeks later came the day of the endurance ride. It was fall now and the weather had turned a bit dreary. We hoped the rain would stay away till after the ride. Pierre had Fig all cleaned up and bandaged. The others had their horses ready and were waiting for their trailer to come. So far we had Kirsten with Sly, Kristen with Calamity, Billy and Kali and Pat and Cherub. We borrowed a friend's two-horse tag-along trailer. Pierre wanted Fig to be comfortable and that way after the ride we could just leave because Fig didn't like to sit in a trailer for long. Pierre pulled the trailer with his truck. All was going all right so far. Pierre decided to remove the center bar so Fig could load easily. Pierre had done professional horse trailering for years and cared for the horse's welfare and he thought this would be better. That was fine. Pierre got him on and Fig decided to pretend Pierre wasn't there and leaned on him. Once Pierre got out he wanted to put the ramp up but this trailer's design meant that you needed to have the center pole in the back half in place. Again, Fig leaned on Pierre but finally he succeeded and we were on our way. It took us time to learn that he did not like being in a tight spot for long rides. He was not claustrophobic. He just like having a box stall and to be loose so he could look out the windows

For the most part the trailering went well until we stopped at the lights. Fig didn't mind the rides but he was not keen on stopping. Thank goodness it was early in the morning and there was no one in front of us or behind us. At the stoplight Fig managed to move truck and trailer two feet forward and two feet back – all just by shifting his weight, all fourteen hundred pounds of it. As the truck moved back all you could hear was a "ping" noise. In all the years I knew Pierre, I never saw him turn that white and go into a cold sweat as he did that day. All he said was, "He is going to kill us."

Pierre told me that in all the years he had done transport, he never had a horse do that. He had horses do some really odd things when he did professional transporting but never had a horse do that. Pierre vowed never to use a tag along again. Gooseneck trailers, which are more stable, were the better choice. (Unfortunately Pierre would later buy a heavier truck as well, a bit too big for what we needed, that only added to our debt – but that's another story that has no place here.)

Luckily, despite Fig's wear and tear, the truck seemed fine and the brakes were fine. We proceeded the rest of the way with no problem (though later, on closer inspection, we would discover that Fig's shenanigans inside the trailer had caused extensive damage to the truck's rear axle). We got there just before the others. Pierre was a very punctual type of person so he was relieved that we got there on time. He looked for a spot to park that would allow him to get out easily at the end of the ride because he wanted to get Figaro home soon after the ride.

We went and got our registration papers. I got Fig saddled. He took it like a pro and did not seem to mind all the commotion. We tied a huge yellow ribbon in his tail. Yellow let other riders know that a stallion was on the trail while a red ribbon signalled that this horse was a kicker. The official came and put Fig's number on his hind quarters with a chalk like substance. The others got ready too in the same manner. With us was our little helper, Katie, then eight or nine. She liked Figaro and wanted to come along and help us as well as the other riders. Pierre got her an embroidered hat to make her feel special and to thank her for her help.

When we were all ready, we went to the vets to get our pre-ride check. Fig was a bit studdy but it didn't help that there were quite a few mares in heat. He was still a gentleman about it. He called the odd time to announce his arrival. Enroute to the vets, we received a lot of compliments. One woman said, "That farm has the most beautiful horses." There was the occasional "what a beautiful horse" as we passed other entrants. We finally arrived at the check point where a male vet came through and said, "I'll take the black boy." I still remember him. He had the most wonderful New Zealand accent. He was a man probably in his late thirties. He checked Fig over and said his heart rate, even with the excitement, was very good.

After that I got on Figaro and waited for the others to finish their vet checks. Pierre led us to the starting area. Pierre noticed Fig's fifth leg hanging out and told him to put it back in before he tripped someone. I heard the odd chuckle. It was funny. Pierre could be quite the character, but he loved the attention as well and with Figaro there he got all the attention he wanted. A bit further up a lady called out to Pierre and said, "That is a beautiful Friesian." He turned around with a serious look on his face and said, "Don't swear." The woman looked puzzled.

Pierre said, "Don't swear. He is not a Friesian. He is a Canadian horse." then smirked.

The woman laughed and said, "That was a good one."

Many would say how they had never seen a Canadian his size and how he looked so much like a Friesian. I can't blame them for making the mistake with his breed because of Figaro's height and the way he carried himself when he was out. He was just a proud horse. It was not hard to look at him.

After everybody was up on their horses, we headed out. When we were out of sight of the crowds, we headed into the woods for the first part of the endurance ride over nice deep sand. The trail meandered though some trees then into open areas on the trails. Pat led the way since she had more experience and showed us the trail markers. At one point, we came to a fairly steep hill. The trail was not a straight run. You had to manoeuvre around trees. To top it all off, you pretty much had to gallop it. My stomach sort of turned because the other horses were much smaller and could do it more easily. After ducking many of the tree branches, I saw why many riders had opted for shorter horses.

This path presented a challenge: it was like pole bending -- but uphill. We each went individually up the hill and when my turn came, all I told Fig was "I am leaving it up to you bud." Without hesitation he went up the hill and for a big boy he moved around those trees like nothing. I was very relieved when we were at the top. We would come back again since we did this route twice for our mileage. The second time he was much quicker.

The ride was going well. The skies were getting cloudier and you could feel the air changing. So far so good. We were coming close to the half way mark and there was quite bit of downhill work ahead. Now we came to a huge tree that had fallen across the path. I mean big! To jump and clear it you would have to get your horse to jump a good two and a half feet. The girls wanted to jump but I advised them not to try it. Just then a girl came whizzing by on her horse. She was adorned in purple, with purple tack to match. She jumped the log but the horse had a rough landing. Seeing that, we decided to bypass the tree and found a way through the trees. It was very tight with many thin twiggy trees. Fig led the way. A lot of horses don't like branches hitting their face. He just tucked his head and barrelled through them.

Pat was a good leader and we managed to get in good gallops on the straightaways. When we were about two hundred yards from the check point, we got the horses' heart rates down. Fig had to let everybody know we were coming and the one vet already knew to get ready for him.

The girl in purple found out that her horse did not pass the vet check and she was reprimanded for reckless riding. There are scouts on the trails to make sure that safety remains a priority for rider and horse. I'm so glad we decided to go around and not jump that huge log.

At the check point, our vet listened to Fig's heart rate and pronounced it very good. Just before we left to give Fig a five-minute break, the vet said, "I have traveled all over Canada and have done many different events. I have seen lots of Canadian horses but Figaro is the best looking Canadian I have ever seen." I remember that to this day.

As we headed to our designated spot to give Fig some electrolytes, a man on his horse passed way too close with his mare -- who was in heat. Fig got really excited, reared and got me in the chest with his hoof as he came down. During this excitement I saw Fig ejaculate, which raised some eyebrows. He showed characteristics of being a stallion. This however now confirmed it. Steward sat the event saw the incident and the other rider got marks deducted because Fig's stallion ribbon was definitely large enough for all to see. His actions were irresponsible considering the rules of the event were quite clear.

My chest hurt a bit and I was somewhat winded but was fine and carried on. I got some bruising later. I did not blame Fig; it was not his fault by any means. When a horse is fit and on an adrenalin high, you have to expect that they may do something.

We carried on and the ride was great. The rain set in. We had to duck a few more branches because they were starting to get weighed down by the rain. Good thing I trusted Fig. Once or twice I had to lean right over into the saddle or do the limbo in the saddle to avoid hitting any branches. He could have bucked but thank goodness he took pity on me. By then we had been riding for about five hours and were feeling fatigued without really being aware it. All of us were having such a good time and the time just passed by so quickly.

When the day finally came to an end, we were all soaking wet. Our part of the ride was done. Other competitors were doing fifty miles and up so they had a few more hours to go yet.

We did our final vet check. It was unfortunate that our vet had to attend to an injured horse. The lady vet said Fig was doing great, prescribed a 10-minute break and told us to continue on. I told her we were done, at which point she said, "What a pity. With his vitals, he could do another twenty five miles easy."

At this point I was tired and was glad to be going home. I didn't realize how tired I was or even how sore. An hour after we stopped riding the trail, I could feel all my muscles and they were killing me. After all that we loaded up. Fig was quieter on the way home. I think the ride gave him an adrenalin high and it lasted for three days afterwards.

Elementary Dear Watson, Elementary

Fig had had his issues but over time he got better about being led and handled. With time as well, he was maturing more and more as well. He was getting taller and thicker. He was no longer 15.3 hands high; Figaro now stood about 16.2 and he was starting to thicken out. A gelding will not get that thick and muscular due to lack of testosterone. Fig had been gelded when he was two years old but I had been wondering for the longest time if the surgeon had possibly left something behind.

The next time we met up with the vet I picked his brain about this. What was the explanation for that fourteen stitch scar on the right side of Fig's sheath? I just presumed it was a different way to geld. At the track I had held many horses during a castration procedure, and 99 percent of the time it was done underneath with one or two simple cuts.

When Pierre came onto the scene in the summer of 2003, he too started to question Fig's studdiness. He had worked in a veterinarian hospital and he thought that Fig's stallion-like behaviour was odd. He started to investigate. Meanwhile, as I say, Fig was really thickening. His cheeks grew and his neck grew -- just like a stud. If you took him up to any mare he would react -- not in any stupid way but he would show interest. He was more polite about it and he liked to romance them rather than scream at them. When I explained his early days of him and his fifth leg, Pierre investigated more. When I showed him the letter from Fig's previous owner noting Fig's studdiness, he, too, found it to be odd. Even a couple vets thought it was odd since if there was only a nerve left during the gelding then there would be nothing you could do.

One summer day when I was brushing Fig, I showed Pierre the scar on the side of his sheath. The first thing he said was, "They were looking for something."

So we had some questions that needed answers. Then fate came into play.

I had a project and needed a piece of leather, which took me into the Tandy Leather store. We ended up talking to this gentleman who happened to be a horse person and we fell into a conversation. He dealt with quarter horses and by a fluke he had a quarter horse who was supposed to have been gelded, but was really, really studdy. The only difference was his horse was mean and aggressive. The gentleman said that after a year they tested him – using the same test Fig got -- and it came back negative. They tried another vet, redid the test and this time it came back positive. It turned out his horse had retained a small testicle.

This is when Pierre took matters into his own hands and got a vet to do another test. It turned out that Fig had cryptorchidism – meaning that a testicle had not dropped normally. He had retained a good sized testicle but due to his age at this point it was too risky to bring it down. We decided to leave it. So that explained the mystery. When we told Frank, he said, "I knew it. He was just too studdy to be a gelding."

The moral of the story? Sometimes a test can be wrong, so trust your gut and get a second opinion. My so called gelding was really a stallion. This explained so much.

Fig and the Fiery Red Stallion

Now that we suspected Figaro to be more of a stallion everything changed somewhat. We now knew what we were dealing with especially with behaviour even though Figaro was not your typical stallion.

Frank had gotten two new stallions. One was the aforementioned Orgy, a grey Lusitano stallion. Later he would be known as Ugly. Renegade was the other stallion and he was a rarely seen chestnut Lusitano stallion with a nice white blaze.

Both were typical boys and were a bit of a handful when they arrived. Renegade was a typical fiery redhead. He liked to turn and bite his rider's legs. Under saddle when he concentrated on his work, and with Frank's help, he got better in time.

Figaro had other opinions of Renegade. Fig didn't pay too much attention to the other stallions. His favourite was Pimpao, his neighbour. For the most part Figaro had gotten better and generally didn't care about most horses but if he felt he needed to he didn't signal with his ears. I could feel his muscles tighten underneath me when I was riding. Ninety nine percent of time he didn't react.

There was something about the redhead he didn't like. I had been in the arena a couple times with him and Fig was just on guard with him. I was never scared of any of Frank's horses. I had met much worse at my job at the racetrack. All in all, Frank wouldn't put anyone in a bad situation or put riders on horses he thought they could not handle. Frank even wanted to do a *pas de deux* (a kind of equine ballet in which two horses move in tandem to music) with Renegade and Figaro. He thought they would be great together because of the contrast in colour. Unfortunately, it never happened.

The redhead at this point had Frank's more experienced rider on him. His main rider was Chuck. The first time I noticed there was tension between the two horses was when Renegade was acting up and Frank asked us to go into the middle so Jessica, a student worker, could gallop Renegade out. Jessica was quite a good rider and did well. But at one point Renegade came in a bit too close at a gallop and I felt Fig's muscles tense and he did pin his ears. Fig, though, didn't move. You could tell he was not keen. Pierre could see what I was feeling from the stairs where he was sitting watching this play out. Pierre advised Jessica in future to be careful of coming that close with Renegade.

The day we really found out that Renegade and Figaro did not care for each other was when I went out for a hack in the field after a ride. It was summer time and it got really hot in the arena. I headed out into the fields. Pierre came along for the walk. We were at the furthest part of the field by the wooded area and were about to make our way back along the mare's paddock. When Fig stopped, I could feel his muscles tense. In the distance by the big hill was Chuck on Renegade. When the two horses saw each other they were a good two hundred metres from each other. Renegade started acting up. Chuck used all his might and experience to get the redhead under control. Then Fig, who had just been sauntering around the field, was now fully awake and pulling my arms. My shoulder popped out slightly out of its socket. It did this on occasion due to an old injury. I kept a hold of Fig but my shoulder was starting to feel like pins and needles. Pierre told me to get off and he jumped on to take him back to the barn. Fig was not about to go easily. He wanted to keep an eye on Renegade. After a bit more fighting, Chuck headed back to the barn. Pierre wanted to hold Fig back till they were out of sight. The only problem was that Fig was still not keen with Pierre on his back and was not amused that he was not allowed to go to the redhead. Pierre was going to bear the brunt of this battle.

Laura Luszczek

As Fig tried to move on, Pierre turned him around along the tree line. It looked like Pierre was succeeding in getting him to move. Now Fig changed his mind, did a small figure eight and took Pierre into a tree branch as thick as an arm and at least four feet long. The branch broke on impact and hit Fig in the back end. He didn't budge and somehow Pierre managed to stay on but leaned back, dazed for a minute before once more getting a hold of Fig and riding him back to the barn. Fig settled down after that.

As for Pierre, he had a headache for a couple days and a small bruise. Later he said, "I think we will just keep the two boys away from each other if possible. Hey, if a human can dislike someone, why can't a horse?"

You Can't Fence Me In

I knew from Fig's experiences with the likes of Renegade that his strength was monumental especially when he was "ready to battle". On the other hand during those quiet playtime moments Figaro's strength was still phenomenal.

Fig was a sleeping lion. You never knew when his mind would decide to wake up. These days he was pretty quiet. He was not up to his Houdini ways and was just content to be outside. He would be the last in the turnout program and had the opportunity to be out longer. Fig was showing much improvement by no means did this mean he was a saint all the time.

One time we arrived at the farm and Chuck told us that Joe the farm hand was going to kill Fig. "Why," we asked, "What did he do now?" Fig had apparently managed to pull half the flex fence off the posts and Joe had to spend most of the day repairing it. I thought it was a joke since flex fence should be pretty hardy. They advertise it with scenes of trees falling on it and it snapping back to normal. What could Fig do to it? Such fencing is held in place with brackets, bolt, washers and screws. Not just nails. A wooden board can be pulled off. That is why the planks are put on the inside. It is less aesthetically pleasing but a horse can lean on it and it won't pop off. This fencing is pretty tough and can withstand up to two thousand pounds of pressure. I guess Figaro did not read the information pamphlet on the fencing.

I have seen Fig bend wire fencing to the ground to allow him to get at grass on the other side. He could have stepped over the wire but never did.

I was a bit puzzled. One summer afternoon we saw for ourselves what the big boy could do.

We came on to the property we passed the house and headed down the small hill toward the barn. Fig's paddock was the first one you saw and in the paddock was an interesting sight. Pierre stopped the truck mid-way down the hill. I had taken a nap and only woke up to hear Pierre cursing my horse. As I looked up I understood why. Fig had his head under the top flex rail and was walking backwards across the paddock. Not in a panic, but with an easy movement. I guess you could almost call it the horse version of the moon walk. I could see the wheels turning in Figaro's head, "Let's see how far I can pull this before it comes off." He was probably a good fifteen feet out. Pierre said something in French, probably not something nice.

Pierre then rolled down his window, switched to an English curse and yelled, "Leave the fencing alone!"

Fig took notice of his voice. He stood for a moment raised his head. He then let the fencing roll down his neck. When the fence hit the ground, Figaro looked up with a look on his face that said, "What? I didn't do it!", then he sauntered off as if nothing had happened and went to graze. Pierre got some tools to repair and tighten the fencing before Joe would talk about killing Fig again. What possessed him to do that? I will never know. Maybe it was to get to the girls at the bottom of the hill or maybe the grass. All I know is strength and brains were not a good combination some days.

From that day on, we decided that if we ever got a farm, Figaro's paddock would feature wood fencing – oak boards. Retailers of the flex fence were surprised that he was able to do that. They suggested using electric fencing, one more line of defence. I was determined to get a farm one day and if I wanted Figaro to be safe and happy I always had to think of everything when it came to Figaro. I wanted the best for him.

The Tsunami Charity Event

All the extra time working in the arena with Fig was paying off. He was improving more and more. Sometimes we would play music while we worked to see what Figaro was interested in. He was catching people's attention more and women especially liked his cuddly demeanour. With him maturing more and thickening out, he was becoming a more impressive animal. I had many compliments about how much he looked like a Friesian.

In the news in late December 2004 the world heard of the devasting damage the Indian Ocean Tsunami caused. People around the world rallied to help in any way they could with the devastation that took place. This event was my opportunity to help along with Figaro.

One day Winnie, another rider riding horses at the farm, was on the stairs and I had just finished with Fig when she mentioned something about the Tsunami Charity, a benefit for those in Thailand impacted by a tidal wave caused by earthquakes registering 9.1 to 9.3. She had been watching me work with Figaro. She had watched us on a couple of other occasions, too, when I rode and was working with Fig on tricks. Winnie would later end up doing liberty/trick training work herself with her horses. Charles, a local racehorse owner, was working with kids from a school he deals with and they had a goal to raise money for an event that Winnie was helping to organize.

Winnie said it was going to be a show about the different horse breeds. I asked if they had a Canadian horse. She thought about it and then asked if we would like to be in it. Since Fig had never been to a show, Pierre and I thought this would be a good chance to see how he would react to a crowd. At the time I thought this was going to be a small event. It turned out this was going to be quite a large event, larger than I could have imagined. This would determine if our goal was going to become real or if it would be just a dream. If he liked the crowds, then my goal to host charity events would be pleasurable for us both. If not then I would scratch it off my list.

I worked with Fig on a small routine. He knew the basics. I wish he was more trick-trained then but still, he looked good regardless. Pierre said he was a flashy looking horse and people like to see that. Fig really responded to some music Pierre found, a Bond 007 soundtrack. He loved the music and eventually learned his routine.

When the day of the show arrived, the trailer showed up and Fig was placed in the middle, with two boys in front. He was getting better about being with other horses. Pierre put a hay net in front of him and placed inside about a hundred pounds of hay, which separated him from the boys in front. We figured out he just did not like being in a small stall. So the middle was perfect for him. It was a bonus to have the trailering paid for and the trailer also had a camera inside. Fig was put on the trailer last because of being in the middle. On this journey was Stacey, Dee, Irene and Dave with their horses Curioso, Roz, Garbosa and Quartteto. We followed them all down to the venue. We could see the driver looking into his camera in the back constantly. Fig was a bit rowdy on the trip but nothing bad happened.

When we got to the performance arena, we unloaded the horses and put them in to their stalls. We were first to arrive and they all settled in nicely. Fig so far didn't seem to care and ate his hay. Eventually all the other horses for the show arrived. They included a miniature horse, an Icelandic horse, Paso Finos, a CARD (Community Association for Riding for the Disabled) therapy horse and more. The therapy horse was beside the miniature stallion. At one point Pierre was brushing Fig and a young blond haired girl with the CARD group walked by. She looked to be no older than six years old. She inched her way closer to Pierre. Pierre told her it was alright to pet the horse. Fig was very calm and relaxed. She hesitated and did that little hesitant wiggle small kids do when asked if they like to do something. Just as she was about to approach, one of the assistants with CARD saw her. The woman panicked and told her not to go near Figaro because he is a stallion. Pierre reassured her and when the girl came closer Fig put his head down. Without any hesitation she hugged his head. He just stood there. Not a flinch or anything. This went on for a minute or two. She just hugged him. She was so tiny she was about the size of his head. He probably could have lifted her up with ease. Fig always seemed to know. Eventually her care giver took her by the hand and she went back to what she was doing. As the little girl walked away she kept looking back at Fig and gave him a little wave goodbye. Later we found out that the little girl had suffered brain damage due to an accident on a farm, leaving her with slower motor skills. Animals know more then we will give them credit for or ever know.

Sometime had gone by since we arrived and now it was time for rehearsals. All was going fine. We did our thing but our rehearsal was mainly for the music timing and getting used to the long dark corridor. It was long and narrow and there were other stallions on the site. We needed to get the timing just right. Fig didn't care and we had to stay off to the side for a while since one of the stallions, Corsario, the showman that he was, could be pretty excitable.

Once Corsario passed Fig, I headed back and at one point got stuck in one of the aisles with stalls where the barn staff was working. When they turned and saw Fig coming their way, they asked if it was alright to pet him. We said yes. Then we answered their questions. Fig even performed a bow for them. When they asked if he was a Friesian, we started to explain that he wasn't and educated them on the Canadian horse. We even had a couple stop us to ask if they could breed to him to one of their horses. Unfortunately, we had to turn them down because there were no guarantees. Up till now Fig was making a nice impression. Once we headed back we came to a small warm up ring where we had a chance to warm up before going down the corridor. The next event was the polo team and the Paso Finos.

The show was all good. I was a bit nervous since I hadn't seen a show ring in a long while. Fig was gleaming. His dapples were showing through. That horse was so shiny it did not take much to polish him up.

We got into the warm up ring and I got him warmed up. At one point one of the other stallions got rowdy and was trying to come close to Fig. Fig was his collected self and stood his ground. Just as the stallion got under control it was our turn to perform. I remember heading down the long corridor. It was dimly lit but you could see the light at the end of the corridor. Then as we reached the light you could see the crowds. We went into the ring and to my surprise the seats were filled. This was going to be our make it or break it stage. As Fig stepped out he bowed his head and trotted in. As we lined up I took a quick look around the crowds. At that moment I thought there must be about 500 people in the stands. I was wrong. I found out later there were about 1,200 people that attended this fundraiser event. The crowd section was very low lighted. As the ring was lit up Fig stood in the center waiting for the music. I could feel his body bulk up underneath me and as the music started he went right into it. He knew this music inside and out. He was a pro at this point. He got a bit strong during the routine but he remembered the routine so I just had to trust him. Part way through, even with all the flashes, he was good. All I could see by the time I started performing was a dimly lit arena. The performing area was bright. The spectator's area was darker. You could make out silhouettes of people. When the first flash happened, Figaro took one minor step over. I didn't care about the rest. He was otherwise quiet during the routine. I know I wasn't doing anything overly spectacular. When the others were performing I could hearing clapping during their routines; all was quiet as we worked. I was trying to stay focused. Figaro had already corrected the routine once or twice and was doing phenomenally. When all was done the clapping started.

After we were done I was ready to head out of the arena. The one problem now was that Corsario was heading down already and I couldn't go down the same aisle. There was not enough room. So I moved closer to the spectators where Fig now had kids petting him. Figaro loved it. There were so many hands on him I could not tell you how many kids were petting him. We managed to make our way back and waited for the performances to be over. After everything was done spectators came to the back to chat about the horses.

After the show, more people inquired about breeding Figaro. One lady from Wisconsin wanted to breed her two mares. Pierre explained that this would only have a fifty-fifty chance of success. But she was willing to pay for Pierre and Fig to go down and have Figaro try to breed her two mares. She would pay all the costs. It was tempting but we turned it down. By the end of the day twelve people wanted breeding from Figaro. Not bad for a first impression. The organizers were happy with him too. All went well the whole day. It was a great experience.

Afterwards I managed to slip away so I went to see a couple friends and my mom upstairs in the VIP room. Like any mom would, she said, "You did great." I told her about how quiet Figaro had been. Mom and another person said all they heard was, "Wow, he is beautiful," and a great many other compliments.

This other woman said, "All I heard were people around me saying under their breath, "Wow."

When I later got the video of the show, I watched it and it was indeed quiet during our performance. For a first impression Fig went out like a star. He was getting noticed. The hidden gem was out in the light now.

Much later I met people who had been at that show and who well remembered Fig. I got many compliments. It was always nice to hear after all those years. I was in awe of him that he left that much of a mark on people. The best part of all was knowing that way deep down I knew Fig liked to show and had the talent for it and therefore it would push me to trick train him more.

This was not going to be our last performance. From that day we were going to do more performances, appearances, and breed demos. We needed to get this wonderful breed out there.

Always Keeping His Mind Thinking

After the event, I figured if Figaro liked to show then performance shows were what we would do. I decided if people thought his presence was nice, impressive and exciting when he did just a basic routine, what it would be like if he was fully trick trained? My mind was full of ideas -- but where to start? So far he had learned a few tricks on the ground. He could fetch, but he was not big on it, come when called, laugh, bow and a few other tricks. Now I wanted to work with him to achieve this under saddle. He was good and did not ever get out of hand with the ground tricks. As for under saddle, he was much better at collection and he had learned the half halt, which would make things easier. I already had a concept for training the bow under saddle. Figaro already knew body cues and generally I would tap his side flank.

This was the beginning. We had still been using the double bridle. The first few attempts he did not seem to quite get it. Once it clicked he would go down a little and then stop. After a moment or two, I realized he did not seem to like the two bits. I thought about what might work, so just to try it I took off the curb bit. It was then that he went down. I was surprised since the bow is a tough trick. Some may not view it that way but it is difficult for a horse. It requires back muscles and the upper hind muscles. In addition, going down on one knee can put a little strain on various parts of the body. This is why when people ask about tricks and training their horse, I turn some down because I do think about the horse. If a horse had back issues, yes, learning the bow might help. It would be no good if the horse is unfit and does not do any regular exercise. It could make it worse. Horses are like us. If you don't do exercises then jump into yoga you will be sore or could even do some damage. Also I look at the mentality of a person as well. Some, as Frank used to say, want to do all the high level stuff but without learning all the steps up to that point. Unfortunately I have seen this many times. As for Figaro, he was fit and had no underlying medical or muscle issues. I even had Pierre check over his muscles to make sure and that his hind muscles were nice and loose. After he went down the first time, I asked one more time to see if he got the concept. I gave a light tug with my left rein and a tap from my left foot and whip and *viola*, he went down. If you have never experienced the bow under saddle it is quite interesting. Half a horse pretty much disappears underneath you. If they keep their head up while doing the bow, not so much. Figaro preferred putting his head between his front legs. However once he got it, deep down I was full of pride. My dreams were becoming a reality.

We didn't work on tricks all the time. It was just the cherry on top of an ice cream sundae. There were so many things I was enjoying with Figaro. At this point, if I could think of something, my attitude was, why not? Some days I took out the small orange cones and would place them on the side of the arena or on top of the pillars. After several visits to Medieval Times (a Toronto entertainment that allows diners to watch jousting), I thought, why not joust? The only difference was that I used a ten-foot garrocha pole as my "lance" but it worked. Figaro could stay in a straight line no problem. Because the arena was smaller I would canter it. It still worked. I gave myself some credit because I would hit those orange cones most of the time. I thought that if he ever did make it to the movies, I better get him used to the clash of swords. We never used real swords. As a substitute, we used a stiff whip or pieces of wood. All of which Figaro did not seem to mind. When it came down to it, he would tilt his head slightly while we clashed our "swords" He was always game and you could get him to side pass or pivot circles around to get closer to "the enemy." He was such a trooper. That was why I called him my war horse. If we ever had to go back to the medieval days, we were prepared.

I continued to test my bond with Fig. One day Pierre suggests that I be blindfolded. No one was in the arena and I thought, alright. I asked him what exactly I was supposed to do. He said he would guide me through some dressage movements and we would go from there. He said, "Don't worry.

Figaro will not hurt you." Which was true. So I put on a bandana over my eyes and out we went. Now when you can't see, your balance is a bit off, well at least in my case. My balance was not too great to begin with because of my back and hips. I found I leaned to one side slightly. Figaro assisted at some moments by moving to one side and once gave me a small bump to get me back into the middle of the saddle. We did leg yielding, we trotted and did a few steps of canter. We did circles and more. It was a weird sensation. In the back of my mind, I thought at least if I were ever to go blind, I know I could still ride Figaro. After all was said and done, we managed not to run into a wall or anything. Pierre would guide verbally and tell me to change direction etc.

That is when Pierre said, "I don't think you need to ride with a helmet on Figaro." I know this thought will get some people riled up. I do believe that a rider should wear a helmet when up on a horse. I had had my share of concussions – ten of them -- and I know I should always wear a helmet. This is not an excuse but my head did get very heated in summer when I rode. Even when I had a helmet with lots of air vents I would end up with heat stress and would feel nauseated and a little dizzy. When Pierre said this I was very hesitant. I always rode with a helmet. I went a few rounds and it felt different. After much thinking, and with some hesitation, I agreed. I still advise people to wear a helmet. I did always wear one on other horses or on trails and all other times when I rode. Only when I was performing with Fig did I not wear one.

My thinking was this: if Fig was ever to get into a movie, the actor riding him would not be wearing a helmet. And if I could not trust him, why would I expect another to trust him? I never had one issue riding Figaro without a helmet. If kids were nearby, I would explain not to do what I was doing and explain the consequences of not wearing a helmet. I am glad that they did listen, that showed me they had respect and listened to what I said. When your ride you never know who is watching. If it took a moment or two I would always stop to explain myself and make them aware why they need to ride with a helmet. One thing I have learned with people if you talk to them with respect most will listen to what you say.

It may sound weird but sometimes giving that little bit of trust can take you so much farther.

photo by Laura Sperduti

Figaro Observing and Learning

Sometimes when you think you have seen it all or think your horse can't amaze you more, something happens to challenge that assumption.

It is amazing enough that you can teach a horse any number of things and that the horse retains that knowledge. More amazing still is when a horse sees something and then tries it on his own. I have only seen one horse do that, and that horse was Figaro. Fig would actually teach himself his own tricks.

This first became apparent when Fig and I were sharing the arena with Frank's younger dark bay Lusitano stallion, Manjerico Jr. Frank was working with Manji and another rider. I stayed out of the way while he taught her. At one point I stopped to listen to Frank give pointers to his student. After a few minutes, I noticed Fig collecting himself more. In a few strides he got a bit of a bounce. If you have never ridden a passage, it is a bounce movement with a subtle pause in between. It was not that prominent with Figaro but it was there. I guess I was not the only one who noticed.

After Frank let his student cool out Manji, he came over and said to me, "He looks like he wants to learn." Without saying a word Frank got us along the wall and told me to half halt. It was then that he gave Figaro a tap on top of his huge hind end and with a little urging Fig gave a step or two of a passage. Again we asked, because his steps were not too high. Frank pushed on. After more encouragement, Figaro gave a few good steps. When motivated he could look impressive. With each bit of collection, Frank would have us stride out as much as Fig could stretch. Frank explained that if you coil the spring, you must release the spring. When you released the coil, you had to sit deep or you would be leaning back when he took off. Figaro had that force.

Richard, a French rider, had come to stay at the farm. He was helping Frank with some of the horses and with farm labour. Richard had done some work with his own horses in something similar to *Cavalia* (imagine Cirque du Soleil, but with horses). He saw me with Figaro and gave me some pointers to improve the *passage*. Sometimes he would watch us play at liberty. Most of the time, Richard would talk to Pierre in French off to the side of the arena near the stairs while I rode. Then later on Pierre would translate some of the conversation. Richard apparently had good things to say about Figaro. In time, and with a little help, Figaro would learn the *passage* and *piaffe*. Eventually I learned to motivate him myself and thank goodness for Figaro's flexibility. I did this by a light tap on his hind end. Eventually he got the idea. It was amazing what you can do with the right motivation and knowledge.

One time when I was cooling Figaro out, the barn's vet, stood by the door with Frank and Pierre. Frank reportedly remarked, "If you could take Manji's energy and put it into Figaro, you would have the perfect horse." Figaro was the heavier, baroque horse. The vet seemed to like Figaro and complimented Figaro a few times. He liked the bigger horses. All I knew was that Fig had a powerful hind end and I intended to use it to my advantage.

After a little work Figaro was improving his passage. I remember Frank saying that once a horse learns the *piaffe,* you go into the *passage* and then from there once they are able to collect themselves then you can perform the *levade.*

He was right. I figured this out by fluke when we were working on the *passage.* I then wanted to work with Fig on the *piaffe* and he got so puffed up he did a small *levade.* This is when the horse collects himself and will have both front feet off the ground at 30 to 35 degrees and can hold the position.

As short as this accidental levade was, Fig held it. It was then that I realized how to obtain the rear. He had the hind end power and he seemed to be at the right point to do this with some work. I took him into the middle of the arena. It was worth a try. So I asked him for the half halt and gave a small prod from my heel. He gave me a few steps of passage. I tapped him again and I sat a bit deeper and sat up a bit more as if I was going to ask him to halt one or two steps and gave me a small hop. It was a start. So that he did not get excited I took him around and went to a different spot. I asked again and he gave me a bit more. So once more I said to myself, let's see if the third time is the charm and it was. He went up for a short time. I rewarded him with a well-earned pat and took him around. In time he would perform it with no problem. Fig would do it with this small cue: a subtle curl of the reins and a slight lean back. I made sure he understood the difference between rearing and backing up. The cues were similar but had their subtle differences. You need to be in control and you don't want him to associate backing up with rearing up because once taught this can be difficult to undo. This was my greatest accomplishment with him and in my eyes he had a great rear up. If you ever want to feel like you are on top of the world, you could not feel it better than on a big black steed.

Fig was capturing more people's eyes. He was no longer just a horse. Fig was the cool trick horse. He was no longer the black sheep in a barn of white stallions. It might sound weird but sometimes I felt like the underdog. I did not have the money to afford a Lusitano or the money to get the same schooling. When given a challenge, I will strive for it and on this account I succeeded.

Just as things started to look so promising, fate always seems to throw that curve ball at you. Sometimes you wonder whether the gods are testing us, to see if we can go the distance.

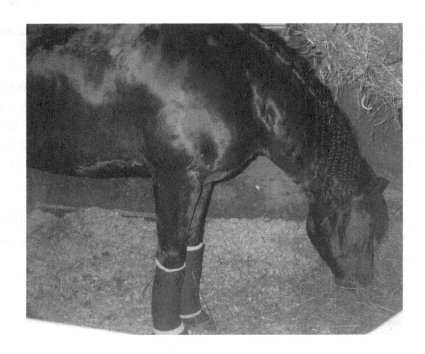

What's Wrong?

It was early in the year when spring was coming and the horses were spunkier. Everybody at the farm was tired from an SPCA show the night before.

Pierre and I decided we might as well head up to the farm because I knew the barn would be quiet. When we arrived I did as I always did: I headed right to Fig's stall where he would always turn around to greet me. But when I called him he didn't move. He remained facing the opposite direction. I called again, still walking closer. When he didn't turn around, my gut was saying something was not right. When I opened his stall door I knew why. He was lathered in sweat, shavings up the back of the stall and he was holding his leg up in the air. The worst part was that his leg was swollen but his ankle was bigger than a melon and hard to the touch. I knew right away this was not good. After working at the track for some time, you know when things are not right and the first thing that came to my mind was that the ankle was broken. Pierre was chatting away with some boarders when I called him over. I was praying he would have a different opinion.

Pierre was a bit slow to react until I called out to him to come -- now. After a two-second look he made a call to the vet. Figaro was in distress and Pierre was afraid that Fig's ankle was broken.

When the vet finally arrived he brought out the x-ray machine and administered some pain killers. From what he saw he wasn't too hopeful. Even worse, the vet said that this didn't just happen. The vet believed that Fig had been in distress for some time. Thank goodness we came up. The usual farm workers had been given time off because of the late night. Some girls and an exchange student were taking care of the barn. Meanwhile the vet took X-rays. I could feel my gut turning inside out.

By then Frank had come down to the barn. When he saw the vet's truck he had to inquire and at this point the prognosis was not good. Even with the pain killers, Figaro still didn't really want to put any weight on the leg and he kept it off the ground. Frank was upset and at this point I swear my stomach turned inside out.

I brought a plastic lawn chair to his stall. He was settling now due to the pain killers. His eyes seemed to soften and he lowered his head. The women at the barn were amazing and were comforting me while we waited for the results. While they were comforting me, to be honest, I don't remember a word they said. I was focusing on Fig. Pierre helped the vet haul his equipment through the big brown doors to his van.

As I sat there with Fig, he brought his head out and for a moment instead of thinking of his pain he gave me his signature bear hugs with his head. I think at his point he was more concerned that I was upset than with his pain and he just kept this head there. All I could say was, "Figaro, I will make this promise. If the pain is too much, the day you don't want your apples and carrots then I will know it is your time to go."

When Pierre came back in, the vet gave us some extra-strength Bute and was going to call Dr. Brad to get an appointment to get an ultrasound since because of the swelling it was hard to get a clear X-ray and he wanted to see what the tissue damage was.

Pierre bandaged him up and when things had calmed down, I asked why he was outside for so long with the vet. Pierre told me the vet suggested we put him down due to the extent of the injury and the fact that even with heavy-duty pain killers Fig did not want to put his foot down.

When Pierre said no to the vet, the vet said, "If he recovers, you will be lucky if he ends up being a lawn ornament." The vet also told Pierre that Figaro would probably be on at least six months stall rest.

Pierre said, "No. I will try everything first. So no."

Finally we got the ultrasound appointment. We bandaged him up as if he had a broken leg to protect him on the journey. Good thing Pierre had experience shipping horses with broken legs. We made it safe and sound to the clinic. Fig was sore but of course a mare was calling to him so let's just say his mind was distracted. This made it easy to tranquillize him and take him in for X-rays and ultrasound. They did the ultrasound but due to the swelling and fluid build-up, it made it hard. From what they could see, Figaro had bruised his sesamoid. That can be just as bad as a fracture. Figaro had torn his flexor tendons, the tendons in front of the pastern, and he had rotated his tendon. He was prescribed more medication and stall rest. Brad was amazed after looking at the injury. He said the last time he saw an injury like this was after a horse jumped a six-foot fence. Brad said Fig had to do that when he was turned out. Brad said he must have come down with a lot of force. Fig liked to play and most likely he did his little 360 degree leap in the air and came down too hard. Probably he had little turn out the day before because of the performance and he did like to play when turned out in the arena. So I think it was a recipe for disaster and a bit of bad luck. He was not out of the woods. Even if the tendons did heal, there was a possibility of calcium developing by the tendons and that would mean surgery with no guarantees. We would have to wait and see.

There was a lot of support from everybody in the barn and we constantly got reports of people giving him pats and checking on him. I think that helped him mentally and thankfully he didn't developed any vices from boredom. Many people walked through the barn and I can't thank them enough. I think Figaro appreciated it as well.

So this was our next journey. Every day I went up to the barn. Figaro was put on a strict diet and had his meds hidden in a small mash each day so he would take it. He hated Bute and no matter what you put it in, he would not eat it. Funny thing: during his recovery, he ate it. I guess the pain was too much for him. We gave him a hay net so he didn't have to bend and put too much pressure on the leg. I have to say, while I sat watching Fig, he did use his head in many ways. If his leg got too sore he elevated his head until the pain subsided. I have seen lots of things at the track, from broken legs and much else. The weirdest thing is feeling no tendon on the horse. Where there should have been a firm ligament was a Jell-O-like sheath. Pierre did the bandaging the first little while but when his work obligations got in the way, I eventually took over that task. If the bandage was not put on right, it could cause even more damage and/or a permanently bowed tendon.

I did not feel as comfortable back then bandaging this particular injury. I had done broken legs and to me it was agonizing. I likened it to a doctor pressed into treating her own child. How do you separate your feelings of attachment? It was so different treating Figaro. He was a major part of my life and I didn't know if I could cope if anything happened to him. You can get attached to a horse at the track but not in any way close to the relationship I had with my own horse.

My goal was to help stabilize the tendon slowly back to its original position. For the first week or two, Figaro did not leave his stall. Rose and Frank took turns checking on him at nights to make sure nothing was wrong and that he wasn't in distress. I think Frank was more upset then he let on. The worst part for him was that he had to go to Portugal for two weeks because of a family get-together. I found out later that he was worried about Figaro the whole time he was gone.

After two weeks, Figaro was bearing more weight on his leg and thought it would be better to cold hose his legs to help alleviate the swelling. My only choice was to take him every so cautiously out of the stall. He would walk a step out and if it bothered him, he would stop and raise his leg. When he was ready he would try again. Sometimes it took 30 minutes to make it twenty feet. I let him do what he needed to do. Sometimes he would lean on me a bit. To assist him as much as I could with each step where he needed to put pressure down, I would lean into him. When we were outside I think he was relieved that he was somewhere else other than in his stall. We sat outside and I would cold-hose his leg for an hour then bring him back in. I would bandage him. This course of treatment went on for about a month and a half.

Figaro was showing some improvement and he would let us know if he was sore or in pain. He would raise the leg. After a month and a half he was able to put more weight down and could go for a longer walk. I put cold water bandages on and kept them cold while he walked. I also still continued the cold-hosing treatment. A concern with horses on stall rest is the possibility of laminitis, which is what ended the racehorse Barbaro's life. Barbaro had just recently passed (this was in 2007) and that put me even more on edge with Figaro's injury. A vet advised us that while Figaro could walk we were to keep the bandage on for support but not too long. Our walks started out for two minutes then we got the raised foot and we would take him inside. In time it increased to five minutes then eight minutes, then ten minutes, to the point we could go to thirty minutes but we would have to take some rest periods in between. I just held onto the lead and he made the decision when he wanted to move on.

Mentally and physically I was getting exhausted since Pierre and I both put in long days of physical work at our jobs. I remember one day when I was so sick. It was 30 degrees outside. Chuck had put a small fan by Figaro's stall so that he stayed comfortable in the heat. I was so dizzy and tired I needed to drink a Red Bull to stay awake. It didn't help. It turned out I had a temperature of 102. Regardless I still took care of Figaro. When it comes to my animals they come first no matter what. I have to thank Liz, a co-worker who drove me up to the farm when Pierre had to work. She was a great friend when I needed help. Thank you Liz.

One day after I had put him in the stall waiting for his legs to dry, I went to the arena to watch Frank giving a lesson to some of the women at the barn. I remember sitting on the stairs wondering if I would ever ride Figaro again. It was then that Frank came to the stairs and sat beside me and inquired about the progress of "the beast," as he called him. I admitted that I missed riding but I told Frank that it didn't matter if I never rode him again I just wanted him with me -- even as a lawn ornament. Riding is nice but it is not everything.

After another two weeks, Figaro was showing yet more improvement and was walking for longer than half an hour. The tendon was in place, just not firmed up totally yet. I continued the cold water treatments and kept him moving. He was not on turn out yet. The little exercise he was getting would help strengthen up the tendon slowly. I did not want the support on all the time because the tendon needed to strengthen itself. Once a horse comes to rely on support, they will always need support. Figaro seemed to know this himself. We would come in and all his stall bandages, save the one on the injured leg, were off. I said to Fig, "Fine but you need at least the front pairs on." If I was not making the decision, he was going to make it for me. He was saying, "I don't need this." At the beginning he would keep his bandages on. Now he seemed to be saying that he no longer needed those other bandages.

When we finally hit the three-month mark, Figaro let us know he was on the mend. We went for our daily walk and he decided to do a mini Spanish Walk and attempted a bow. The tendon luckily was almost as strong as it was before the injury. We got extremely lucky and he did not develop a bowed tendon. We got even luckier in that he did develop a calcium bump, however, when the vet looked at it he said Figaro wouldn't need surgery.

After about two weeks, Figaro was given the okay to be turned out for short, supervised durations. After an exhausting three and a half months of daily visits to the farm to care for Figaro, I have to admit staying up was hard. He had been doing alright with his mini turn outs. One day I was watching him in the arena from a chair. There was a mini gate preventing him from going out one side and there was a pole up on the other side. Every other time he was in the arena he was behaved. I must have dozed off. My mistake. When I woke up he wasn't there. I felt the panic a mother does when her child is out of view. I panicked. I looked: no gate or pole was down. Where did he go? All arena doors were closed. I looked out the one side. Then I ran to the side with the pole. There I found Figaro at the end of the mare's barn driving old Manjerico, the main resident stallion nuts, grazing on some grass. What does he do? Look up at me with an expression on his face like, "What? I wanted grass." I found out he was a very good limbo artist. I made sure to block the doorway with barrels to prevent further escapes.

Finally after he was able to go out in the paddock again and the tendon was stronger, Fig was able to do light lunge work. The next test was the true test. Could he handle a rider's weight? Or was he destined to be a lawn ornament? With Pierre supervising, I finally sat up on his back. Pierre stayed by his side and he led him a couple steps. It went well. Figaro did have the odd ouch moment but he moved on again. I guess his way of saying; I am not done healing yet. We began the weight training. Over time we were walking around the arena with a rider on for about twenty minutes. Within another week he was able to do a light trot, stopping if it got too much. He always let us know.

By the next year, Fig was back to his old self. We were back to doing our arena work. We worked with polo wraps on for the first while. Then one day he stopped and pointed at his leg. He did this three times. I thought something was wrong. Then he was trying to get the Velcro off. So I got someone to take them off. He knew what he needed and hated having stuff on that he didn't need. So the pro let me know.

It was at this point that Figaro became somewhat more accepting of Pierre and did not terrorize him as much.

photo by Laura Sperduti

Back on Track

With Figaro on the mend, things were looking up. I never would have thought I would be able to ride him again, never mind do what I always dreamed of doing. This was where I always tell people: learn about your horse and always check your horse over every time you see him. Fig was doing well and the ligament was getting stronger. It would take a few years before there were no flare ups. Luckily even when there was a flare up with the tendon, it never seemed to make him lame. I could tell he was a bit off and did not want to do too much.

This is where I knew when to read him. To confirm, the tendon would get somewhat hot and swollen. He was easy on himself and in listening to him we seemed to have an understanding. Even with liberty work, which was not too hard on him, we would keep an eye on him.

Sometimes I stopped working with him altogether. Like standing on the stool, for example. We minimized him doing it at the time since stepping up and holding transfers his weight to the front. This is what tends to be forgotten. It is no different than having a horse lie down on his back. Yes, it can show trust but a horse was not built to be on his back for any extended amount of time. If a trainer does it right and works with the horse slowly, then a horse can build up his strength and back muscles for this. Most people have a tendency to want to rush. Likewise teaching the sit or rearing on a hard surface. A horse may do it many times and have no effect but tricks like that over time if done repeatedly can cause hock issues (sitting on a bean bag made for horses can alleviate this). Turning while on a stool imposes different risk: should the stool have a gripping material? If the horse's foot cannot slide a little the ankle will not turn. So if you don't have a stool that rotates you must insure to give the horse time to correct himself or you can wrench his ankle. Sometimes I will put a little sand on the stool to allow some give. Like any trick if you take your time and the proper steps were taken in teaching, then the horse should be calm and will not get over zealous when performing that trick. Anything can pose a risk but proper measures should be taken to ensure safety of both parties. No different than any other discipline. We should not get over cautious or you would never do anything. Just use common sense and do not over do one thing and a horse will not get sour mentally or physically.

Of the fifty tricks Fig learned, only five actually required extra physical strength. He was generally fit and those particular tricks were not worked on as much. The other forty five I thought might prove useful if he were to go on a film set. There were many tricks he knew that only required little refreshers to maintain. I also wanted tricks that Figaro could perform even at the age of thirty without stressing him. He liked to perform and it would be a shame if I could no longer perform with him. Some people think when their horse gets old, you can do this but you can't do that. In many cases they can do certain things, so you just have to be easier on them and give them longer warm ups. They just need a bit more time and after all the years of service, they deserve it.

One lady I know tried to retire her trail horse when he was 26 years old but had more problems because he moped. He had lost teeth and had other issues linked to his age. But one day something told her to put the saddle on and he was happy. He could no longer go twenty miles but he could do twelve. He came back to life. Horses are like people: after working for so many years it is hard to just go cold turkey and do nothing.

In Figaro's case he loved to perform and I had every intention of letting him continue to perform for as long as he still had the desire. Why not? So we did as much as we could do while still thinking about him and his welfare.

Meanwhile, Winnie, another resident rider, was inspired and started doing her own research on liberty and at times she would ask me my views. She began working with Frank's younger Lusitano stallion, Manjerico Jr. At this point her tricks were as simple: she had taught the horse to pick up a brush or find the treat under the cones. Winnie would later purchase two horses from Frank and go on to teach them liberty tricks and further her knowledge on liberty training. She now hosts charity events with her horses and fellow boarder's horses.

For Figaro and me, liberty work was a part of our routine but it was not everything. Sometimes we would just play. Just run around with each other and just have fun and play our game of tag. I wanted him to be as accomplished under saddle as well on the ground. This is what made him a great jack of all trades. Sometimes I think people get too caught up in ground work. After a while, more excuses are made not to get up in the saddle. I have seen it happen many times. For Figaro, at least, our routine never got boring. I always changed it up. Even after a ride, sometimes I would sit behind the saddle and undo his tack. Then I would drop the saddle on the stairs and ride bareback for a cool out time. If he felt good, he would go for a roll. If it was warm out, Fig would get a nice bath afterwards. Even if he was out of your sight, I could always tell that Figaro was rolling by the loud grumbling noises he made as he rolled. He almost always rolled from one side to the other. He had good back muscles. Once he went to roll and seemed to get stuck mid-roll and had all four feet in the air for a moment. We waited to see which side he would roll to but he opted to let gravity choose and in slow motion he fell to the one side. Then he got up, shook himself off, and did some leaping.

Figaro was just a character. He seemed to grow on people. His antics generally brought more people to his stall or to the barn so they could watch him. One boarder and her daughter would strike up many conversations with me about Figaro. Some days I would spend the extra time and just make him look super good and that is when Figaro got another nickname -- Fancy Pants. The daughter walked up to Figaro and said to him, "You are Mister Fancy Pants." I asked her why and she said that he was just beautiful and she liked his tricks. Over time Figaro acquired other nicknames -- Fig, Hoover, Fancy Pants, Mick Jagger, Mr. Fig, Mr. Figaro and the common one at the time, Figarama.

Mr. Fancy Pants was going to have a chance to shine but first we had to audition.

Time to Shine

Spring was in the air and everyone – horse and human – could feel it. Figaro and I had done much work on minor tricks, such as untying hands, raising each leg and holding items longer. We had perfected his rear up and Spanish Walk and just needed a chance to move to the next step. Frank would host the Old Gala show but he also did outside performances as well. This spring they were having a gathering, a fun show. Sometimes the students had a chance to show off their accomplishments. This time they decided to open it up and have a costume class and talent show.

I decided, why not? I never really cared to show Figaro for ribbons. I know he was good and the reason I never showed him in a breed class was because he was oversized. Some judges would mark that against him. A small handful that disliked oversized Canadians. Figaro was considered a freak for the breed (a freak was a horse bigger than normal for the breed) many others never seemed to not have anything against the size. What might have been used against him in a breed class, it seemed to me, was the very thing that made him stand out. Years later many people came up to me and said, "I remember that Canadian, the big beautiful one." So it worked for him and me and that's all that counted.

Many thought Canadian horses were not capable of performing high level dressage. At the time there were not many Canadian horses and it is hard to say with accuracy how many Canadian horses did higher levels of dressage. At least we were at a barn where we had a chance to show it being done. Now you can go on many Canadian sites and see lots of Canadian horse enthusiasts doing high level dressage and more with their Canadians.

A week prior to the show, the barn was being prepared and a tent was set up outside. It gave me enough time to decide what costume to wear. As I was riding around, Figaro stopped by the gazebo-like tent. He sniffed it and investigated. The two ends were open and luckily I ducked in time because he thought it was a good idea to ride *through* the tent. He just walked through that tent, with the wind blowing at the sides (a lot of horses would have been spooked by that). As we walked through the other side he seemed content and we continued on our way. After he had done this I started thinking about movies for ideas and then it sort of hit me. I remember seeing an old photo of Frank dressed as Zorro and riding his black Lusitano, Negrito, pasta bonfire. Why not Zorro? I borrowed a hat and someone loaned me a real French sword, long and slender. I had a black Shakespearean shirt and my mom made me a mask and cape. The riding boots and breeches were perfect. I later got some small fake roses to put in Fig's mane to make him look better for the part.

The day of the show the girls did their dressage tests while a small gathering of people looked on. I got Figaro ready. He was just so black and shiny. Pierre insisted on doing the roses, which was fine. He did that while I got ready. When the time came we went into the arena with a couple others. We did a small routine and received a small gift bag of goods. Then there was a talent section. Winnie had gone in with young Manjerico and did some small tricks she had worked out. Since this was last minute for me, I had some music put together and got Figaro to perform some tricks at liberty. Our finale was a bow and a rear up.

It was not till after that we found out why Frank and his daughters had put on the talent show. It was to see who would come out to do the talent portion of the show and to see who could be in future shows. It was sort of an audition. Figaro made the cut. Luckily there was an event coming up soon for the Orangeville SPCA. They wanted Figaro to do one act. They had thrown a couple ideas at me in time. We would see what we would end up doing.

Clever Boy

I was looking forward to being part of one of Frank's performances. This would be the first time riding Figaro with the students and horses from Frank's farm. Until then, Figaro, of course, was Figaro in the meantime.

I was not the only one to have fun with Figaro. Many others started to enjoy Figaro as well. Brenda, one of the fellow riders told me once of the games she used to play with Figaro. She described her habit of wandering through the barn, packing her usual stash of carrot pieces in her pocket. Brenda would generally stop to pet the odd horse or see who was interested enough to stop munching hay for a moment to accept a carrot. Figaro was generally one of her stops. He knew the sound of the carrot bag and in mid chew he looked up and would give Brenda a look. She opened up the stall door. Fig had a cross bar so he could not escape from his stall. Yet it gave him more freedom to move his large neck and head around.

He would immediately check out all her pockets just in case there were more goodies. Fig was a big boy. He can put you off balance with just a nudge. Most would be intimidated by his size when first meeting him, but Brenda never thought too much about it since she was so used to his size. When he leaned toward Brenda, she backed off a bit since he was frisking her pockets quite thoroughly. When she reached into her pocket to get him a carrot, she came with a handful of jellybeans. Figaro had a sweet tooth. This was her own personal stash for a quick snack for when she worked in the barn in the mornings. I should know. With all that physical work, you do need a cheap sugar rush sometimes. However, in Figaro's eyes, he thought he had hit the jackpot. So she gave him one. She thought, "One jelly bean can't hurt. I've given him jujubes before."He liked the black liquorice ones best. He loved black licorice and on special occasion would go to the Dutch store to get him the salted black licorice.

That one jelly bean was sucked up in seconds, like a vacuum. After Fig had finished bobbing his head up and down with delight, he started nuzzling again, a little gentler than before. This time, Brenda went into her left pocket to get him the appropriate treat...a piece of carrot. Of course he took it, but instead of the head-bobbing, Brenda got another look. As he was crunching, he nuzzled again, going back and forth from the left to the right pocket, several times over. Brenda reached into her left pocket again and gave him another piece of carrot. He of course took it again . . . unamused. Fig immediately started nuzzling her right pocket, insatiably, still gently, but with purpose! So Brenda gave him another jelly bean. This didn't stop until he had consumed the fourth jelly bean. So Brenda decided to challenge his brain, is it just routine now? Brenda then turned her back to him and switched -- jellybeans in the left pocket, carrot-pieces in the right. Brenda then faced him again and when she approached him, gave him a pat on the head. He looked at her as if to say, "What are you up to treat lady? I want another jelly-bean!" Brenda stood there and he started the nuzzling again, back and forth from the left to right pocket . . . favoring the left pocket. After a moment or two, Brenda gave him the fifth jellybean.

Now their game had begun! Brenda went out of Figaro's sight, emptied her pockets of all treats and put only one jellybean back in her left pocket and only one carrot piece in her right. She walked back towards him . . . he was waiting anxiously. She stood in front of him, and with only one sniff for each pocket, he went for the left pocket. Bingo! Sixth jelly-bean! She made sure yet again to be out of his eyesight. Switching the treats again, she then walked back to Fig, stood in front of him again, and wouldn't you know? He went directly for the right-hand pocket, without as much as a test sniff! Seventh jellybean found and devoured! Brenda did this yet again. Why not? Fig seemed to be enjoying this. So one more time, just to be sure . . . but this time, Brenda kept a jellybean in the right pocket, with the carrot in the left.

Brenda said "OK smarty-pants. They're not just being switched back and forth. Let's see if you can guess." As Brenda told me, this freakishly smart giant was enjoying every minute of this game. This time she gave it some thought and said, "I got you this time Fig. I've got you now."

Without hesitation, Figaro moved to the right pocket for his eighth and final jellybean. Brenda laughed out loud, scratched his forehead and thought to herself how totally impressed she was by Fig's sniffing abilities. Only afterwards did it occur to her: not only did Fig enjoy the jellybeans but he had just lured Brenda into spending some time with him.

Once the treats were done, he seemed to have had enough of what Brenda called the "impress-the-human-game." Most horses really do enjoy our company but Brenda felt at that moment she had just been conned and when the treats were done he was quite content to go back to his hay.

If anything Brenda had a good time and a good laugh. Thank you Brenda for keeping his mind sharp.

A Lasting Impression

Figaro always enjoyed an impromptu visit from Brenda. She always had a memorable time with this clever boy. Who would guess that Figaro would also have a lasting impression on her brother too.

It had been some time since Figaro's injury and this was the day he was going to have an impact on someone's life.

All was well and he was being quite a good boy. This particular day it was warm. It was early in the evening when students were coming up to the farm for their lessons. I was just finishing with Fig. Generally for a cool down, sometimes just to work on my seat, I would take his saddle off and leave it on the stairs. Best part I never had to get off his back. I would just sit behind the saddle and undo everything and slide back into position. Never once did he ever buck me off doing this. This day, as per usual, a couple people came to watch the lessons and sit on the stairs. I was used to it. Some were new faces and some were people I knew. I do remember a man sitting near the top of the stairs. He was mid-sized and had a pleasant smile. I was just riding around and working around the students as they came in. Fig was cool about it. We walked, trotted and did a little canter. We moved between the horses and riders with ease.

It wasn't till the next day that Brenda came over and said her brother Ron was impressed with Figaro. He would have bought him right there and then. I thanked her for the compliment but I said Fig is not for sale. I did tell her that if her brother came to the farm again, she should let me know.

Later Pierre and I ended up meeting Ron and his wife Louise when they visited the barn. Ron paid us a compliment years later and said we were the first people who welcomed them to the barn and made them feel at home. We always liked to meet new people and in time Ron became a good friend of mine.

This was a start to our long friendship. One day I even let Ron ride Fig. Unfortunately, it was a hot day and Fig was less than keen on being ridden. His best effort was not there. Still, Ron got the experience of riding the big boy and that made Ron happy and ecstatic.

Fig must have made an impression on Ron since he would later get his own Canadian horse, a gelding named Pax. Eventually Ron would pursue with Pax the same things I did with Figaro. He now has his own Figaro.

SPCA Charity Show

We were finally getting closer to the SPCA Charity Show. Frank asked if we wanted to be in it. Frank's daughter Rose was going to do the coordinating. I was hoping to end up in the women's quadrille. It was not in the cards. I was at the in-between age. I was younger than most women there and the next group was a bit younger than me. I ended up in the younger group, slated to be the opener. There were three other girls and their mounts, Garbosa, Roz and the black cross mare, Tia and there was Figaro and me.

Rose wanted us to carry flags. Of course, I was the guinea pig. So a got a towel and a large wooden pole and we attached the two together. I placed the pole on the top of my foot and started at a walk. To keep it balanced on my boot was a challenge since I have small feet for my size. Fig reacted in the way I thought he would -- no reaction. After we tried it, Rose decided to try the others, and while it took they a bit longer but they were alright with it. I am glad Figaro was ok with it because we were going to carry one of the two larger flags.

Meanwhile we worked on our simple routine. I just wanted to do something a bit more. It seemed to me a shame to come this far and not display Figaro's true level of talent. While Rose was up in the viewing room with another party working out details, I practiced with the flag. We went around easily and I even went through the routine with him. I did this mainly to see how the flag moves and feels. Sometimes you needed to grip it harder when the flag started waving and exerting a pull. When I stopped, I was thinking about putting the flag down. Before I did that I wondered if I could rear up with the flag. You never know till you try it. It was then that I faced the viewing lounge and Figaro obliged. We did it. We reared up with the flag, no problem. I guess Rose had seen it. It was then that Figaro was going to have his moment. At the finale Figaro, was going to at least perform the rear up. Even better news, we were going to be the leader of the group. The only downside of that decision was that we had to convince the other horses to get close to him. Figaro never did anything to any of them. His size and thundering hooves intimidated the other three. When we did the rear up in the finale, two of the horses would do side passes -- not from panic but from intimidation. So we rehearsed a lot. The routine also changed a few times as well. In the end all was well.

My next step I wanted to get him a lyrca snuggy– a horse hoody to cover his head and neck. It was easier to braid his mane the night before and then strap on the snuggy to keep his mane tidy. We needed to do a Portuguese braid, which are two long singular braids down the center of the neck. Then you can weave large ribbons through the two braids and it looks really nice. To distinguish the mares and geldings from the stallions, the mares and geldings had red and silver and the stallions blue and gold. Figaro got blue and gold. I got him a nice light blue snuggy. I had tried it on Fig to make sure we got the right size, and of course he did not mind a bit. Later, Richard asked Pierre in French if Fig had minded it and Pierre said he didn't even flinch. It was then that Richard said something and went running up the stairs. In a moment or two he came down with a large suitcase. He opened it up and brought out a large white caparison (a one-piece cloth that was used in medieval times to cover a horse's body), with red and black trim and designs. Richard asked if he could try it on Figaro. We said sure. We wanted to see what he looked like it in it. Once both Pierre and Richard had negotiated the head piece, the rest followed easily. He looked good once they put it on him. Right then Frank came around the corner. Richard started to speak to him in French while I waited for Pierre to translate. He told Frank how neat it would be to have four stallions do a routine in medieval gear. Frank said it would indeed but doubted his horses would tolerate the gear. So that went out the door but at least I knew Figaro would pretty much wear anything. I had already ridden him a long dress, no problem, for a Christmas party. This would be good if he ever got into a movie.

In any case, our routine was down pat. The only thing our little group disliked was the seven dwarfs' music. At least we knew our routine and all was well.

We got Figaro all cleaned up the night before and he was all braided and did not seem to mind the snuggy at all. The next day we got here early and loaded Figaro up. We had bought our own three-horse trailer at a good price from someone Pierre knew. Figaro had his own limo. The rest had a large transport coming. Once we arrived at the fairground, they were offering as a promotion pet photos taken by a professional photographer named Paul. When we arrived we found Figaro's stall. Beverly, one of the helpers, had made signs that gave a little information on each horse and the breed. Since Figaro was the only Canadian horse there was a write up about his breed. When we took Figaro off the trailer there were not too many people around but Figaro always walked off proud and would give his grumble call to let everybody know he was there. I guess he made an impression. Paul's girlfriend was a model and she had seen him. Since everything was quiet, we took advantage. The rest of the horses had arrived but they were settling into their stalls, which were located in one building, with a 50-foot aisle leading to the arena where we would perform. I gave Figaro a nice warm up in the arena. Pierre, as usual, was talking to whoever would listen to him and now he was talking to Paul and his girlfriend. Pierre then called me and I brought Figaro over, at which point Paul's girlfriend mentioned how much she liked him. Paul said she had been talking about your horse since you got here. She had seen the others but she really was drawn to Figaro. It was then Pierre said, "Show them some of his stuff." So I performed a bow and a rear up for them and Paul took photos.

Paul asked many questions. Could a model sit on him? Would he stand beside a motorcycle? I said, "Yes, nothing fazes him and when it comes to inexperienced people he would be a perfect gentleman."

He mentioned how he would like to do a photo shoot with some models and maybe there was a chance for a possible commercial. There was one coming up and the idea was on the table for a Mustang car commercial and they wanted a black horse.

Doors were opening up.

After that I was about to take the saddle off when Melissa asked if Figaro could do a little something with a few others for a TV station – as a way of publicizing the event. So I headed outside to the two large outdoor riding rings. There I joined up with Darcy and her stallion, Corsario, with Rose on Orguluso and me on Fig. We did a small routine and in the end we lined up and gave a few words announcing what we were doing. So Figaro got his few minutes on camera as well. He was a star that day and took it all in stride as if he had done it for years. As we cooled out, Ron and his wife Louise took some fantastic photos.

After all that we took Figaro in and let him relax and eat some hay.

When it finally came time for the performance, we all got tacked up and waited for our turn. We waited in the corridor while Suzanne and her mare did her small routine. We waited patiently. Figaro was ready to go and as the curtains opened, in we went. We headed toward the left while Beverly announced us each by name and each horse. It was then our music began and our routine started. Chuck, our handy man, had made flag holders for our stirrups so we didn't have to balance the flags on our feet, which made things easier while we did small intertwining circles, leg yielding and more. When the cameras were flashing as we went by, Figaro would slow up on his own, wanting to stop and pose for the camera, but I urged him on. There would be lots of time for photos afterwards. Despite all the practices, the three other horses still did not want to get too close to Figaro. I slowed up Figaro as much as I could. He knew the timing and where he was supposed to be, so it was hard to convince him otherwise. When we lined up for our finale, Figaro knew his part: he walked forward a couple steps and up he went like a pro. He got a lot of applause and it was then that Beverly asked for one more, with Figaro obliging. Once we left the arena I gave him a good pat. He had deserved it and he seemed to enjoy it.

When all was done, the public was able to come back and meet the horses. With most of the stallions, their stall doors stayed shut. But of course most people were happy to talk about their mounts when asked. Pierre, however, had Figaro's door slightly ajar while he was rubbing him down. It was then that someone asked if she could have a picture taken with him. Pierre said no problem. He held the shank while they got a photograph with Figaro. Other people saw this and they, too, asked. Next thing we knew we had a line-up to Figaro's stall. Figaro was living it up; at one point there was a group of ten people taking a photo and Figaro just stood there. Chantal came over and was giving us a hand. She was only fourteen but we had involved her in as much as we could. Figaro had lots of patience. People who knew horses were amazed at how quiet he was for a stallion and for those people who did not know horses we tried to educate them about his breed. We even mentioned what he had gone through with his injury and how he turned around. People did say they felt the love. An elderly lady at one point had come up while her grandchildren got photos. Pierre told her to come in to the stall but she did not feel confident with a cane and was leery. After some persuading she walked in. We let her have her moment. She had never touched a horse in her life. As she walked in, Figaro was a pure gentleman. It took her a couple pats but once she became more confident the fears just melted away. It was then she hugged him. She said he is so soft. She even came back a second time. We accommodated as many people as we could. We had our own transport for him so we were in no rush.

Eventually the crowds died down and it was time to head home. We had to help load some of the stallions on the transport trailer. When our time came, it was already dark and of course Figaro took his opportunity to lean on Pierre while he fixed his hay net. Once it was up, we were on our way home. We visited Fig the next day to make sure he was alright and gave him a good massage and rubbed his legs with alcohol. Then I gave him a week off. We still visited him and played and he just enjoyed some rest and relaxation.

Figaro was a professional now, a true showman.

Time to Move on to Bigger Pastures

Figaro seemed to be turning a new leaf in life and around that same time I, too, embarked on a new path.

Figaro was always a class act with the ladies. I could ride outside and there would be no problem. Our rides had been uneventful and we continued working and improving our riding and tricks.

One day, however, something was not right. I had had a great session in the indoor arena and as a cool out I decided to ride outside. We went to the far side of the arena and as we approached the top half and his usual paddock by the mare's field and the parking lot, things changed. Fig got puffed up and went suddenly from Mister Laid Back to Mister Attitude. So I took him in a circle and the same thing happened again. He was not hollering or anything but something was not quite right. There were two mares up in his little paddock. They had been shipped in to be bred but generally we had passed these mares many times without incident. The mare field was right beside him and there was no problem ever. This time just before I reached the top corner again Figaro went into black stallion mode.

He went straight up and I mean 90 degrees to a massive buck and back again. Good thing I had a good seat. After four times of this, enough was enough. So I sent him galloping full tilt. After a turn or two he came back to his senses. I was more baffled than anything. What on earth had gotten into him? I had no problems with him in a long time. Something was saying this is not right. So not to let him win, we cooled out finally with no more commotion.

There had been many upgrades on the farm and one was a nice wash bay in the outdoor arena. After I cooled Fig out I wanted to give him a good bath. It was then a next set of riders had come out. Rose came over and started chatting with me and another boarder.

We had been talking about some of the stallions when Rose said, "Yeah, that is why my dad likes Quartetto and Figaro, they are such stallions. They make the ladies want them (she was referring to the mares)."

So now I knew why he reacted the way he did; it was not his fault. He was enticing the mares who were probably coming into heat. Generally this would not be a big deal since he mellowed out a lot. However a teaser stallion is meant to get worked up to entice the mare for another stallion. This was not meant for Figaro and would not be an asset to further his talents. This is where after much discussion I decided he needed a quieter atmosphere to keep him focused.

Figaro had just recovered from an injury that almost finished his riding days. This is why people said I may have obsessed or worried. I knew this horse like the back of my hand; he did not need to talk for me to know something was up. He was not acting normal and I got my reason. This is why it is important to know your horse and how they act. This way you know when they are under the weather or if something is not right and yet again I was not wrong. This is why it is important for a horse owner to have his or her eyes open. You don't need to be paranoid but be aware. If you had a child you would react no differently if you thought someone taking care of that child was mistreating them. This is why when you take on any animal; remember that you are that animal's voice. For any of my friends or family, human or animal, I am not afraid to speak up for them.

This latest incident with Figaro told me it was time to move on. The farm was changing. Too many stallions and too little turnout and now with more breeding happening I felt it was time to go. Pierre and I had talked about relocating Fig so he was closer to us. The long drive to work would not be so bad if at the end of the day the drive to Fig was shorter and we could go check up on him more.

We found an apartment in Orangeville and luckily a farm down the road that was willing to take a stallion. Also it was quiet with only a handful of boarders. The best part was that Figaro could be out all day in a good sized paddock. With less people using the arena, I had more opportunities to work with Figaro in peace.

We had had great times at Frank's place and many great experiences and we loved the people. Figaro needed to be a horse. Riding is not everything. We had to think about him. He was no longer any worry and was being handled by children. He was going to be alright.

New Day, New Farm

The first day we arrived at the new barn, the road had been closed due to construction. We had to take a detour. We were able to find the barn pretty quickly. Since it was a big rounded roof barn. At least it made it an easy landmark for people to find.

Either way, Figaro seemed to blend in just fine. The owners, Greta and Rob, took the time to learn about him and ask about his likes and dislikes. I think Greta was more on edge the first while since Fig was a stallion. After being in a barn that was more laid back and more care free, it took a while to adjust to the new place. We played by their rules and were just glad to be able to see Figaro more.

We even met some of the other boarders and their horses; some were interested and some nervous of a stallion. In time, they realized there was nothing to worry about. I found I had more people to ride with and we started having small riding groups that included Heather and her chestnut gelding, Lancelot, and there was a Jenny and her pony, Speedy, and a few others. It was a pleasant place.

I worried in the beginning since many barn owners say they can handle stallions and then you find out they can't. These owners had knowledge but I believe much of it was learned through their daughters. They seemed to have no problems with Figaro and complimented us on how Figaro was so polite when putting on his halter and shank. Once you put the halter on, he would let you put the shank through and he would turn his head so you could clip it to the other side. Once Greta and Rob realized he was not a hormone-crazed stallion, all was well.

To see Figaro happy in his new surroundings was so relaxing for me. He could just enjoy being himself. If anything, he seemed to develop a new friend in a crow that started to hang out by his paddock. Fig never seemed to mind him there. So at least he had a paddock buddy as well.

The Stare Down

It was late fall and it would be our first winter at this Farm. Pierre and I were working weekends at the farm to give the owners, Rob and Greta, some time off. I quite enjoyed it. One particular day it was a bit foggy and there was a light dusting of snow.

After we fed the horses, Pierre took Figaro out first, as he always did. To his surprise this day there was another creature in Figaro's pasture. As he took Figaro into the paddock and was latching up the gate, he noticed Figaro looking toward the middle of his paddock. The fog was dense that day. When Pierre looked to where Fig was staring, he saw what had grabbed Fig's attention -- a large buck. He was a fair size and was well developed. His thick neck and large antlers showed his maturity. Pierre had to watch. He wasn't sure whether Fig would chase him or just watch.

The buck and Figaro just stared at each other. As the buck stared at Fig you could see his thick neck rise. He was gazing at this big black beast trying to figure out if he was friend or foe. What felt like an eternity, after a minute or two the buck decided to break the staring contest and turned to the side did a couple leaps across the paddock and over the fence. Figaro then moved from his standstill and did some leaps in the air and then a 360 leap in the air and went to the back of his paddock to see where the buck had gone. I think he would have enjoyed the company and play companion.

Pierre said it was quite breathtaking to see this large buck and Fig standing there. He said it would have been a fantastic picture. I might have not seen it with my own eyes but I can see Figaro's big black silhouette in the fog, the big buck standing there, the two animals staring into each other's eyes.

The two majestic and proud animals together for a moment in time.

Figaro will be Figaro

Due to the many times the barn was quiet, I had lots of opportunities to work with Figaro. There were plastic barrels in the arena and this is where Figaro's tricks would start to broaden. One day he was loose in the arena and I was looking at the barrels. Out of curiosity, I took one to the front half and let him look at it. He walked up to it with no hesitation and sniffed it all over. Then he pushed it with his nose. I rocked the barrel and he pushed it again. I rewarded him and he seemed to get the idea. In time if I brought the barrel to him he would roll it. When we were done, I would let him roll it back to the corner and put it away himself. This was simple. I repeat: sometimes you have to think outside the box. One day he decided to roll it, and then roll it back. The first time he let it roll into his legs and just looked at it. It was then that I signalled him to roll it. When he did, I rolled the barrel back to him again. It took a few times but he seemed to get the idea. This trick would become a favourite for children. They loved rolling the barrel to him and Figaro rolling it back. There was no end of possibilities for the barrel. Figaro figured out another trick -- knocking the barrel over. Even better, he could flip the barrel end over end and he got pretty good at that.

Between rides, we worked more at liberty -- just because it was so quiet in the arena. Given the time to just lie back often means you see things and have a chance to relax and learn more.

After a fun session with Figaro and playing tag one day, he seemed to be in a playful mood and he set his sights on the lunge whip I had put on the ground for the moment. He walked over to it and started moving it around with his lip. By now he wasn't as much of a mouthy horse as he had been when he was younger. I still remember when he would pick up a whip off the ground or the odd branch he had found in his paddock.

I think mainly he just out grew it or matured. Once in a while he would play with a branch or grab my whip while I was mounting, carry it for a bit and drop it, making me dismount to retrieve it. He knew how to pick up items and would do it if asked but it was not really his thing. This was a good thing. I have seen horses asked to do a lot with their mouths which is good in a way. It can become a nuisance when they won't quit grabbing everything in sight. It is not their fault. They are just doing what they have been told to do.

To come back to my story of the lunge whip, Fig seemed at this moment quite intrigued and he picked it up, and then put it down. After looking I realized what it was he did not like. It was all the sand sticking to the saliva on the handle. So I picked it up and wiped it off for him. It was then that he took the handle and started, not tossing his head, but swaying it back and forth. It seemed as if he was watching the long tassel going back and forth. It was then he went a bit faster and started to make the whip snap. He was already bombproof to this and seemed to be getting a kick out of this. His first attempt he managed to get my leg. So I moved out of range. Fig had taught himself a new trick. All you had to do was hand it to him and he would snap away.

Some days I think he found it amusing that he was now the trainer and wanted to see if he could make us dance. Always the character.

Good Ole Jake

When spring came around, it brought new boarders.

In this case, a good friend. Sandra, a solid girl with black hair and glasses, had come with her quarter horse gelding, Jake. Jake was in his late twenties and he used to be a chestnut but due to age he now looked more like a roan. Yet you could still make out his three white socks and the star on his forehead. His stall was right across from Figaro. It seemed Figaro and Jake clicked from the moment they became neighbours. They became such good buddies that they would alert each other when either Sandra or I had treats.

One day I was mystified by something. It seemed to me that Figaro was looking through the cracks of the feed room. When feeds were being made up (each horse would get a particular amount of grain along with whatever vitamins and supplements the owner called for), the door was closed sometimes. Sandra was too occupied chatting to notice Figaro starting to grumble. Jake would make a small nicker and then it went back and forth. It seemed as if Figaro was relaying the information – supper's coming--to Jake. If either Sandra or I had treats, we could not just walk by. If you tried to sneak a treat by one of them, one would snitch to the other. No matter how sly you were when you left or came in, you had better have two treats on hand. Jake was no rookie and Figaro was too smart for his own good sometimes. Through these small things, Sandra and I bonded more and more. Eventually we started to ride together more often and are still good friends. Sandra would come to share in many of my adventures with Figaro. To this day when you need someone to just chat about horses Sandra is always my number one person I turn to.

Ron and Louise Visit

Sandra was a fairly new friend. A new farm, a new friend. We kept in touch with some of our friends from Frank's farm after we moved. I was glad about that. So often when you move to a new farm old, long time friends can seem to drift away. Then again, somehow horse people seem to follow in the same circles so old acquaintances tend to remain friends.

Even though we had left Frank's place, people there did not forget Figaro, especially one person in particular, Ron. We had chatted off and on. He wanted to come out and see Figaro and did so several times. The first time he came out, his wife Louise, was pregnant. When we did the SPCA show she had found out she was expecting. So when she came to visit the first time she was pretty close to giving birth. Louise and Ron stayed long enough for us to catch up. Figaro took his chance to nuzzle Louise's belly. He always seemed to know and was extra gentle. Ron and Louise both said when their son was born they would come out again and let us see the new addition and of course, let Figaro meet the newbie.

When Aaron was born they came back. The weather was so nice. You could not ask for a better day. When they came up Fig was in the paddock and we took Ron out to see him while Louise was getting Aaron set up in his carrier.

When we went to the paddock Fig would, as he always did, perk up for guests. This time he just turned around and ignored us. Most likely he was enjoying the nice weather so we went into the paddock. He then lifted his head and finally showed some interest. He came to see Ron and say hi while we chatted. When Louise came to the gate, Fig seemed to wake up. She stayed outside the gate. Ron told her to come in but being a new mom she was nervous. I can't blame her. Ron encouraged her to come. Louise was still not sure and the classic saying came out of Ron's mouth, "It is Fig. There is nothing to worry about. It is Fig."

I never worry about Fig and kids. He really liked anything baby -- whether animal or human. When she opened the gate and came in she was barely even a couple feet in. That is when Fig just walked between Ron, Pierre and me like we were not there and walked up to Louise. Figaro ever so gently put his nose right by Aaron's hand. His interest was Aaron and the infant was probably not sure what he was looking at. He then did what any baby would and moved his tiny fingers around Fig's nose. Fig never flinched while Aaron explored Figaro's nose. Figaro enjoyed every moment and let him do what he wanted. It was then Louise relaxed more.

Later I brought Figaro in, groomed him and saddled him up. We showed off what he had learned since they last saw him. After we were close to being done, Ron took a couple photos. Ron asked if I could hold Aaron up on Fig. I had no problem though I have to admit I was a bit nervous -- not because of Fig but holding a baby that young. Aaron was only nine weeks old at the time.

Louise was very nervous. Ron said, "Don't worry Fig won't do anything." So he handed me Aaron. I just had the reins draped over my saddle and Fig never moved an inch. If the barn was collapsing down around him he might slightly react. He would not budge when there was a child on his back. This was Aaron's first ride on a horse. He would not be the only child to have his or her first ride on Figaro. Just goes to show you can't judge a book by its cover. Not all stallions are evil and if anything Figaro broke that stereotype for many. People felt safer around him than some mares and geldings and if this did not prove it, nothing would. It was a great day and was so good to see them again.

It was not long after this visit that Ron told me he bought himself a Canadian gelding from Quebec. Pierre and I picked him up and did the trip in one day. Pax was a good example of the breed and would be tall himself, maturing at about 16 hands. He was black and had a very sweet, calm disposition. He was somewhat similar to Fig in that he was "a rig" (short for ridgling, a gelding with an undescended testicle). Pax, though, got the surgery and had his testicle removed. Ron definitely wanted something like Fig and he got his wish. Ron is trick training Pax as I wrote this.

When we got back to the farm, Ron, Brenda and Ciara were there to see Pax. After we had settled him in, at one point during the conversation, Brenda said that Ron really liked Fig and fell in love with the breed.

Brenda said to Pierre, "I told Ron that he wouldn't get another Fig."

Ron knew that but he still liked the breed. He was able to find something relatively close in size but with a calmer demeanour. I told him that Pax would be perfect for him and for Louise, who wanted to get back into riding. I told Ron that Fig is a great horse but I don't want anyone to go through what I did at the beginning.

I know deep down that Fig was one of a kind and that even if he were to produce an offspring, that colt or filly would never be what the sire was.

Let me help you

Things for the most part at the farm were quite relaxing. Where Frank's barn featured constant movement and activity, this barn was laid back and quiet. Figaro more and more seemed to like the quiet atmosphere and people really had a hard time imagining my stories about his earlier years. Figaro never caused any commotion and was the perfect gentleman. Even the barn owner had a hard time believing he was a stallion but he respected Fig regardless.

Even though he was laid back and happy, Figaro was still a thinker: his mind never turned off at any point. There were times when I could see him apparently napping or grazing by the fence line. I knew better. He was happy where he was but old habits die hard. While he looked to be snoozing, if you watched for a bit you could see him lean toward the fence and listen for the hum of the electric fence. When the fence was turned off, he could have easily bent the thin coated wire fence to graze and I think he did once but fortunately that was the extent of it.

Figaro had not unlatched gates in some time but he was still the escape artist in waiting. He figured that since he could not get past this fencing, he would try the gate. The gate had a good latch and I did not think he could get that one undone, but Figaro had the smarts of a ferret. (I can vouch for this since I had two ferrets as pets for many years.)As much as you think they are not observing, they are. In this case, whoever turned Fig out did not make sure the latch was all the way down. Figaro seized his opportunity and managed to jiggle it free. He then decided to go on a walk about and visit the other horses. Luckily he did not decide to go down the driveway. This farm was not fully fenced in, had Fig trotted down the driveway the story might not have ended as happily as it did. Luckily Figaro just went visiting. Rob and Greta figured something was off when they heard the sound of hooves right outside the barn. Fig seemed content to graze and they caught him easily.

After that escape, they added an extra chain that wrapped around the pole at the gate, with another ring it could be attached too -- just in case. They admitted this was probably their error. In the end, there was no harm done. I told Rob that Fig was good at opening gates and stalls. His new stall, though, was secure. It was a sliding door with a latch. This he could not open.

Still, Figaro kept poor Rob busy. One day Figaro decided it was a great idea to take off his halter. I should have remembered to leave an extra halter on his door, just in case. It had been a long time since Figaro had taken his halter off and it must have not been on the top of my mind. I had warned them about Figaro and his elaborate galloping to the gate and stopping in front of you. They were okay with that because they knew what to expect. Most days, though, he would saunter in if the weather was nice and he wanted to bask in the sunlight. This day he wanted to be halter free. When Rob noticed him without his halter, he decided to go into Figaro's paddock to find it. Rob was not frightened of horses but he could be a bit nervous with them maybe more so because of Fig's size.

However, he went in and started to look for the halter by the fence line. Figaro had been grazing contentedly, he must have thought it would be fun to go visit Rob. Rob was so focused on finding the halter that he did not see Figaro coming up behind him. Finally Rob felt a presence and by the time he turned around, Figaro was behind him. In a graceful movement Figaro had leaped to the side. He never touched Rob, but I think Fig caught him off guard and he took a misstep and fell over. He told me afterwards that Figaro wanted to play. He wasn't ready and it threw him off his game. He said he did not feel threatened at all. He said if Figaro wanted to he could have hurt him but he didn't.

When Rob fell Figaro came back to check on him. Rob did end up finding his halter and all was well. I told him I would leave an extra one handy for future events. Rob was not fazed at all and would even cut the grass in Fig's paddock while he was in there. Pierre had shown Rob this one day and it made his life easier. All Figaro would do is sometimes follow behind. One day I watched him follow Pierre back and forth on the riding lawn mower. Pierre would cut the grass on occasion when I rode. Rob and Greta did not mind at all. It gave Pierre something to do and it gave me peace while I worked with Figaro. Rob and Pierre would do various projects together and we even helped with haying and much more. We believe in helping others.

Fig likewise. One winter day, Rob went to bring in Fig. However, if you have ever worked on a farm in the winter, you know the joys of frozen snaps on horse blankets. The snaps this day were frozen. Like any good Canadian, you take your gloves off and try to warm up the snaps till the small bit of ice melts. Most times it takes a second or two.

Fig was getting a bit impatient waiting for Rob to open the gate. So he thought he would help him out. He grabbed the top of the gate and lifted it right off the hinges. Then he backed up with the gate in his mouth and dropped it. Then he stepped back a few steps. He thought he was being helpful.

Greta had a good laugh telling me all this. Rob was a bit unnerved but he, too, was chuckling so I don't think it bothered him too much. I think they respected his strength. Of all the horses I have handled throughout the years, I still had the most respect for Figaro. I can say I have dealt with some of the best behaved to the worst behaved horses. When I say worst I mean when a horse flips for no reason in a stall, attack with hind end and front teeth and I don't mean nipping. I mean biting and kicking with intention to hurt. Some of these horses were so bad that to deal with them daily, they needed tranquilizers so a human could get close enough to handle them. Regardless, I did deal with them and could work through their problems.

Figaro had real strength and intelligence. This is what made him who he was. He could have used his strength against us but he never did. Deep down he was a kind old soul.

Winter Entertainment

Figaro did not bow down to the seasons. He always seemed to be awake no matter the time of year. Even in winter, I never slowed down seeing him. It was rare for snow to stop me from seeing him. Only times during extreme cold did I have to be careful. Because of my bad circulation, I was a big candidate for frostbite. For any animal, especially horses, there is no need to get them sweaty. If it was tolerable but too cold to ride, we would just do some liberty work.

Sandra was doing the weekend work at the barn now, not Pierre and me. This was fine because Pierre wanted his weekends free since he worked all week in the cold. I still went over to the barn to see Figaro. I was always thinking about him and wanted to know he was alright. I never regret any time we spent to together and therefore never had regrets that I should have spent more time with him. Most days we spent more time doing liberty work than riding owing to the cold and miserable winter. One particular day we were just playing around. Sandra was in the barn and we would stop and chat for a bit. While she took her time cleaning stalls, I would get Figaro and bring him straight to the arena most times because you never knew if he wanted to have a good roll first. It was his signature move. Then we did some work with the barrels and he was right on target and did everything he was asked. In the end the little lazy part in me came out and I wanted to see if Figaro could put the barrel away himself. Once I asked him a few times to roll the barrel, he seemed to catch on to what I was asking. The next time I asked, he gave the barrel a good push and it went a good twenty feet toward the corner of the arena. He pretty much figured out what I was asking since he had seen me take the barrels to the corner many times. Sometimes he would even follow me. When I was with him I always talked to him and I would say, "You need to put away your toys." A small part of me thinks he knows what I was talking about. Fig just seemed to know.

I was figuring out what to do next. I noticed that he would follow my body movements and especially when I was working on the Spanish Walk. He seemed to take direction from the whip so I stood still in the middle of the arena and just moved the whip in front of him. He followed it till he did a semi-circle. I then did it again. This time I wanted a bit more and he went around me a few times. While he did this he would bow his head and face me. I watched his body language. To those who don't know stallions in the wild, horses send messages to each other. They come in close, always keeping their attention on their opponent. I don't recommend going into an arena and playing with a stallion unless you have control. Even in liberty shows, you will see the head trainer always keeping things in line and if a stallion starts to move out of turn you may notice him stop and rearrange his stallions. Regardless of all the training, horses will be horses sometimes. You know one is going to charge you when he faces you and tosses his head back and forth. I had a stallion do this to me once and he meant it.

It took time for me to make him understand. He got it in the end when I made him move away from the small circle and I would not let him back in till I said he could. This is where respect is vital and I had his respect. As for Figaro, he postured a bit, yet it did not go any farther than that. Then I needed to try the other side. He was not as keen to work going to the right, with a bit of encouragement he seemed to get what I was asking. It would take a couple sessions before I could get him to switch directions by turning my body and he would do a small figure eight and go in the other direction. This later became an asset when I used to lunge him in small circles with just the reins before I got on. Some days if the arena was empty I would do it with no reins and he was the same.

Our liberty work never ended with just one thing. Usually I would pick a day and put him through his paces. When all was well I would stop and play with him or Pierre would and I would take a break. Sometimes afterwards, as a reward, I would let him walk around and have a good roll if he had not had one yet. I was glad to have a witness to some of his antics. Because no one would ever believe what he was capable of as he did his thing.

Figaro had learned how to make a lunge whip make a snapping noise. Perhaps he thought I was talking to Sandra a bit too long and was not paying attention to him. It was then that he picked up my training whip, walked over and proceeded to tap me with the whip. Not hard but in the cold it stings no matter the pressure. I asked him, "What are you doing?" This was not the answer he wanted and he then proceeded to whip me again. As I moved away, he came toward me and did it again. Sandra said to me, "I guess it is your turn to do tricks." The master had become the pupil. Instead of taking it from him, I knew he was most likely in a playful mood (and he would have probably made me pry the whip out of his mouth). Instead I took off running with Figaro doing some little leaps in the air and a few bucks in between the whole time, with the whip still in his mouth. And we went back and forth. I would change direction and he would do a beautiful rein-back manoeuvre (a graceful reverse) and come after me. After a few minutes of this, he let me take the whip out of his mouth. By his clever use of the whip, Fig had simply been asking me to play with him. I'll say it again: he was not dumb and he knew what it took to get your attention or to make a point.

This horse knew me too well. After my dog Sarah died, I could not hide my emotions from him and as a good friend he seemed to know what I needed. When I walked into the barn after Sarah's death, he took his chin and drew me into him and then bear hugged me. He would not let me go and if I tried with all my might I could not escape his big neck. It was like he knew and waited till a single tear ran down my cheek and then he released me. Sometimes the things we need most are no words to be spoken, just understanding.

Christmas Party

Greta had noticed that the boarders seemed to be coming out more and were always hoping to have a Christmas Party. She had a couple ideas for some riding games such as Musical Stalls and an Egg and Spoon race. I brought up the idea for a Command Class or better yet Simon Says. The Christmas party happened. The games were played and we all got prizes. You got to pick your mystery box.

We had a decent crowd. We had Speedy and his young owner, Jenny. Rosie and her owner, Elora, Heather and her thoroughbred, Lancelot and Ascension and her owner. They did not participate in too many of the games since she was pretty green. There were more horses and riders, too many to mention.

It was a cold day but for the most part, everybody seemed to be excited. We started with the Egg and Spoon race. Luckily the eggs were hard boiled. I don't think one person actual finished the course with the egg intact. We finally had to base the winner on how far the egg made it. Next we did the Command Class. Speedy the little white pony and his owner Jenny were my competition for this class. It came down to her and me. My advantage: Figaro was very good when it came to his cues and was on the ball. Jessie tried very hard but Figaro managed to pull through.

The next game was the Musical Stalls. During this game, you stay to the outside while riding to music. It was just like musical chairs: when the music stopped you had to get to your stall. Whoever was left without a stall was left out. Again it came down to three of us. Figaro for his size was not scared and could turn quickly and sprint if needed. At one point, Amanda and Teddy were at the one end and I was at the other. As the music stopped, I turned Figaro as fast as I could and galloped. Amy, who could be timid at times, seemed to have the inner warrior in this competition. She came galloping as fast as she could on her bay mount. As we got closer to the stall, Teddy was all brave till he saw the big black stallion coming at him and his inner warrior said no way and ducked to the side and we got into the stall. Everyone was laughing, even Amanda.

The games went on. It was down to Speedy and Figaro. As I passed by Pierre he told me that Jessie had not won anything all night and to let her have this one. I hate rigging a game. Fair is fair. Jenny was young and it was the right thing for me to do. As the music went on, Greta played it a bit longer. I could see the intensity in the young rider's eyes. When the music stopped, I was less than thirty feet from the stall. One quick turn and a short sprint and we easily had it. Jessie was just then making the turn and was a bit farther from the one remaining free stall. Figaro knew what to do and instead of letting him go, I held him back a bit and forced him to turn slow. I was trying to make it look like we tried. Jenny, meanwhile, was galloping as fast as that little pony's legs could go and she made it just as I slowly trotted to the stall. She had a smile on her face from ear to ear. I was going to hear it for the next week or two how she beat me. To see the smile on her face was worth it.

After all was said and done Pierre had gotten his hands on some big sleigh bells and wanted Figaro to go around the arena with them. We had fun experimenting with the bells. We trotted around and did the Spanish Walk. They sounded beautiful but they were loud when you are on top of the horse. It was just a fun way to end the night.

All the horses got a prize. They were hung in their stockings on their stalls and we then all enjoyed a nice pot luck dinner and did what I enjoyed most, just hanging around with your barn mates. I had not seen so many people in the barn since my days at the previous barn.

After that evening whoever had previously been nervous to ride with Figaro lost all doubts. The stallion was a perfect gentleman the whole time and if anything more people would come out to ride or have ride dates after this Christmas Party.

Trail Rides

Riders at the barn had enjoyed many group rides but when summer came around people started going on more vacations or were otherwise away, so many of my rides were just Figaro and me.

One day around mid-afternoon I felt like riding. So I tacked Fig up and rode outside. I did a little leg yielding and worked with Fig on his *passage*. He did it but with no oomph. He just decided he did not want to lift his legs up. He did it but not with the same enthusiasm as the Andalusians. He would sometimes not exert himself unless he had a crowd or filly (on occasion) nearby to impress. That or just to drive me nuts. You have to love a horse with a sense of humour. I could read in his eyes what he was saying. As for Pierre, he was as usual helping Rob and Greta with their outdoor jumping ring.

After I did my ride, Pierre shouted out to me that I should take my time because they had a lot of work to do in the ring and we wouldn't be going home any time soon. So I decided to walk Fig around the property. After our short roundabout I felt adventurous so we rode in the woods at the back of the property. It was beautiful with the light shining through the trees and the bugs dormant thanks to the breeze and cool air.

As we walked through I was memorizing landmarks so I could find our way out. After some time, Fig and I came to the end of the wooded trail and arrived at a field. We continued our sightseeing. When I came back to where Pierre, Rob and Greta were still working, I noticed two of the neighbour boarders riding around in the fields. Something told me they may be cutting through Rob and Greta's woods but I thought they would not because we were there. You may think, why would this matter? It is a simple matter of common courtesy. We would not ride on a neighbour's property unless we asked and the same should apply to us.

Just to change the scenery, I thought I would go back to the field and enter the woods where I exited previously. Just as I hit the field I saw the two riders come out of the woods. So I thought maybe I would be courteous and inquire if they had asked Rob and Greta if they could ride on their property. Greta wanted people to sign a waiver. This is good for the average horse farm owner to know: If any rider falls off on your property, you could be held liable for whatever reason. Just as I thought that, Fig had his head up in the air and let out a loud deep neigh. Last time I heard that was when he announced to all the mares he was there at the endurance ride. It was his stallion "I am coming and I am serious" call. For Fig to neigh that loud was very rare because even around fillies he would only grumble. The ladies must have seen us, heard Fig and turned around and headed back to the woods.

Fig was not content with that. I knew he was not happy that these strange horses were on the property. His muscles tensed up and he started doing the most extravagant *passage*. At that moment I thought, if Frank could see him he would be proud. I had been trying to get Fig to do this very thing earlier. (I knew he wasn't tired).

I knew if I let the reins relax he would have chased them. (He loved to chase. I swear I had an over-sized dog sometimes). We caught up for a split second even though he did the *passage* the whole way. When they got out of his sight again he was not amused. So he decided to leap as high in the air (he basically did a *capriole* like it was nothing). Thank goodness I have a good seat. After he did that he just resumed his *passage* and we continued.

Just as I thought I lost the other riders, I saw them again -- back on the farm property side. Fig decided that was not to his satisfaction. He did a beautiful turn on his haunches, found the path (the one I had to try to remember landmarks to find and still can't find on the way back, smart horse) and *passage* even harder. Just as we came out he saw them. He stood there and watched. I was hoping they were going to go back in to their outdoor arena but they didn't. I guess they knew they were in the wrong.

After Fig saw them heading to go back towards their barn he stopped. He looked at the farm mares whose heads were over the fence in the field beside us. They were taunting Fig, as they did commonly time and time again, and I told them, like usual, that Fig can't breed them. So to make Fig feel like the man, I let him get closer but not where he could get too studdy. He would grumble. In his mind they were his girls. Then we did the *passage* in a not so puffed up version he was displaying for the trespassers but the toned down one for local consumption. I figured he would be tired after a half mile of doing the *passage* so I just gave him a pat and took him back to the barn.

That is why he was such a good horse. He was the real Black Stallion. He listened to me even though his instincts told him to do differently. Also he knew -- when his job was done -- to be gentle enough that when a baby was near to use the gentlest touch. Figaro was my pride and joy. He was never trained for the majority of the things he did. He just did them. No trainer could teach a horse to use his discretion like Fig does. I tip my hat to him and hope that anyone reading this can understand my respect for Fig.

Walk with Me Awhile

It was one of those nice summer days but too hot to ride in the arena. So we decided to walk around the property. We went around the field and did our smaller walk around the barn and paddocks. Rob would mow the path ways to make riding a bit nicer. The outer edge of the property had tall grass amongst the trees.

As we were finishing around the last paddock by the woods, something went by us. It didn't see us but Fig was ready to investigate. I thought it was another rabbit. We had had a couple cross our paths before. To my amazement I looked over and saw a young deer looking our direction. It was just getting small antlers and so it must have been a yearling. It stood no more than ten feet away. Fig just watched it. He must have seen the innocence in his big brown eyes. He wanted to chase it for a second but just relaxed and watched it. Figaro changed his mind about chasing the young buck. There was no movement from the young buck at first.

We must have been there for at least five minutes watching the little buck. Of course you never have a camera when you need it but I decided to just enjoy the moment. After staring at us for a few moments. He took a bit of grass then continued to look at us.

After some time I thought we should continue our walk about when I noticed the little buck was following us. The grass was a bit longer and he had to lift his thin little legs a bit higher to get through the grass. However the little buck seemed too delighted to have a friend to stroll with. We walked a bit and stop and each time the yearling would come a little closer.

After 15 minutes of this he was about five feet away. Fig even tried reaching out for him. After a couple mouthfuls of grass the buck did the same. Their noses almost touched they were so close that could have passed your hand between their noses. Then just in a split moment he turned around and with a couple graceful leaps he was back in the forest. It was a beautiful moment, one that will stay in my mind. Innocence always brings out the best in Figaro.

A Promise

Jenny, owner of Speedy, was pursuing jumping as her thing. When I was young, jumping was also my pursuit -- until I discovered dressage. It all depends what is introduced to you and how. Sometimes you just need inspiration. Jenny would say that dressage is boring, which was generally the same response from most people. I remember Frank saying that most people don't pursue dressage because it takes time, while jumping can be learned much faster. Some say it is the thrill of vaulting a fence but I got the same thrill from other disciplines. Maybe it comes with getting older but for me the biggest thrill was having my horse work with me and performing dressage moves such as the Spanish Walk or the bow. It was always a thrill and great accomplishment to me since I learned and did it on my own.

Jenny started to come around to dressage. She would watch me perform some dressage moves and others times some tricks. I don't know what exactly changed her mind but I knew that Figaro and I had made an impact on her. Her mother, Anne, told me one day that as a part of her lessons Jenny and Hugs were starting to learn dressage. I said, "Good for her." Anne then mentioned that she had a growing interest in it and soon she would be doing her first dressage test.

When she came into the arena with Hugs, I said to her, "So I hear you are going to do your first dressage test."

She said, "Yeah." She told me how she was hoping to do more in time.

I said, "Good. This will also help you with your jumping. Dressage teaches your horse to be more supple and responsive. Also you will learn your horse's strides better as well."

I explained to her there is more to jumping then just getting over a jump. You should know your strides before a jump. Control your horse's speed and know when to ask for more. She listened. I always tried to explain myself and especially to young riders. You may not think they are listening but they are. That was why when I did stunts with Figaro in the arena with young riders watching I always made sure they understood not to do what I was doing or try it with their horse. Figaro was trained.

Afterwards, I talked Anne first and broached her with an idea. If Jenny did well in her dressage test, would she like to ride Figaro? Anne was fine with the idea. When Jenny was done riding we both told her. She was excited.

Over the next couple weeks Anne kept me informed on how Jenny was practicing harder and studying her material.

When the time came, the next day, Jenny told me how she did. Her score was good and she placed high. I believe second. By then I had finished my ride on Figaro and I told her to get her helmet.

When she came back I put her up on Figaro. They walked around at first and then after a bit you could see she was trying to ask him to leg yield. She was not overly tiny. She was about 8 or 9 years old at the time but her legs were not long enough or strong enough to make an impact on Figaro. He must have had an idea of what she was asking and he tried to do what she asked. She then trotted him around a bit. You can tell after her pony, Figaro was a big difference. She did not seem scared in the least.

I stepped in and I got him to do the Spanish Walk for her and even the bow. She worked hard and she deserved it.

I remember Greta coming in later and expressing concern because I let a child under 18 ride Figaro. The arena was empty and I told her I would not put anyone in danger. I reminded her that the under-18 rule is for the show ring. I have seen many riders under the age of 18 ride stallions. Anne even contacted the insurance company but they were not concerned. They said that clause was for the show ring and this was a one-time ride on a trained horse.

This was one of many small things that made me always feel a bit unsure about Greta. She was computer literate and only had come into the horse business more recently. Sometimes you have to trust your gut. The absolute truth would come to light sooner or later.

Regardless I gave a young rider something to remember.

Possibly A New Career

Jenny had drive. I felt that she would go as far as her dreams could take her. Who knows, one day I might see her in a dressage competition. It would be awesome if she remembered her motivation was to ride on Figaro when she did so well in her dressage test.

Funny how opportunities arise out of the strangest places. I had gone to a local tack stores usual to pick up Vetrolin (a conditioning detangle) for Figaro's mane, some treats and whatever else I needed.

Pierre and I would start up conversation with people at such places and why not my favourite place, a tack store? As I was looking for items, Marie asked me about Figaro and how his training was coming along. I told her how he was doing and how he was learning more and more tricks each day.

It was then she said, "Have you ever considered him for movie work?" Marie and her daughter had done some work with a movie wrangler named Richard. She mentioned how they had done background work and how shows and movies were looking for horses with potential. She gave me Richards email address. Maureen said just to pass on her name and to send as many photos as I could of what Fig could do. When I got home I sent Richard photos of Figaro rearing up, with the flag, bowing and much more. At the time Fig knew about twenty five tricks and was learning more. Figaro was also quite bombproof and since he had matured he would be fine for anyone to ride. I have ridden him around like a dead soldier hanging off the saddle and doing all sorts of weird things. Figaro also had lots of patience and could catch on quickly if needed without getting excited. Plus he was safe to ride around other horses. I'm positive that he could do anything he was asked.

I always check my emails and there was nothing for about a week. Figaro unfortunately seemed to get an abscess that week and was a bit lame. I was kind of relieved there was no email yet. That weekend the Can Am event (an all-breeds equine expo) was on. Pierre and I decided to go. We had a great time looking at all the stuff. I saw some things I would love to have if my dreams ever came true. I watched some of the demos and performances. I have to admit my mind drifted a few times to email messages. After chatting with some friends I forgot all about it.

Something told me to check my emails that night. I saw Richard's name pop up. His message was brief but to the point. He said he liked what he saw and would like to come out and see him any day. *He liked what he saw.* I was a bit excited. I could not believe this was happening. I emailed Richard. He wanted to come out in the next couple days to see him. I was excited but then I thought -- this is not good. Figaro was a bit lame. He had gotten a small infection in the abscess. I talked to the vet and he gave him some antibiotics. For two days I did more work on his abscess. I had soaked his foot in Epsom salt and warm water. Then I wrapped it up with Animal antic to help draw out whatever was in it then wrapped it up with vet wrap then with some duct tape to make a more solid bottom so he could go outside with it.

Figaro seemed to be getting a bit better. I emailed Richard again saying Fig was still a bit sore. He said that was fine he wanted to come out and see him. So the appointment was still on.

When the day arrived we had to get Figaro all cleaned up. Rob and Greta had come down to the barn and seemed a bit excited themselves, even though Greta tried not to show it. Figaro seemed to know something was up. He always seemed to know when we were going somewhere or something was happening. He was at the gate ready to go. He was still a bit off. He seemed to be forgetting it. Once he was cleaned I put him in the stall and we waited.

After an hour or so we saw a black dually (a truck with dual axles on the rear wheels) driving onto the farm property. Out of the truck stepped Richard, a tall man well over six feet and his wife, Suzette. As they came into the barn, we put Figaro out in the cross ties. After some handshakes and greetings we headed to the barn so as not to waste time. When he walked into the aisle the barn was somewhat bright because of the coverall letting in the natural light. Figaro was facing toward the arena. When he heard us approach he turned around – or as much as he could in cross ties. Richard stopped, took a look and said nothing. He then walked to the side then to the front of Figaro.

It was then he said, "I wish I could have a whole barn of horses like him. He is larger than most Canadians." Richard had worked with some Canadian horses in the past." He liked their disposition but added, "The only downfall is they tend to be on the shorter side. That is why Friesians are more popular for films, also the Andalusian." He said, "They are beautiful but they tend to be a bit high strung." He looked at Figaro and said, "He could do well for so many roles."

It was then we took him out to the arena and let him loose. He played around a bit. He was a bit off. I turned to Richard and asked him if I needed to demonstrate anything. He said, "No, that is fine. I have seen what he can do from his photos."

Richard asked a lot of questions about what he would tolerate, for instance wearing armour. The only two things he does not like, I told Rick, are riding double and pulling a carriage. Other than that he couldn't care less. Pierre snapped the whips to show Richard how bombproof Figaro was.

After everything Figaro came over to Richard and Suzette and investigated them. They did not seem nervous at all.

Richard said, "I may have something coming up for him. Maybe two things." One he mentioned was a horse running between paddocks and another was a medieval film.

He did say directors change their mind constantly so you may have something one minute and the next minute you don't. What mattered most our foot was in the door and Figaro seemed to please them.

Richard even told us about the money Figaro could earn. It was good money and even a commercial could involve a week of filming. Depending on the horse's experience and what the horse could do, a day rate ranged from a couple hundred dollars to a couple thousand dollars. A rider could make at least a couple hundred dollars a day.

I didn't really care if Figaro made a dime. This was just the "the cherry on top" for all our hard work. Looking back I guess a part of me hoped that we could finally get out of debt and we could get our small farm for Figaro. I promised if he earned it I wanted to make sure he had a nice big stall and a huge paddock and possibly a couple girlfriends so we could try for a Figlet.

Hills of Headwater Tour

A month or two after Richard had come to see Figaro; a photographer came by and took some beautiful shots of Figaro. Linda had met Pierre at a dressage clinic for dressage and she had mentioned her work, which included some magazine covers. Pierre must have talked about Figaro and what he did.

Linda came out and Figaro provided her with some amazing shots. This came in handy later when we hung one on his stall when our town was hosting the Headwater Tour (it's a tour of horse stables in our area). With the help of some people I knew, we got in contact with the organizers and asked if they had a Canadian horse represented. They said no. They had Lusitanos, Belgians, Gypsy Vaniers, miniature donkeys and the police horses coming in. After a few minutes of conversation we were in. We were going to do a small demo and I had to do a write-up on the Canadian horse. No problem. I got Figaro ready in the next couple weeks and my write-up was ready.

When the day finally arrived that September day in 2009, it was a bit cloudy and it rained off and on most of the morning. Our routine was the last seminar of the morning till the afternoon demos started.

We got there early to let Figaro settle in. He realized where he was and seemed to settle in much quicker. When we first entered the building, we passed the bleachers and there was a section sectioned off by ropes for the police horses that had come in already. Figaro walked in all proud (only hollering once) to announce his arrival. After we put him in the stall, we got my trunks out and had his stall set up with information and pamphlets for people to take with them. While Pierre went to work on getting him cleaned up, I took my opportunity to go take a look around. When I got back more horses started to arrive and the people started to trickle in.

Later on some more of the other breeds of horses came in. Frank had brought two of his horses. We gave each other a hug and he asked how the big boy was doing but he couldn't stay long because his demo was coming up soon.

As we waited, many visitors and spectators came around. Of course Pierre would jump in and start telling them about the breed and then about Figaro. Many visitors to Fig's stall had a chance to take their picture with him. One lady came around a couple of times to give him a hug and comment that he was "soft as a bunny." He didn't seem to mind all the attention. He just munched away contentedly on his hay bag.

Many of the other horse owners and breeders commented on how well-mannered he was. The Belgian owner even inquired with Pierre if we had a farm and if we would teach his two-year-old horse some manners.

We explained we were hoping to get a farm in time and open it up for boarders and for some horse training. Wherever we boarded or met people at shows, many of those we talked expressed the hope that we would get a farm. They liked the care we gave Fig and they felt comfortable with our knowledge and our horsemanship. Many said they could relax if their horse was in our care. This was and still is my goal. One day I will get my farm.

The best compliment of the day was from the head groom/officer who came with the police horses. He shook our hands and told us that Figaro was the best mannered stallion he had ever seen. He said he is very classy and then gave us compliments on his shiny black coat and his overall health. He compared Figaro to the other stallions that had come in, noting that while they are beautiful but they are also too high energy. He said if it was not for the trainer handling them he would be concerned. He said under saddle they are very well trained, but he did not seemed impressed by their constant hollering and prancing around on the ground. This is why we always tried to look professional. Figaro was a comfortable showman, a class act who loved the atmosphere of the show grounds.

We still had some time till Figaro performed and the rain seemed to be letting up. We were scheduled to do our routine in the indoor arena. However, due to technical issues it would be easier if we could just go outside. We said no problem. I had looked at the one ring and it did not seem too bad. I should have taken a closer look at the other ring.

When our time came we saddled Figaro up and I got on him. We headed out to the warm up ring. The barrel racers where finishing their run in the other ring. You had to manoeuvre around them galloping out of the chute. Figaro didn't care a bit. We did what we could in the small corner of the arena. I was glad Figaro was so warm. Out in the open was pretty cold and all I could think of was that I would be sick as a dog after this and I was right. Breeches in the cold are not that warm.

When our time came we headed into the arena and that is when I realized Figaro probably should be a seahorse right now. Most of the arena was flooded only a few areas had a relatively dry area. As we made our turn into the arena I could feel him slip here and there. Other than that it was not horrible. I tried to manoeuvre around most of the giant puddles. I realized it was going to be hard and I had to make the arena work more in my favour. Figaro was not scared of water and there was no sun reflection.

I opted to just go through the puddles. Figaro trotted, cantered and even *passaged* through the puddles. At one point we tried a rear up on the drier area, his hind end slipped a bit and he did not go as high. He was watching himself. We later found a better spot and we got a better rear up. We even brought out the barrel and Amanda who owned Elora at the farm came in and assisted with the barrel trick. Our finale was the Spanish Walk and bow. We answered questions while waiting for the next seminar to come in which was the carriage miniature donkeys. This was the first time Figaro saw donkeys. As the children in the crowd petted him the donkeys brayed, he looked up for a moment and went back to the children petting him. Even some adults a came over and got some pets in and some photos too.

When it was time to go, poor Figaro, after trying to keep his footing seemed a bit stiff. When we got him back to his stall Pierre went to work on his muscles. Between the cold and slipping I can't blame him for getting stiff. After this I gave him a well-deserved week off. While we took care of him more people came to see him, ask about him and if he was available for breeding. If I had a 100% guarantee I would be rich after that show. We had offers of up to $2000 to have Figaro breed their mares. One couple wanted to try and they were willing to give us two of their mares. I would have had ten bookings easy. Unfortunately, until we got our own farm I did not want to try on another farm. That and I wanted him to have the opportunity to have his chance with a couple mares out in a field, which a couple vets said it would be worth a try. They have seen rigs with testicles higher than his produce offspring. One good example was a farmer not knowing his donkey was a rig and he ended up with a couple mule babies.

Figaro made his impression on people. I know because four years later we would meet a couple at an Upper Canadian horse auction to raise funds for the club. While we were bidding on some items, we started to chat with this couple.

When I said Figaro, they said, "Wait a minute the big, black beautiful Canadian. We remember him, how could you forget him? You don't see too many Canadian horses his size." They said he was just gorgeous and was so well mannered. They had seen him at the tour. As much as the one critique disliked tall Canadians, this is what made him stand out from all the others. He was big but he did not get the draft horse look about him. He was just well proportioned and with his long mane and tail. He just looked good.

I remember walking away feeling good. It is nice that he made that kind of impression. I owned the freak and I loved it.

The Need to Leave

Anyone who has ever boarded a horse has very likely experienced barn politics – friction between owners of the place and boarders or among boarders or even between the vets and farriers coming to the barn. Horses don't always get along; neither do humans.

For some time, Pierre and I had been aware of some underlying tension between us and Greta. We always helped with haying and tried to help them in any way we could. Others came to us for our opinion or advice and I think that is what truly bothered her. So we backed off. We were not there to cause tension. However, with the uneasiness, even though you play by the rules, it does not make for a comfortable setting.

The tension finally broke one day when we had to stand up for a fellow boarder who was doing everything in their power to help their horse. Greta had some of her own personal issues toward the girl and could not put it aside to see she was doing everything she could for her horse. Unfortunately with us standing up for the girl, the anger turned on us.

We did what was right and did not feel out of place. We had helped and played up to the rules to the letter. In the end we were not going to be treated like that. We decided to leave. The boarder left shortly after as well.

So we started searching for a new barn and then we remembered we had to consider the six horses that were coming for the winter that had boarded there the previous year.

The owner of the horses said, "My horses go where you guys go." After we told him the story, he said, " My horses were only going there because of you guys."

We made a couple phone calls. People would have taken us in but they couldn't because their barns were full. When we called Frank, he told us that young John– a former pupil of his -- had just built a barn and had some room. He welcomed us with open arms. Best part: I had a winter job and could spend time with Fig too.

We moved Figaro and he settled in quite nicely. He was now back with his old rival, the redhead, but we kept them separated. Regardless, I finally got a good night sleep.

photo by Laura Sperduti

The Reunion

We had a new start and the first couple weeks at John's farm were fine. Figaro had a nice-sized paddock to himself. The barn and some of the paddocks were still in the building phase and the indoor arena still needed doors. The stalls were all 10' x12' and were cozy. The walls were wood and the aisle-ways were laid out in brick. If anything, it was nice to be back in a carefree atmosphere. John had ridden at Frank's farm for years. He bought the redhead from Frank and horse and rider were a great pair. John loved his fiery personality and the challenge. Renegade, the redhead, was a great ride and John was always teaching him. His goal with his farm was to eventually breed Renegade.

Since John did snow plowing in the winter, he needed someone to take care of the horses. I was off for the winter and at least I was working off board. I helped him out and he helped us out. I just like spending time with Figaro.

Also John loved having the barn full, with six more horses. He also had another boarder come in with two donkeys, Silver and Soldier, and a pony Tucker. Tucker was a plucky one. The two donkeys were friendly. The only down fall was they did not have a lot of handling in the last seven years. They were my greatest challenge. Donkeys are not the same when it comes to training. Their owner, however, was the sweetest woman with a very kind heart. She was very petite in size.

John's cousin was also there with her thoroughbred mare, Dancer. She was new to horses and she wanted to learn. She was a nice woman, outspoken, to the point and a good soul.

Eventually Stacey came as well with Loki, her bay Lusitano. He was the same one Figaro used to play with along the fence line as a baby. Loki was now an eleven-year-old stallion. He was not mean but his hormones ruled him and he was going to make my winter interesting.

Interesting Times

For the most part the winter was very quiet. Pierre would drop me off at John's farm because we could only afford one vehicle and that was the dually. All the times I had to wait for Pierre to finish work gave me great patience. Some days I could be waiting for six hours or more in everything from extreme cold to extreme heat. I always told people, there are laws for dogs and children. What about wives? If you can't laugh, you would cry.

The barn was pretty well insulated, though some rooms were not. My general routine was to feed the horses and then wait in the room till they were done. If they were still eating, I would go put out their hay in the paddocks. Then when it was time I would turn them all out. The donkeys were my second greatest challenge, next to Loki. The donkeys were stubborn and would rip the ropes out of your hands. When they tried to take off, I outsmarted them. A small donkey is stronger than the average horse and it is near impossible to stop them. So before they would try to drag me through the gate I did the quickest slip knot around the pole. I let the donkey fight himself. I never moved so fast. I should have gotten into roping. I had tried offering them treats. Nothing worked. The rope around the pole did work and eventually the donkeys learned they can't drag people any more. Once we got over that hurdle they were sweet as pie.

As for Loki, he was a different story. He did amazing work with Stacey through natural horsemanship and he was responsive. However, for everyone else he was a handful. It got to the point I had to turn him out first thing in the morning by himself. If others were out, he would run himself into the fence. He just seemed to go into a trance. Then it was a chore to get him in. He had a rope halter for the first while. After he tried to breed me, I asked for a leather halter and a chain shank. He was not mean but his hormones were going to get someone hurt. Our next dilemma was leading any horse by his stall. He would climb over the top or get stupid in his stall.

There was only one horse he did not do a thing to, and that horse was Figaro. One day I had no choice but to take Figaro by Loki's stall. I intended to move him by quickly. It was when Loki was up by the stall front that Figaro stopped and turned his head sharply to the bars. To my surprise, Loki backed up and said nothing. I intended to ride. So I thought, huh..., and I put Figaro in the cross ties. The whole time Loki did nothing. Figaro had no real contact with Loki up until this point and the last time he saw him was as a foal. Pierre said maybe because Figaro is older. Yet you could pass Renegade, the redhead, by Loki and he would start up again. We told Stacey and she was intrigued. She suggested that one day we would have to ride together.

Finally, after a few more incidents, we all figured it was in Loki's best interests to be gelded. There is a saying a good stallion makes an even better gelding. Stacey then arranged to have him gelded. He calmed down considerably. He was soon able, once healed up, to go outside. We decided it was best to slowly introduce him to being beside another horse and Figaro was the boy. Figaro did not mind and Loki was calm enough around him. He would pace a bit along the fence line but was settled by Figaro. The only problem was this: if we brought Figaro in, Loki would get upset so I tried to time it so I was bringing Fig in when turnout was ending. In time Loki calmed down enough to be turned out with other horses and is now enjoying being a horse.

Aside from the horses, donkeys and ponies, we met new people as well. Figaro had some new friends and admirers. The neighbour next door, Lisa, had seen him and admitted she would love a baby from him and her Clydesdale mare. Even Nancy, the owner of the donkeys, loved him. She used to have a big black Percheron whom she had lost a while ago. Figaro reminded her of her horse. He just seemed to be growing on people. He had many admirers because of what we all grew up with -- the image of the black stallion. There is something so captivating about a black horse. I guess this is why so many loves the romance of the Friesian horse breed. Nancy became a good friend of ours and though she had a lovely big place of her own, she had decided to board out her three little guys as she was getting older and this was much easier. Nancy said that if we ever needed a place, she would let Figaro stay at her farm.

Around this time I sent out an email to close friends, a living will that set out what I wanted in terms of health care should I become incapacitated. I had even thought of what might happen to Figaro should I predecease him. When she first read the document, Nancy said, "I thought you were going to leave Figaro to me in your will." I said, "You never know." It got me thinking. I would rather have Figaro go before me. That way I would never have to worry about him. If I did go first, it was nice to know that someone would take care of him. Nancy would definitely give him the best of care.

I knew he would get along with the donkeys and Tucker the pony. When the donkeys first came to the farm, most of the horses would not go by their stalls. Because of the ice at the time, I had to let the horses out individually or in a small group into the arena. I had to use the other door since most would not pass the donkeys. Luckily, there were two doors to enter into the arena. Figaro, the first time, I just opened his stall door and let him walk into the arena himself. He would stop briefly to say hi to the odd horse. When you asked him to move, he would just walk on. With the donkeys, though, he actually stopped and seemed intrigued. Fig seemed to like Silver the most. He even put his big head over the stall door and sniffed Silver all over. I let him stand there for a moment or two, just long enough to say hi. He did have his limits and I did not want him to get excited or pushy. I stood behind him and gave him a pat on his great behind and he went into the arena without protest. Once I closed the door he had a big roll. I could tell by the groaning. Of all the horses sometimes I would leave him out a bit longer since he was the only one I did not have to worry about doing anything. When the time was right, he came back in and went into his stall himself.

Even the barn cats had a good time with Figaro. One day as Figaro was walking back to his stall he stopped and looked into the corner. I could not figure out why he would not go in. He was looking at his hay. It was then I saw it move and I noticed something black and white. I was hoping it was not a skunk. On closer examination, Milo the black and white cat, jumped out and ran by Fig. He just watched the cat as it ran by and then went in and ate his hay, as if nothing had happened. Another time, when Figaro was in the cross ties, Milo jumped from the rafters onto Figaro's back. Figaro moved a step or two, nothing more, while the cat sat there on top of him. After a few moments, Milo jumped off and proceeds to chase the other cat Cleopatra around the barn.

These cats were too adorable to get mad at. Even when I was working with Figaro in the arena loose, they thought it was fun and entertaining to go after the tassel at the end of the lunge whip. After a couple minutes Figaro would watch and I would end up playing with them for a bit. During the winter we all needed a bit of fun.

When the weather got warmer, I would even wash him in the indoor wash bay, loose. When the barn was quiet, he would stand there no problem. When the odd horse was in, he knew his manners and would just stand there. He knew better than to move. In the warmer weather he just appreciated the cool bath.

At one point the neighbours ducks would came into the barn. Figaro always seemed curious and wanted to investigate them.

Nancy and so many others saw these things and this is how Figaro would grow on people, from his manners to his personality.

When John's sister Nicole first met Figaro, John told me how much she loved him and wanted him to be in her wedding photos. Later I would meet her to discuss her plans. She wanted to sit on him for photos. Once I found out she was pregnant, I said no. Just for safety reasons. I would have said it was alright to do a photo shoot on the ground.

Nicole told me she liked Figaro out of all the horses. He was just so pleasant and such a character. She felt very comfortable around him. She even wanted to do a "destroy the dress after the wedding," with Fig in the role of destroyer. Figaro would have obliged. I could signal him to paw and he would do it. He could even pick the dress up if needed. Unfortunately, she was not that lucky. On the day of her wedding it was raining cats and dogs. So we decided maybe we could do it another day. Meanwhile, John had proposed this long time girlfriend and was thinking of doing a wedding on the farm and he could ride Renegade with wife to be on Figaro. Unfortunately, the best laid plans sometimes get derailed. In time I would find a way to give Nicole what she wanted.

Omer Meets Figaro

At this time I had the good fortune to meet someone who would become a dear friend. For all his earlier mischief and shenanigans, Figaro must still get credit him for most of my friendships and new connections in the horse world. Omer was to be another one. Omer was Figaro's pick of a truly good being and Fig was never wrong. Omer is still one of my dearest friends.

If you saw Omer you would see a tall, older gentleman with a hoodie or jacket on. At the moment, I can't recall which one. If he were in a tee shirt, you would have noticed his tattooed arms. You would be apprehensive if you saw him walking down the street but when you actually met him you discovered what a happy guy he is, with a great sense of humour. To know Omer is to admire him. With his rough exterior, he was a man who had been through so much, including war and just about everything that life can throw at a human. Yet he still had a smile on his face and love in his heart. Omer is a great example how age is just a number. He still worked and coordinated events at a nightclub in the city, where he had previously worked as a bouncer years before.

I came to meet Omer through my mother. He was a neighbour mom walked with when they took their dogs out for an evening stroll. Ever since I left home, I rarely had a chance to see my mother. Funny how life changes things and how some people come into your life. Everything happens for a reason and everyone crosses your path for a reason -- sometimes to guide you, help you or offer a life lesson. Omer brought my mother back into my life again and he would become a good friend. Our friendship began in 2009 when mom emailed me to say that she had met a new friend when taking out the family dog, Sandee, for a walk. Mom and Omer would chat on their walks and she discovered that he knew Melissa, Frank's daughter. Melissa worked with Omer at the same nightclub he did while she was going through university. Mom told him I used to ride at Melissa's father's farm and that I had a horse. Omer said he had always been interested in draft horses and was interested in getting into horses himself.

That was where I came in. Mom had asked me if I would give lessons on Figaro. Figaro was bombproof and kind enough to beginners. However with work and my hours, whatever spare time I had I wanted to spend it with Figaro.

Omer came up one nice warm winter day in December to visit Figaro, Pierre and me. I put Figaro through his paces. This was the beginning and not the end of our friendship or Omer's horse education. I had lots of stress at the time with debts, truck payments and Pierre's constant injuries and sickness, and I was getting mentally tired. Figaro was my stress release.

Even during a first meeting, when Figaro was loose, you could tell what he thought of a person. Though he liked to put on a show, he had his signs. If he walked up and in moments walked away from you, that meant he couldn't care less. It didn't mean he didn't like you, he was just neutral. This was a sign you needed to earn his trust. If he came up and hung out and smelled you over, you intrigued him. At the next encounter, he would give you more of an indication. If he did not like you, he would play but he had ways to intimidate you and he would posture or come up behind you and leap away to throw you off. He would not harm you. It was just his way of communicating. If he liked you, he would nuzzle you, check you over for treats and be the great personality he was. In time, though, the more he trusted you the more he would let you do. Some things he would mainly do just for me. During Omer's first encounter with Figaro, he was intrigued and smelled him over.

In time and with Pierre's and my help, Omer would eventually learn more and get a big white Percheron named Little John, who with his antics would be Omer's greatest teacher. Omer was never left on his own. I was always there to guide him when needed. In turn, he would show his gratitude in other ways. From that first day, Figaro grew quite attached to Omer and you could tell that Figaro liked who he was. In all the years that Pierre was with Figaro, Fig never licked him. After just a few visits to the farm, Omer would stand beside Fig and that stallion would lick him like a human lollipop. The only other person he would lick was me, but in a kiss form. I always asked Omer if he bathed in applesauce before he came.

One hot summer day the flies were out in droves. There wasn't a place on the farm that you could get away from them. You just had to make the best of an uncomfortable situation. Omer took a break from spending time with Little John. Omer had just hosed down his horse who was in his stall drying off while enjoying a snack of hay. Omer went outside to treat Figaro with a few carrots. While standing there with him, Omer noticed how bothered Fig was by the flies. Figaro stayed by the fence. He almost had a look in his eyes that was beseeching Omer to help. Omer sensed Figaro's discomfort and stood by him shooing the flies from around his eyes. The sun was unforgiving. There was no breeze. Figaro's paddock had no trees and no shade, just flies. Figaro shook his head and swished his tail but no amount of action was alleviating the swarming of these flies. Omer continued shooing the flies from Fig's face. The occasional treat of a carrot was welcome. Figaro was not only grateful for the treats and relief from the flies but the mellow tone of Omer's voice. Omer loved to talk to Little John and he was now soothing Figaro with friendly conversation from a soul who cared. By the time Pierre and I got to the farm Omer had spent over an hour keeping the flies at bay.

The summer had been unusually hot and I had told Omer how Figaro did not like the heat. When we got to the farm on the day of the fly onslaught, I was beside myself because not only had Figaro endured the bugs but he was close to having a heat stroke. Omer felt badly about not recognizing that the signs of heat stroke. If he had known that Figaro was prone to the heat, he would have taken him into the barn and hosed him down.

I taught him about the signs of heat stroke in horses: shortened strides, head hanging low, heavy breathing and slight staggering. Omer had been up one weekend and noticed the signs Figaro would normally come to the fence to see Omer but this time he didn't. Omer brought him in and hosed him down, focussing as I had taught him on the underside of the neck and between the hind legs, even the head.

In time we would call Omer "Uncle Bob". I considered him family and Figaro gave his lick of approval to this decision.

photo by Laura Sperduti

Photo Time

Many days at the farm were quiet, and it was nice to have the freedom just to enjoy Figaro. We spent many hours in the arena working on liberty as well as riding. We even went riding down the road with my friend Laura. She took over my role at the farm when I had to go back to the track. It was comforting to know that Figaro had someone I knew and trusted looking after him.

I knew that Laura kept a good lookout and when we were up at the farm together we had fun in one way or another. One day she got on Renegade and we went for a ride. To hit the trails you had to ride a good way down the road. We thought it was a bit closer and by the time we got there we basically just headed right back. It was further than we thought. Figaro was great on the road way; he was like a fine wine, getting better with age. He never seemed to care if a car raced by or about any of the scary mailboxes along the way. Renegade, however, kept Laura on her toes and was half passing pretty much the whole time back and forth along the road. He would spooking at the odd mailbox or fence post, luckily he settled on the way back. I stayed behind to keep an eye on her and to signal to drivers to slow down or to wait while she got Renegade to settle and get back on the path.

Once we were back to the barn, Laura mentioned she had gotten a new camera. Figaro's birthday was coming up and I asked her if she would mind taking some nice photos of Figaro. She agreed and in the next couple days we had our photo shoot.

The day of Figaro's birthday the weather could not have been better. It was warm, yet it was cool enough for both him and me to enjoy. We had played in the arena a bit. I did not really want him to do too much since it was his birthday. He had just turned fourteen. In human years he would have been 42. He just looked great. He had matured mentally as well as physically. He was well muscled and broad. Many mistook it for fat. On closer examination, he was a big boned boy. He had a great thick neck. You could hang off his neck. I was 5'11"with a long reach and my arms just reached around his neck. His mane was at least two feet long. His crest was solid and did not jiggle. He had nice big round jowls and his shoulders and hind end were firm and toned. On top of that, he was doing well and showing no signs of slowing down.

When Laura showed up, I wanted to take Figaro to the nicest spot on the property as back ground for the photographs. At the front of John's property, he had built a nice water fountain and the trees provided perfect lighting as well some shade. I had another idea as well. John's sister Nicole did not get a chance to have her wedding photos taken with Figaro and I was hoping that maybe she could have some shots edited and combine the two. The one photo she wanted was Figaro bowing to her on her wedding day. So I got Figaro to bow and Laura got some shots. I then wanted to have some nice body shots and head shots -- two of which I still have and cherish. Then we got some fun photos. Since John worked in landscaping, he had many solid decor rocks around the perimeter of the water fountain.

Figaro stood up on them as we got some more shots. He loved all the attention.

It was then John came out and he asked if it was alright to put his daughter Annie on top of Figaro. She was only six months old at that time. This was John's first daughter and he was enjoying everything about being a new father. His fiancé and a first-time mom, was leery about putting Annie on Figaro.

John told her not to worry and said, "It is Fig. He won't do anything." John was already talking about Annie riding Figaro when she got older.

I said, "Maybe." I promised Figaro, who had been used as a lesson horse in his early days that he would never have to do that again. He had the ability to teach many but at the same time he was not the type to enjoy doing the same task over and over and the lesson life would have soured him. Only on occasion would I let someone sit atop him for a bit, mostly children.

John held on to Annie while we got some shots. He ducked down behind Figaro so as to not be in the photo. Figaro just stood there like a pro and never moved. This would be Annie's first time on a horse.

Later I sent Nicole the photos so she could get them edited if she wanted. Afterwards we gave the birthday boy a good rub down and a nice warm bran mash full of carrots and apples pieces. He was my buddy and I was going to let him enjoy it to the fullest. Pierre even had a Guinness with Figaro to commemorate the day. In three years away, Figaro would turn 51 in human years and we planned a big party because Pierre was going to be hitting a landmark number himself.

I was just enjoying every moment with Figaro, intending to be with him to the end of his days and giving him the very best. I was just hoping that one day we would have our farm.

Figaro and Loki's First Ride Together

It had been three months since Loki had been gelded. He had finally calmed down and was becoming the lovable horse that he could be and was. Figaro first met Loki as a baby by his mom's side many years earlier. The mare's paddock was right beside the outdoor arena, which made working with stallions quite interesting at times.

They first met when I was riding outdoors and baby Loki was beside the fence being the curious little guy he was. His mare was with the other mares.

Figaro and I noticed him and I thought it was cute that he was watching us. After some time he was still there and Figaro seemed curious so I cautiously approached since I didn't know how he would react. He showed no signs of aggression or anything. He was up beside the fence nuzzling baby Loki. After a couple minutes I took Fig around the arena to go back to work. Loki was still by the fence. When we came up beside the fence trotting, he came bucking and galloping beside us and would wait till we came around again. That was when I discovered that Fig loved babies.

The second encounter was when Loki was two and he was just being started on the lunge line. Even then when Fig would come up beside him and he would duck in. Loki came up close and only then realized how big Fig was. The young horse wasn't scared but it was funny.

It is absolutely amazing that even though the two of them hadn't seen each other in all that time, Loki still respected Figaro and Figaro knew who he was. Loki– both when he was intact as a stallion and later as a gelding - alwayss held his tongue with Figaro. Figaro was the only horse who commanded that respect from Loki. As a stud and as a gelding, he reacted loudly to all other horses – stallions, geldings and mares.

Up to this point he had not been with another horse in the arena because of his studdiness. So Stacey and I decided that since Figaro was the only horse he had never reacted to, we would try them together.

So I brought Figaro out into the arena. Then Loki came out. Not one sound came out of Loki. After Stacey mounted up, we tested them from afar. No reaction. We thought we would play follow the leader. Both boys handled themselves well.

Our next test was to bring them up beside each other. Loki, being the lover not a fighter, was apprehensive about coming next to Fig. Even though he is 16.1 hands and Figaro is only two inches taller, Loki knew that Fig was the alpha. Loki was also a much more slender build and two hundred pounds lighter than Figaro. That is one thing about animals: they know and are not stupid. In this instance Fig knew his place and Loki knew his. Fig was being a gentleman. He knew Loki was not a threat and was very calm and laid back. He was ready to change position if needed to help guide him or to move out of the way.

There was no problem. By the end of our ride, Stacey and I were stirrup to stirrup, knee to knee. The two boys were close enough to do damage to each other if they wanted to. They held their own. Fig, however, did get one little nibble on Loki but that is pretty good for a stallion. Figaro tolerated it when Loki bounced off his side like a little rubber ball. Stacey would laugh when he did that. She said she was using her outside leg to get him closer and he would bounce off Fig again and she would have to convince him to get close again but being built like a brick house, Figaro didn't budge.

Then we did the most beautiful *Pas de Deux*. What made it more wonderful was that Loki was so relaxed and seemed very comfortable with Fig and that Fig helped guide him. He made this younger horse relaxed and there is nothing more beautiful in this world then seeing two riders, and most of all two horses, be so at one with each other.

At the end, I had to say it. I turned to Stacey and said, "It is days like this that Figaro reminds me I will never have another like him."

Times Are Changing

You can just get comfortable and think all is going smoothly, and then life throws a wrench at you. This time it was Granny going into hospital for heart surgery in late August 2010 to replace a faulty valve. We thought it would be wiser to move Figaro closer to her end. We had been living in the country and John's place was a forty five minute drive east of us, so the traveling, we knew, would get too hard for us. Especially since my Granny was near the Fergus area – some 35 kilometres away.

So we went searching for a farm in the Fergus area. Omer said wherever we went, he was going to follow. So the challenge became finding a place that would take a draft horse *and* a stallion. As quiet as Figaro was, many places simply will not take a stallion. After much searching, a friend recommended a farm they used during the winter months.

The farm was just minutes away from Fergus. It seemed this was going to be the place. Once we met up with the owners, Elizabeth and Rudy, we could tell they could handle horses and the facility was perfect for what I wanted. So off we made arrangements to move to this farm.

Looking Out for Better Times

This farm was situated fifteen minutes from Fergus. Once you passed through the small town and crossed the bridge over a river, you could see sitting on a hill an old bank barn and a great big arena. This was going to be Figaro's home for the next year. While we unloaded the horses, Laura came to take photos of Figaro and Little John. We put Little John in one paddock and Figaro in the other. Figaro gave us a show and quite a few photos.

Then Elizabeth arrived to show us to our stalls. John had a large stall close to the tack room and Figaro was on the other side, near the broodmare stall. It was also a very large stall. His side was nice and quiet. One thing I love about bank barns is that they are cool in the summer and warm in the winter. It was quiet the day we arrived but in the next few days we would get to see more people.

I also warned Elizabeth and her "right hand man," as you would call Katie, about how Figaro liked to gallop to the gate. Other than that, instructions for his care were pretty straightforward. For the winter, he was going to be in one of the smaller winter paddocks so he would not gallop toward them. In the spring, Elizabeth was going to let him have the 2-acre paddock behind the main house and near the road.

In the following days, we met Vicki and her mare, Chelsea and Tara and her bay gelding, Jake. Everybody was friendly and outgoing. We got to know most the boarders. Our true test was going to be in the arena. Since this was a new set of people, some people did not know Figaro and they got apprehensive about the word *stallion*. In time, Figaro won them over, especially when they could see what he could do at liberty and some of his tricks under saddle. I would demonstrate his wonderful demeanour and would let them see me getting on him even with horses in the arena. I could go direct him to the mounting block and while I was getting on the mounting block he would park himself in front and wait there. I could put my foot in the stirrup and mount without ever touching the reins. It took a while but when others realized he was not a threat, many boarders actually started to ride with us. Tara and I made fun days together. One person even commented that they felt safer with Figaro than they did the other mares and geldings. Tara and I would ride together and sometimes do some ground work with our two boys.

She watched what I did and we experimented. One day she brought up an empty feed bag and showed it to her horse, Jake. He wanted to see what was inside. When we gave it to Figaro, he decided to destroy it and stomped on it. I remember Tara saying, "He didn't even hesitate." Figaro was pretty exposed to everything at this point. It was at this farm that Figaro probably learned most of his tricks. He was just at that point where he seemed to be picking up things even faster. At the same time I wanted to try as much as I could with him. This was when, for example, he learned the trick of untying my hands -- just in case he needed to know that for the movies, as well as picking up and dragging a tarp, holding items and more.

It was just great to have a fun group of people to ride with and hang out with as well. When Christmas time came, Elizabeth wanted a chance for her students and boarders to have fun. They had done Christmas parties in the past and had not done one in a while. So they asked if I knew of any games and that is when I found out we were going to have the Annual Farm Christmas party.

photo by Brendan Kelly

Fun Times

We decided to do the Christmas party a bit earlier so as many people as possible had the opportunity to come out and join in. The turnout was great. More showed up than we expected. Vicki with her mare, Tara and Jake, Anna and her mare, Katie and Homer were all in attendance. Elizabeth had let her students ride her horses. Ellen was on Dillion a nice bay gelding. Elizabeth rode Fancy and her one daughter, Alice, rode Kisses the pony. The arena was packed. The games in store were musical stalls, obstacle course, barrel racing and a few others. Most of the people liked the barrel racing and the best part was that people could go at a pace they felt comfortable with. The favourite game had to be musical stalls.

Pierre was the one and only judge. He enjoyed tormenting poor Katie. She managed to get out at least two times for going over the rails.

As for barrel racing, Elizabeth and I went head to head. Fancy was fast and Elizabeth was booking it around those barrels. She may have been mostly a dressage rider but she had game. As fast as Fancy went, what cost him was his really wide turns. Figaro was not as speedy as Fancy but what saved us time was his ability to get close to the barrels.

In the end it was close but Figaro came out on top. For a big boy I gave him credit. When it came time for the obstacle course, you got marked on the completion and the time. Most riders completed it just fine. Some even wanted a second turn. Figaro and I became the judge on horseback.

Before we went down to partake in the potluck lunch and goodies, we did a mini-show for some of the kids and got some real nice photos of Figaro. After this event, people felt much more comfortable with Figaro. It did not take us as long now to warm up to people.

When all was done, we went down to the barn for the potluck and for the adults some festive drinking and some famous butter tarts.

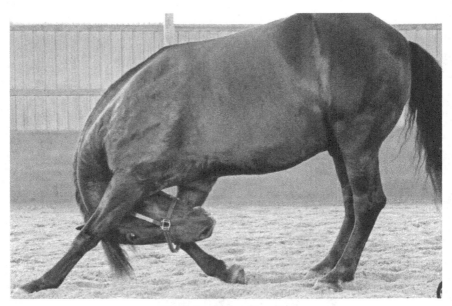

Photo by Laura Sperduti

Magazines

Winter melted away and with that spring brought fresh new life—blossoming flowers, new foals, everything was green and it was a time for a new start for many things.

Spring came around and the warmth of the season was welcomed by all. I had been doing more work with Figaro. It was right around the time of the Wellington Tack Swap – a trade show in Fergus that also features seminars and, of course, the chance to trade gear. It was here that after talking to one of the representatives of a horse newsletter that I had an idea. After talking to her about Figaro, she wanted to do an article but she also led me to more avenues. I ended up contacting an editor. Figaro got his first magazine article in *Equine Wellness* magazine (published out of Peterborough) and had two pages to him about our training and our views. This magazine came out in August 2011.

This just felt wonderful and it was around this time that I decided to open Figaro his own Facebook site called Figaro Canadian Stallion (it has now been renamed to Figaro's Amazing Animals), which led me to make many more friends from around the world. These friendships and contacts opened up yet more doors for me. Nothing was ever just handed to me. I had to work and do my part as well. What helped me most was Figaro himself. He was a good looking boy. Looks aren't everything but it was Figaro's first impression to everyone. Then when he captured their attention he got to display his smarts. He was a well rounded boy. Never mind the fact that the Canadian horse was slowly getting more recognized. In addition, Figaro's abilities were also what made him stand out. He was the whole package. So before anyone thinks this was easy, it was not. I was just fortunate to have a horse that had what it took. I swear with all the dreaming I did as a kid, I dreamed this horse into life.

Would I do this for all animals? No. Will I do this for my next horse? No. Figaro was a one of a kind, unique horse. He just had that something about him. I was grateful to have him and I felt he needed to be known. It was this drive that made me who I am and opened up more avenues than I thought I would never know.

This experience led to another. I spent a considerable amount of time with a journalist who looked at some pictures, did some research and educated themselves about the breed. Figaro became the poster boy for *Horsepower* magazine in the December 2011 issue.

I could not be any prouder of this boy. His popularity was rising. On Fig's Facebook page I offered a contest to receive a copy of the magazine.

I remember going down to the barn that day and giving him a big hug around his neck and just brushing him for an hour just to make him shine head to toe.

One boarder's daughter got a copy and she said she had the poster on her wall. Figaro was one of her favourites. After one of her lessons, I put her on top of Figaro and let her do the Spanish Walk and the bow. When I was that young I know I would have loved to have an opportunity like that. I wanted to give the chance to another, to see the smile. It was well worth it.

I just felt a great sense of accomplishment and even better it was Figaro's and my achievement.

Apple Picking Time

Figaro loved the crowds but he also enjoyed our alone time together. There was a time and place everything. Figaro seemed to know the difference.

I went for hacks on the best fall days when the leaves were still quite abundant but starting to change colour. I love to hack and it is a great way for Fig to have a change of pace from arena work.

I am glad we are both the same when it comes to things like that.

As we headed out I told Pierre we were going out. That is one thing I always do -- let someone know I am out there. Pierre never worried when I was on Fig because he says if there is a horse I don't have to worry about it is him.

I always love to explore new areas we haven't been before and try to change fields so that Fig doesn't get bored. We had been out for some time. There were so many new areas to explore. It would be a long time before Figaro could or would get bored.

Fig wanted to put his head down and like usual I said no because I thought he wanted to graze. I don't mind once in a while. I chose not to let him this day or I know he would take advantage of it. So I brought up his head and proceeded. Then I heard some crunching. When I finally looked down I noticed the apples. I didn't see them when we came down because they were still well covered by the leaves on the tree.

I let Fig eat some of the fallen apples and while he did that I decided to pick what was in range of my reach and stuffed them in my pockets. We moved on and there was another apple tree a bit further up. These apples were much sweeter. I knew because Fig grabbed a small bunch of apples off the tree himself. I grabbed a few more and my pockets were full. I didn't have room for one more apple. Fig also assisted at one point and decided to grab the tree branch and shake it. I was caught up in the moment and forgot that a branch can sometimes come back to hit me. This one did. Luckily it wasn't a big branch.

The branches were thin and very tangled but Fig obliged and pushed his way in and stayed for me to get a couple more. I didn't know where I was going to put them but I just had to have a few more apples. Some horses would have panicked with the branches rubbing and poking the face and neck and would have backed up promptly. Fig tolerated it for the moment then I backed him out and gave him a pat. He trusted me because he knew he was in no danger and I wouldn't put him in harm's way.

I remember looking up and seeing a branch with a lot of apples. Maybe it wasn't the brightest idea but while Fig went back to eating the grass and the odd random apple on the ground, I dropped the reins and stood on his back and stuffed my jacket full of apples till I looked like the Michelin man. I slowly got myself back in the saddle and we headed back to the barn. I know it is foolish to do something like that out in a field. I know one thing. I wouldn't dare do that with another horse. Fig I trusted with all my heart. He proved I can because he never moved. I would not suggest doing this.

With my jacket full of apples, we headed back to the barn. When we got back I realized my dilemma with a jacket full of apples it made it quite hard to get off. After three attempts I managed to not so gracefully dismount and stumble backwards. At least I stayed on my feet.

I put the apples in a basket for the barn to enjoy. We all had a good day.

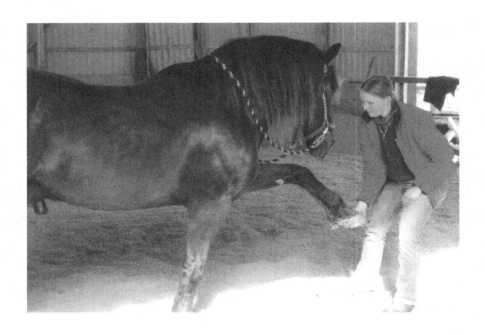

The Learning Never Ends

Around this time, new tricks came to light. Figaro, for example, learned to shake hands. This was not me. This was all him. I went to turn him loose in the arena as I usually do. I had noticed my shoelace was untied so I bent down to tie it. When I looked up Figaro was holding his front leg up in the air. I got up. He was still doing it. I reached out my hand. He somewhat extended his hoof out. It was then I grabbed it as a joke. I thought and said to myself, "What buddy? Do you want to shake hands?" This was exactly what he was doing. In time I learned the dynamics of this trick and many others with the help of Figaro.

Even what seemed the silliest things, I had to try with him. He had, for example, learned to hold objects. I had him hold roses and bow his head. I also got him to hold a marker in order to draw. This was not his thing. He learned it for a purpose. I repeat: I did not want him to lose his dignity. I wanted him to learn but still be a horse and have his pride. To teach him to sit like a dog or roll over was not the goal. He was going to learn what he needed to know. If they required it for film purposes.

However, I did teach him to roll out a carpet. I did not have a carpet but a boat-sized tarp and it worked just as well. He figured it out in a few minutes. If anything things like this kept him thinking and could apply it to different tricks.

Then I taught him to back up on cue. It took two sessions. Between the body cue and voices, he got it and could back up twenty feet if needed. I could even cue which leg I wanted him to lift up first, by pointing to the leg. He already knew how to march and Spanish Walk. The march involves more of a knee bend in the front legs whereas the Spanish Walk involves more of an extended leg – again in the front end. I then incorporated his hind end. From there Fig perfected his *piaffe*, which is a trot on the spot. He already knew this under saddle.

Now I needed him to perform these movements in liberty. Thankfully he was already fit and he was thus able to pick up the concept much faster than expected. If the horse's muscles are not used to it, it may take longer. In time all I had to do was cluck and he would do them on his own.

He also knew how to untie my hands (I had watched the film, Hidalgo, about a trick rider in a Wild West show in the late 19th century and picked up some pointers). Could this trick come back to haunt me? Yes. Fortunately, it did not. He knew when he was supposed to do things and not to because that was the biggest part of training. You don't teach a horse to paw when he does it all the time. Your horse needs to know when and when not to perform.

Since winter can be unbearably cold at times, liberty was the best thing to work on because some days it would be too hard to work him in the saddle in that cold, not only for him but for me too. If it was hard on my lungs it would be hard on his.

In time I wanted him to learn to go to his mark. This would be good for the movies if he was to do something at liberty and then go to a specific mark. I used a pylon. I would throw it and wherever it landed I would tell him go to the mark and he would do it. I even got him used to hand signals so he could see a signal and come when needed.

He knew how to smile. I was brushing him in the cross ties one day and he wanted a stud muffin treat. I said to him while still brushing him, "You have to work for it." He knew the cue with my fingers and in a moment I noticed him following the fingers as I opened and closed them. In time I could make him mimic talking. As I mentioned before, he could have been the modern day Mr. Ed.

Best was when he had to show me up. We finished riding one day. In the barn, the light switch was on the left-hand side as you walked in. I always seemed to turn on the wrong light. I brought him in and turned him around in the wash bay. Due to the wind, I did not want the door to swing and hit his back end. I took off my glove and fumbled for the light. In one swift move, Figaro turned on the light switch. Fig hit the correct switch on the first shot. I told him, "This is our little secret, smarty-pants." He did this a few times. He would turn and look at me as if to say, "I did it for you again, mom. You silly human."

Fig even learned to invent his own games. One day I still had his shank on (a new rule in the barn meant that we were no longer able to turn horses loose in the arena). I always left the shank on just in case. Fig stayed close to me. On his own, he went to where the whips were stored. There were some dowel pieces in that cupboard because we had some ideas for some game for the next Christmas party. I stood and watched as Fig pulled a piece out of the holder by himself. He walked a couple steps. I went to take it out of his mouth but he insisted on holding it. So I gave him a moment. It was then he decided to start twirling his head and the shank started to wind around the dowel. When it was fully wrapped around, he twirled his head in the *other* direction and did the same thing. He seemed to be enjoying himself quite fully. He was always full of surprises. I'm just glad I caught this one with the camera!

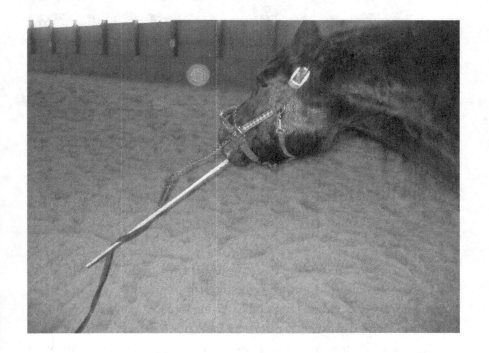

Character Antics

Fig was a trickster but equally evident was his sense of humour. Yes, that's what I said, a sense of humour. One day I brought him in and he was covered head to toe in dirt. I remember telling him, "You must be proud." I had chatted with my friend Sandra who had gotten herself a second horse--Betty, a flea-bitten mare. Sandra was now at the same farm again with me. Many times we had grooming sessions together and Sandra would be laughing. After about an hour and a bit, I got Figaro shiny head to toe. Then he started to smile and put his nose up to the air. Sandra was my witness.

I turned to her and asked her, "Is he mocking me right now?"

She said," I believe he is."

Sandra was my riding buddy and we always seemed to end up together in the same barn. As I was getting my stuff I asked her as she passed Figaro if she could hand him a mint when she went up to see her old boy Jake, who had come along as well. Figaro and Jake seemed to hang out near the fence line. Sandra stopped and looked at me with a look of shock when I put the mint in her hand.

I said, "What?"

She said," Really? One mint?

I was curious about her reaction, "What?"

She said, "One mint? He will vacuum my hand up." It was not hard not to laugh. The look on her face was priceless. The look of you are kidding me. She was right.

Fig's lips were so strong he would suck your hand in sometimes. So I gave Sandra more mints. I should have known better. It was because of this that Tara ended up giving Figaro his next nickname, Mick Jagger -- because of his lips. Around this time (2011), the song by Maroon 5, *Moves Like Jagger*, came out. As a joke I had Figaro do a routine to the music of that song. I was glad he did not forget how to sway his hips under saddle. I then got him to side pass sideways and do some backups.

Even in his pasture he was never dull. Sometimes he would saunter in and sometimes he was dramatic. Katie and the others had gotten used to all this by now. Figaro was Figaro. New people, such as Katie's boyfriend who did not know what Figaro was like, was in for a surprise. When he went out with Katie to bring Figaro in, he went to the bottom of the paddock. Katie called for him. Figaro perked his head up and did a great big rear, and then as he came up from the far end of the paddock, the big black beast galloped toward the gate. Katie's boyfriend said to her, "He is not stopping! He is not stopping!!" He moved back a couple steps, Katie told him not to worry and Figaro came to a stop a few feet from her and waited for the shank to be put on. There was never a dull moment.

Trouble in Paradise?

Aside from ground work, many of our rides were just as educational as our ground work.

Sandra was my main riding partner in those days, along with Tara and her horse Jake.

One of our most memorable rides occurred in the winter. A boarder had come in with their horse who was still pretty green and because of the cooler weather was feeling a bit fresh. So they decided to lunge there horse first. I lunged Figaro in small circles around me with just the reins. Katie had been riding already and was working on her project horse, Cricket, a chestnut thoroughbred mare. Things were alright until all of a sudden I saw the horse on the lunge line bucking out of the corner of my eye. The girl tried to keep a hold of her horse. It was the way the horse bucked. She had managed to twist her body almost in half in doing this. She got her hind leg over the lunge line. The poor girl tried to keep a hold of her. I got Figaro to stop because I had a sense things were not going to go well. It was then the horse ripped the lunge line out of girl's hand and proceeded to gallop around.

Number one rule in a situation such as this: go into the middle of the ring and stay still. Figaro's ears were up and he was thinking. I told him, "If you do anything, you will be in deep trouble." Poor Katie was tired after her ride but now she had to go after the loose horse who was showing no signs of stopping with this twenty foot lunge line dragging behind her. Katie, still on Cricket, tried to cut off her path, with no luck. Katie then got off

Cricket and tried to catch the lunge line. In one attempt she accidentally let go of Cricket. And now we had two mares running around full tilt.

I could not do anything because I had Figaro in-hand and that is all we needed was two mares and him running around. Figaro waited patiently with his ears perked forward. Finally Katie got a hold of the loose horse's lunge line and was dragged a bit. She managed to get to her feet. In time it took a bit but she got Cricket too. Once everybody had their horses again I got on Figaro. He did not do anything out of turn but he had a bit of pep in his step. Most likely a bit disappointed he did not have a chance to run with the ladies.

Not every ride was as eventful as that. Sometimes it was a learning experience. Tara was always fun to have around. It was during our rides that I showed her that Jake knew how to be ponied. This is when one horse with a rider up leads another horse around, with the two horses side by side and almost touching. I showed her with Figaro and leaned over and Jake leaned over, just as he did when he used to race. Tara was a bit leery about Figaro getting close but Figaro did nothing and I led her and Jake a few steps.

Later, Tara described this to Elizabeth, who asked me if I wanted to pony some of her horses. I turned that down. I had two reasons. One was that while Fig was a good boy, he was not a pony horse and I was not going to do that to him. Secondly, he was patient but that was not something I was going to push with him. Every horse has his limits and I was not going to push it with him. The pony story offered further proof that he was almost always good. The only downfall was because of his good nature people wanted him to be the guinea pig to test things out. I had someone once ask me to put Figaro by the roadside with a nervous horse on the inside while we were walking on the road. I had to turn it down. I was not going to endanger him, especially on a roadside, to benefit another horse. He was a tough boy but he had earned his dues and I was not going to put him in harm's way. A better solution would be to do more work and bombproof work to a nervous horse before introducing him to the roadside. I would only pony another if the circumstances required it. Like someone's horse would not cross a creek as an example.

The Protest at the Fair

Working in the arena or going for trail rides was good. A change of scenery every once and a while was a treat. Figaro and I took opportunities to venture off the farm too.

It was a Saturday (August 28) when I was going up to see Fig, as usual. I wanted to go earlier than normal that day to see if any of the early morning boarders were around to go out for a ride.

When we arrived, I saw Elizabeth getting Kisses ready to go out. I thought her daughter was going for a lesson.

She then informed me that in order to help their campaign against wind turbines, they thought to get people's attention by bringing a pony. That was not a bad idea since the turbines do affect animals as well.

Elizabeth asked if I would like to take Fig. Of course I jumped on it. Fig loves crowds and I could keep the pony and Nicole company. We got him cleaned up and rode two miles to the event . Figaro easily handled the traffic and crossing. He even slowed up when we had to cross any pavement.

All in all it was a good idea I went too because Kisses did not like the cars passing her and would get antsy when they passed, especially noisy trailers and tractor trailers. Occasionally she would get nervous passing signs. When Fig led the way, she settled down.

We arrived and there was lots to see. There was a great display of tractors and tractor pulls going on, with lots of people walking around and a pig roast on the spit.

Unfortunately Kisses didn't care for the tractors back firing, the noise or the farm equipment doing their demos. So we took her to where the booth was set up, took off her tack and let her relax. She was quite content to just eat and let the children pet her.

As for Fig, he took no notice of the noises or the crowds. He would occasionally nicker to see if any other horses were around but other than that he took everything in stride. We were even able to hang signs off the saddle. All in all, he did most of the foot traffic and went around to the crowds. We even displayed the odd trick to the crowds. Then to give Figaro and Pierre a break, they would get refuelled then go back out.

I ended up watching the pony, voluntold so to speak, since we also had haying going on at the farm. Elizabeth and the gang had to go back and forth. I didn't mind too much. I was in the shade and would occasionally answer questions about the pony and the turbines to the best of my ability.

Fig was the highlight of the event. Pierre did a great job promoting our campaign and Elizabeth's farm. She never asked for that or expected it. When they saw Fig and how well behaved he was, people inquired about lessons.

Fig really turned some heads when Pierre decided to watch the tractor pull. Pierre had Fig right up against the barrier and Fig never flinched from the noise. The kids watching even got into it when Fig would start nickering. So Pierre jumped on the band wagon and said that Figaro thinks this or that tractor will pull further. When he was right, the kids got more involved.

At the end of the day both Fig and Kisses were tired so we headed home. Kisses did not like seeing the traffic come toward her and had an incident with an inconsiderate truck driver who almost pushed her into a ditch. Both horses came home unscathed. We made sure we put her on the other side of Fig so she would relax and not see the traffic.

You could almost see the relief on the horses' faces. When they both saw home I think it was a sight for sore eyes, as the saying goes. Fig was quite tired but I think he was happy to get out in the public eye. He loves the attention and sometimes he needs the reminder and a pick me up.

Overall Elizabeth was happy. Pierre and I enjoyed the outing and helping Elizabeth. I guess one benefit out of the event was that the committee was so happy with Figaro that they were considering doing more events with him. They needed something to push the campaign tenfold and from what we got back in reviews, Fig helped do it.

Other than that it was a great day and Fig yet again showed his class.

Godiva Makes a Return

Early in October, Elizabeth asked if I would be interested in Fig leading a protest against the turbines. Since Fig had experience carrying a flag, I of course said yes. I was considering wearing a t-shirt while carrying a flag.

A week or so later I missed an organizational meeting because Pierre had to work late. A note to all: if you don't attend a meeting, guess who gets voted to do things? You guessed it; the person who was not there.

Elizabeth and others on the committee were thinking of ways to best catch people's attention. That is where I came in later that night and Elizabeth phoned me. Her voice had a slight hesitation. She said they were talking and they thought I would wear a costume. I said, "No problem. What is it?"

Elizabeth then proceeded to tell me about Lady Godiva, the famously naked horsewoman of the 11thcentury. She said that Fig was more than capable and would handle the crowds and flashing lights from cameras.

I said yes to be Lady Godiva, adding that if I had to ride naked I wanted free board the rest of my life. We both laughed. She said I could wear a body suit. Why not? It might be fun. I don't mind sticking up for a cause for the better good. Personally I wanted to move out to that area eventually and I really did not want to look at those turbines, but I was also opposed for many other reasons.

It was decided. Fig and I were going to be the leaders of the procession and the special guest of that night.

The day finally came and Fig had been cleaned up the day before. Fig was ready to lead his mini-cavalry for the protest against the turbines. It was later in the fall and the weather was unpredictable. It was nice all week. Our luck, it decided to rain on the day of the protest. Our crew was going regardless, even with the threat of a tornado. We had two trailers delivering and I was the last one to go. My hearts go out to our clan and everybody that attended because they braved the rainfall and the cold weather. At this point we thought our horses were going to be the only ones there. To my surprise, even my granny came to the protest.

Finally after a bit of a wait and change of plans for Fig's transport, we arrived. It was cold but Fig took it in stride. There were more horses and thanks go out to the other horses and riders that attended. There were many, many people to support the cause. I got dressed up and went with the procession, trying to keep warm. Thanks to Fig for being so warm. He didn't care about the weather or the signs, the traffic and all the other sights and sounds, or even the mares that were around. We joined the other brave souls and paraded in the pouring rain.

After a while we proceeded out. We listened to the speech by Elizabeth. She had a strong conviction, which was powered by her powerful argument. Fig and I responded at the appropriate points with a nice rear and did a couple other tricks for the crowds. All the time Fig loved it and was more than happy to do rear up and bows for the press and other spectators. I was freezing and shaking at this point. I tried to layer as best as I could under the body suit, however I was still cold. When the time came I walked beside the mayor to the building, with Fig and Pierre following behind. I went back and took some photos for the press, while the others went back to their trailers and tried to get warm. When it was my turn to go back and change my clothes I streaked across the parking lot somewhat laughing because I remembered the song "The Streak" by Ray Stevens. Once I changed I was never so happy to be in nice dry clothes.

After all that, everybody went in to the building. Mother Nature decided to stop the rain. Other than that we were more than happy with the turnout. There had to have been a least a thousand people there. It definitely was a successful and peaceful protest.

For the Love of the Canadian Horse

It was near the end of August when I received a message from Debra. She was wondering if Figaro could come and help out at a demo they were going to do at the Fergus Fair. The one Canadian horse she had coming was older and would not be able to handle jumping. I knew Figaro could and was just thinking it was a small jumping demo.

Of course I couldn't resist and said yes. The one catch: we were going to be jumping double and then in fours. I trusted Figaro to the fullest and knew he could do it (we had, after all, managed a four and a half foot jump), but we definitely had to do some practice since the last time we jumped was about five to seven years before this.

Next was to see how he would handle jumping after all this time. To my surprise he handled it very well. I guess because we have worked on free jumping and he can go over a jump with my cue. That was not chasing him. He took it all in stride. We started small. By the time we were done we managed a foot and half with ease. The only thing I was not sure of was if he could handle jumping as one of a double. On the other hand, we had handled quadrilles with six and sometimes eight stallions. So I wasn't too worried about him being able to do it.

I had a chance to meet the girls and the other horses. I was going to work with them one day and saw a mini preview of the routine. It was still in the works. At least I had a chance to introduce myself. Everybody was so pleasant. We decided we would do a run through of the routine before we went out. I think some of the girls were worried that I could not learn the routine quickly. I do have a good memory so I was not personally worried. Debbie had seen Figaro before and knew what he could do. When I met the other Canadians, they were all very nice. Figaro was definitely the tallest of the group. I knew it would still work out. Luckily one of the Canadians was 16 hands high so we had a good match that way.

It was Saturday August the 17th. Pierre and I had organized all the tack and whatever else we needed the night before. Figaro was out for a bit and when I went to get him from the field, he knew something was up since I generally never go out that early to get him. When I called him half way to the gate, he came up galloping and bucking. Then walking to the barn he was walking with a mission. When we got to the barn, Pierre was ready with shampoo and gave Figaro a nice bath. Figaro stood patiently as Pierre got him cleaned up and ready.

Lillian, our good friend, arrived with her trailer and we were off to the Fergus Fair where there were already many horse trailers, with the fair rides up and going. Figaro walked off the trailer without a fuss and just took it all in. He always walked with pride when out in public. He was like a star on the red carpet. I had to run ahead to find Debra while Pierre grazed him for a bit. I found Debra and the rest of the gang. They were finalizing a warm up ring in which to practice. Once I knew what was going on, I went to get Figaro tacked up. By the time I got Figaro tacked, the girls were back at their trailer waiting for a truck to arrive with their tack. I had to laugh when I came around the corner. The girls were a bit in awe, I think. Figaro walked quite proudly.

It was silent then Kyra said, "Oh my God!"

Then Lindsay spoke up and said, "That's not fair. His mane is longer than on our horses." Figaro's mane was about two feet long, which made for a lot of work but it was stunning. All the horses looked dashing with matching blue saddle pads and polos.

When the truck arrived, the girls started tacking up their horses. I decided to warm Figaro up a bit and at one point during that time I had Figaro do a rear up. All I got was "Wow! I didn't know he could do that." At this point

I think Figaro assured them he would fit in. He took to the other horses no problem, which was even better. We were definitely off to a great start.

After we all tacked up, we headed to the warm up ring with two jumps, with the tractor pull not too far in the distance and the fair rides no more than twenty five feet away. He never flinched at all the noises that could easily have distracted a horse. Not even when strollers went by or the tractors were pulling. One man, I was later told, buzzed passed on a small tractor and spooked a few horses but I never noticed because Fig didn't react. Been there, done that, don't worry.

We just did our warm ups and did a jump or two. Next came the one part I was not sure of -- jumping double over a jump. My partner was Lindsay on her horse, Neo, the 16-hand high Canadian. We decided to test it out. Somewhat surprisingly, Figaro went side by side, no problem. Neo was nervous after the first jump -- possibly from not knowing Figaro -- but Lindsay was in control. After the second jump, no problem. Next was learning the routine. After a quick run through, we had it down pat. Figaro had not worked in a group like this in about six years but he acted like we just did this yesterday. We did everything from pin wheels (two to three horses side by side with another two or three horizontal to each other and doing a uniform circle) to a carousel (five horses trotting in a circle to riding two - three abreast, then passing opposite directions between each other.)

Soon it was time to perform. Debra did a liberty act with Ferro, the 26 year old stallion, and another gelding. Then I went out and did a two-minute solo routine while they did a tack change. Figaro did very well and at one point very subtly snuck in a bit of grass while bowing. We did a rear, bowed, showed off some dressage moves and even did a circle around a man on the ground while Figaro's back end was facing him, which is full trust on all three of our parts. When Debra was saddled and ready, we joined up and proceeded to perform with the whole gang. Debra even announced to the crowd that this was Figaro, performing with this group for the first time – and having met them just minutes ago. Later we got quite a few compliments from spectators about Figaro's demeanour and professionalism. I couldn't help but be proud. We did our quadrille, which went smoothly. Then the four off us then proceeded to do the jumping. I managed to lose my stirrups at one point but I collected them quickly and all went well. Even when all of us went over the jump four astride it went very well. Then we finished the performance and answered questions from the crowd.

After we had some group photos taken, I had to thank Debra for the opportunity. I even got some compliments from my fellow riders who suggested I take Figaro and put him into some dressage classes. But I had promised I would not show him for ribbons. I knew he was more than capable of winning a ribbon and I didn't need a judge to tell me he was good. I knew it and I got compliments from others. That was all I needed.

That day I made some new friends and met some great horses as well. I was hoping to do more demos in the future and thought that maybe we would go to the Royal Winter Fair or the Can Am one of these days.

For a day or two Figaro was as happy as can be. I got back in the saddle after a day or two off and he was virtually dancing in the arena. He even did a beautiful *passage*. There is nothing more beautiful than that -- a horse dancing underneath you out of happiness.

Apple Picking with the Farm Kids

One beautiful fall day I couldn't resist going out for a hack after riding in the arena. I told Pierre I was going for a ride and he said fine and proceeded to play with Alice one of the farm kids I figured I would go to the upper field.

Fig and I had been out for half an hour and were descending a small hill. Fig started to munch on the apples that had fallen off the tree. I looked up. This apple tree had so many apples ready for picking. I couldn't resist.

I picked as many as I could that were within reach and put them in every pocket I could cram them into. After I reached all I could, I decided to go to the adjoining field. When I was just finishing my ride in that field. I saw Pierre, Alice and Sadie, the faithful farm dog, coming down the hill. Pierre must have remembered the day I came back with a jacket full of apples and decided to bring Alice for some apple picking.

So I came back around and Fig was quite amused watching Pierre climb the apple tree. Pierre climbed as high as he could without killing himself. I could not help laughing every time he had a branch stuck in his clothes. Poor Alice was worried for Pierre and kept telling him, "Don't fall."Alice was only 5 ½ years old though she seemed like an adult at times. It was cute. Finally, once Pierre got himself in a good position he told Alice to collect the apples he had thrown down. Sadie assisted Alice by pointing them out. Alice was quite the trooper and collected all of the apples tossed down. Fig was content eating apples that went astray. He was not bothered by the branches rustling or when Pierre shook half the tree to get the apples down. That method was quite effective when he wanted to get lots of apples to pour down. Poor Fig was hit the odd time as they came cascading down off the tree. He wasn't fazed at all. He just ate the apples. To make things easier for Alice, I gave her my outer coat so she had something to put the apples on.

After Pierre got as many apples as he could without falling out of the tree, he made his slow descent to the bottom, with the occasional French curse coming out when he got hung up on a branch.

After that we headed back to the barn. Poor Alice. The trek was a bit much for the little tyke. Pierre carried her for a little while but he couldn't do it for too long because of his back. I noticed their struggle so I turned Fig around and went back. I got off and let Alice ride Figaro back. I held onto the reins and she got a ride back to the barn. Figaro was very careful with her and went on the most casual walk he could do. When we were almost back at the barn, I turned around and I could see Alice was enjoying herself by the big smile on her face. When she finally got off, she was more than happy to show everyone all the apples they had picked and of course, she ate an apple, her own reward for all the hard work she did.

It is times like that I wish I had a camera. It would have been a beautiful shot. A girl collecting apples with the farm dog, Pierre up in a tree and the black stallion eating apples no more than a couple feet from Alice. What a great day it was!

A Glorious Ride

Apple picking seemed to be the thing that fall. I was heading out for my ride and Pierre figured it was a great day to bring Elisa and Leo, the farm owner's children. He had promised them he would take them out apple picking one day and decided to take out the ATV and the small wagon for the kids to ride in. As they went around the field in the ATV, I was riding behind with Figaro. When we got to the apple trees, the picking and fun began.

As the children picked the apples down below, Figaro took his opportunity – once again -- and stole the odd apple out of the wagon. Pierre decided to show off and climb the tree to shake down more apples – even though there were enough down below. I just prayed, as accident-prone as he was, that he did not fall out of the tree. Even the kids told him to be careful. After the apple picking was done, we went around the field. The day was just perfect and this time I had brought my camera along. It was then I went up on the hillside and we took time to take a few pictures of Figaro and me. Lately I had had this feeling like I needed to cram in all the things I wanted to do with Figaro into a short time. One of those things was to get a shot on the hillside. I got a few great photographs.

The hay fields were firm enough and it was then that I decided that I always wanted to gallop up a hill and rear up at the top. This I did and do have the video on YouTube. It just felt great. Figaro galloped up the hill and you could feel the great force of his hind end as he propelled himself up the hill. When we reached the top, he seemed to know what I wanted and gave me a rear up. When all was done and I was walking down the hill with Fig, I remember putting my hands in his mane and just feeling great and then saying to myself, these are the days I will remember.

As we traveled along we came to the creek and I rode Figaro around in the water, letting the current dance around us as he pranced through. It was just a great day. I remember falling asleep that night saying this day was fantastic.

Photo by Laura Sperduti

A Friend from the Past

I have said it many times about how weird it is that some people come back into your life. Everything has a purpose and a reason. This could be applied to Michelle and Ron. Michelle and I had worked together at the racetrack many years before. She used to groom and hot walk. She decided to learn the skills and life at the racetrack. The racetrack is a great learning experience. The downfall? The work is seasonal and there are no health benefits. So Michelle decided to work for herself and learned blacksmithing. Since she had left the track, I only had some contact with her occasionally. I'm not sure to this very day what made me contact her but once we started talking again, I mentioned Figaro. She had met him in the early days when he was more of a handful. I liked the farm's blacksmith but I figured -- why not give the business to a friend?

When Michelle and Ron came to the barn, it was just like old times. We reminisced about the old days. Then when it came time, Sandra had also decided to have Michelle do Betty and Jake because she had a hard time getting her blacksmith to come in. So they did her horses first. When it came to Figaro, he was a good boy for his trims. They took turns trimming his hooves. The whole time we chatted. Michelle asked what breed of horse he was. I said he was a Canadian horse. It seemed to come up a few times. I thought maybe she thought Figaro was sport horse.

When all was done, I told Ron and Michelle to come to the arena. I could see the look on her face. I knew that look, that "oh dear God" look. I think she thought I was going to just lunge Figaro. They both were in for a surprise. After some prodding, they followed me up the hill. When I got inside the arena, I could see them being polite but their eyes betrayed their impatience. I got Figaro to bow, then put him through his paces. A few minutes after, I think Ron was in shock. Again, Michelle asked again what breed he was and I told her again that he was a Canadian horse.

She said, "Really?!" in a curious and pensive manner. "We have met a few Canadian horses but none like him. Generally they are pushy."

I said, "I know. They have the reputation. They are not all like that. The breed was getting stamped with that reputation, just as thoroughbreds all get labelled as being crazy. Any horse can be pushy. Canadians just have more body behind them. Like any horse, if they learn they can get away with it, they will."

When they told me of their experiences I was not surprised. Too many people, when they learned the breed was near extinction, started to go out and get them. The only problem was that some made them lawn ornaments and didn't do anything with them. Ron still could not believe Figaro was a Canadian. She said, "I have to say this. He is the best mannered Canadian I have ever met." After meeting Figaro, Ron grew fond of stallions and one day wanted one of his own. He would later get a lovely rescue miniature stallion that needed a well-deserved forever home. He is now a happy little horse and enjoying his life with some donkeys and other fellow minis. I told Ron not to expect to meet too many like Figaro. He is a one of a kind.

Bomb proofing Put to the Test

These were the days when I just enjoyed riding out on the trails. There is only so much arena work you can do sometimes and Figaro was at the stage that he was already doing well under saddle. He knew his transitions. He could canter sideways, do flying changes, canter from a standstill and more. With him seeming like he was more sluggish these days, trail riding just felt good. However, this day was not going to be one of those days.

As we headed down the long path, we made a turn to the first hay field where we headed up a steep hill. Once we were almost at the top Figaro slowed down. I took a look around and saw nothing. I stopped him to make sure. I thought maybe a rabbit was going to pop out of the bushes. The hay was not that tall yet and was maybe a foot high at most. He still seemed to be on alert because I could feel his muscles tighten a bit. Once we took a few more steps, a flash of feather was suddenly in front of us. A bunch of turkeys had been laying low in the grass. One flew up in front of Figaro, with a bunch of others not too far from us. One came so close I could have easily grabbed its wing.

Luckily Figaro stood there like a champ. After all was calm and the turkeys flew away we continued on. We went down the other side of the field and down the steep end of the hill to go toward the corn field in the back. We went to go across the field and a coyote ran in front of us. Figaro wanted to give chase but he seemed to give up as quickly as it happened. We almost finished walking to the back of the property where the creek was when six kids on ATVs came up out of nowhere right behind us. I moved Figaro aside and their caretaker told them to slow down. They apologized. We continued. I figured it was time to turn back since I did not know where the ATVers were going to turn up again.

We exited the corn field and traveled along the back half of the field. Just then a bunch of young turkeys started to run in front of us. They looked like tiny grey velociraptors running through the grass. Figaro seemed quite inquisitive and would lower his head to get a better view from behind of them. They went a good fifty feet till they ducked off into the woods. I remember telling Figaro, "Let's hope the rest of the ride does not continue like this."

The next field was no better. We continued down the back and all seemed well until we passed a small pond. As we passed a tall bush a blue jay flew out of a tree and hit Figaro in the head. Fig shook his head in protest. The blue jay was fine as it squawked away at us. Then I took Figaro by the apple trees and let him munch away on the fallen apples. I think, I said to myself, *he deserves this*. I know deep down any other horse would have dumped me at any or all of these points on the ride and run off. My war horse deserved his treats more than ever.

Something Is Not Right...

The last trail ride was not fantastic. Even after some of our rides in the arena, we hit the trail. This was Figaro's and my time together. Things in my own life were a bit stressful at this point. This was my time to just let go and relax. Some days I brought out my camera and would take beautiful shots to put up on Figaro's Facebook site. I enjoyed taking photos of him he was very photogenic. I was not a professional photographer. However in my experimenting I learned a lot. I even took a photo of his pet crow. Figaro had seemed to acquire another pet crow and sometimes the bird buddy would follow us for a bit down the long path to the hay fields.

Sometimes I would even think about opening a pub or coffee house called The Stallion and the Crow.

As for photos, I even got one of him rearing up. This is how much I trusted him. I had the camera in my hand and hung off his side slightly to get a shot of what it was like to be on a horse when that horse was rearing up. This is how much faith I had in Figaro. This was the bond and trust we earned together. Some would say it was stupid, others would say I was a show-off. My own feeling? There was some envy and jealousy. I couldn't care less. I had a great horse. If people felt they had to put me down because of my bond, showmanship or training, I didn't care. The only thing I never tolerated was anyone bad mouthing Figaro – or my partnership with him.

Someone, for example, attacked one of my photos on Facebook. The photo showed Figaro being a bit over zealous in his rear up and he had his head tucked in. I was accused of reaming on his mouth and spurring him. I explained the scenario. I never needed to spur him or pull hard on his mouth. Later I showed a photo of a young rider performing her rear up with slack reins and no stirrups. After the explanation, everybody backed off and apologized. Unfortunately, these are the things you have to deal when you start to get noticed. There will always be someone trying to bring you down or put you down. In these times you have to ask yourself-- how strong can I be when times get tough? Do you stand by your buddy in battle or run the other way? I always believed in don't assume, ask questions.

When it came to Figaro I always chose to stand beside him.

In the next few months I noticed Figaro was not himself. The one thing I always tell people is to spend time with your horse so when the slightest thing is off you will see the signs. Figaro had been showing small signs like being a bit sluggish then the next day he was fine. Or his weight was fluctuating. At first I thought it was the weather, but I took mental note of it. Even when a good friend of ours came to visit Figaro from the track (Lisa and her daughters), I found Figaro was not one hundred percent that day.

On following rides I would find myself trying to take in every moment. I would put my hands in his mane more, trying to savour every movement. When grooming him, I would run my hands all over him, feeling every bump and blemish over his body. Fig, for example, had what horse people call a "prophet's thumb" -- a small indentation on his neck. Legend has it that the Prophet Mohammed tested his horses by depriving them of water for several days. He then released them near a waterhole while sounding his trumpet to summon them. Five mares heeded the call, and they were kept for breeding. The prophet pressed his thumb into their necks, leaving an indentation that was passed on to their offspring.) Fig also had a chestnut (a bony growth on the inner side of the leg above the knee) in the shape of the Playboy bunny symbol. Finally, he had a double whirl on his forehead that some books allege is unlucky. I always told myself when I saw these marks that I was in for an adventure. In time, we would see which one won.

Now my gut was telling me that something was wrong but I just could not put my finger on it. Every time I made plans or thought about the future, it was like my mind stopped me from going further. It seemed as if I could not look past 2012. When I thought about Figaro's age (he was then 15), for some weird reason, after I worked down the years and reached 20, I stopped. I was hoping it was just me being paranoid. I could only hope he would live a long and prosperous life.

In the coming winter months, I noticed Figaro dropping weight. That seemed strange but as quickly as he lost it, he regained it again. I figured maybe his age was catching up to him or maybe the cold was getting to him.

I brought this to Elizabeth's attention. When she felt his ribs, she would run her hands up and down when most people would run their hands sideways across the ribs. Due to his hair you could not see much. I knew he was dropping weight by his girth. He was usually on the last few holes on his girth strap when I tightened it but lately it was almost to the top. Elizabeth said she felt nothing.

She had a friend who represented a special supplement. A few of us decided to split the cost. Later, Figaro seemed to have a bit more energy so maybe, I told myself, he was just lacking some minerals in his diet. In the arena though, some days he was enthusiastic and others he was not. One day I was asking him to do a *piaffe* at liberty and instead of a steady rhythm he seemed to be more like a statute. He would raise one front left and one hind and hold it. In a way it was kind of neat. He looked like a plush toy that you could pose. When I clucked he changed legs. Still, we made our session short. I knew something was up.

Even our rides changed. He now needed to stretch at the beginning. I thought he had some issues in his back and I had Pierre look at him. Yet he could find nothing. So I went out and got him a memory foam half pad to help alleviate his back. It helped a bit. He seemed to need to have that stretch. Some days even as we cantered he would not extend himself and refused to get out of a collected canter. I did not argue with him and just kept our sessions short.

Even his mane was becoming brittle. The winter had a lot of cold wind and I thought maybe it could be wind damage and got some Vetrolin Detangler with SPF in it to help replenish the mane. That seemed to help a bit. So things were looking up. In the summer it seemed his coat got oily every once in a while, so I gave him a good bath to try to get the oil off. When I brushed him I started to notice skin tags in places where there were none before. He was getting older. So who knows when these things would develop?

What came to me one day while I was working on the computer and watching Figaro in his paddock from the window (we lived on the farm where Figaro was boarded) was a dream I once had. A few years back when I was coming from my grandmother's, I pointed to a farm and for some weird reason I turned to Pierre and said, "I had a dream that Figaro died at that farm." At the time we knew nobody on that farm. I found it odd. I knew the exact spot where he died as well. I remember Pierre turning to me and saying, "Get that out of your head. Why would you think something like that? It was only a dream." I did not want to think something like that at all. Yet why did it come to me?

I even found myself talking to others and saying I would never have another horse like Figaro. Michelle told me later they had noticed it and thought it quite odd as well. I think my mind and intuition were trying to tell me something. I chose to ignore it. Nobody wants to face the inevitable.

A New Place and a Time to Shine

With everything changing and granny on the mend from her heart valve replacement surgery, the drive back and forth drive from Fergus to the track was getting to be too much. It was fantastic to be on the farm with Figaro but it was far too much driving and it made our days so long. Then, as it often does, fate intervened.

Omer had moved his two horses down to a smaller farm near Erin run by Steven and Leah. They ran a carriage business and did wedding events, parades and wagon rides. Steven was a blacksmith. Leah taught children lessons on the farm.

When Omer had moved, we visited when we could because we were no longer on the same farm. We had so much in common with Steven and Leah. We considered the distance we were travelling and we discussed moving closer to the track yet staying close to Figaro. We had found a nice quiet apartment to rent in Erin so we would be much closer to work and still be close to Figaro. Moving to Erin shaved about a half hour off our travelling time each way. Plus, on the upside, they had a very large stall and a paddock available for Figaro. After I had talked to Leah, she said it would be no problem -- especially after I told her how easy Figaro was to handle. Steven and Leah were both very capable of handling Figaro.

Leah told me afterwards she talked to Steven about boarding Figaro. At first he was a bit apprehensive about having a stallion on the farm. When she mentioned Figaro was a Canadian horse he did not seem too amused. Steven had dealt with the breed while shoeing and like so many seemed to have bad experiences. I guess the combination had him a bit worried. However, Figaro would quickly change his mind.

The day of the move, unfortunately, Pierre and I got held back at work. Luckily Omer was there to go with Steven to load Figaro. Omer felt honoured and if I trusted anybody with my horse, it was him.

Steven came to pick him up with his two-horse trailer. Omer loaded Figaro with no problem. Figaro loved Omer. Omer being the great friend he was brought Figaro to his new paddock and made sure all was well with him till we arrived.

When we arrived he seemed to be enjoying his new paddock. After I discussed his needs with Leah she said Fig was going to be getting a bit of extra hay. We were still not a hundred percent sure why he kept dropping weight. He was put on a better feed. Morgan, Steven and Leah's daughter, an accomplished rider herself, was there and already asking questions about Figaro. I told her in the next couple days I would show her Figaro's tricks. At least he had a little admirer already.

In the next couple days when we went up, Leah told us about Steven's experience bringing him in. I am so used to Figaro and his surprise gallop to the gate. He didn't do it as often during this time, Steven got the experience when he called him in. Figaro did not disappoint. Steven went on the other side of the gate just to be safe. Once Figaro was there, he waited for the shank to be put on. After I had told Steven it was Figaro's thing, he seemed more relaxed. He told me he was not scared just unsure about whether Figaro was going to stop. Other than that, Steven said, he was a pleasure to work around. Figaro really showed his manners being next to Beauty, Omer's big black Percheron mare. There were no problems at all. Beauty was one of Figaro's girlfriends and when they grazed together, Figaro liked to rub his nose in her mane. We used to graze them side by side. Fig had been beside both mares and stallions in stalls with no problems. Leah and even Steven had to say he was really well mannered. l totally relaxed now. It was something I hadn't done in a long while. All was well. Things could only look up from here.

More Fun Times

When Figaro was settled in, I took him into the arena. He seemed to be filled with life again and ready to perform. When I brought Figaro into the arena, Morgan was right behind us. Some of Leah's students and Morgan's friends were there too. Why not put on a show for the kids? So I put Figaro through his paces. We did the Spanish Walk, he bowed and reared. We even brought out the stool and Figaro stood up on it. He even played with the kids with the barrel. Pierre was my stunt man and he would stand on Figaro's back for me because my knees burned when I tried to stand up on his back. Pierre did not mind doing it, especially for a crowd. Figaro was a class act and he stood there with no one holding him. Next Pierre would snap the lunge whip behind him to demonstrate how bombproof he was. The children were delighted and nobody worried about the stallion stereotype.

Figaro and I would even ride out in the outdoor arena when the kids had their lessons, without problem.

As for Morgan, she was a good rider and she was always near me when we visited. And always a pleasure to have around. I did promise her and her brother that one day I would let them up on Figaro. One day after their lesson was done, they had done well, so that was when I got Cody up on Figaro first. They were both good riders so I let Cody experience the Spanish Walk, then the bow and the rear. The sensation of the bow always throws people off since it seems like the front end of the horse disappears. Cody did well. Morgan seemed to be a natural. When it came time for the rear she just knew how to sit the rear and to do it with pride. With loose reins and no stirrups, she was all confidence.

I think I ignited the spark for her to want to do tricks. However, I encouraged her to keep up with her riding. One day I was going to teach her. Leah said she was already talking about teaching her horse to bow.

Figaro was ever the highlight. When Steven and Leah had a function at the farm, they brought out their carriage and Figaro enjoyed galloping alongside the fence line when the carriage went by. When he was out in his paddock, he would watch anybody riding in the outdoor sand arena or he just graze. When there was a crowd, he enjoyed showing off.

Leah noticed how he was. Leah had her connections. She even brought up the possibility of Figaro doing demonstrations for the pony clubs and possibly being a flag bearer for an event.

Figaro seemed to want to do more and things were looking up. Deep down I felt as if he needed to retire. Though his coat was gleaming and he was back to his normal weight, something deep in my soul and intuition was saying that something was not right.

Figaro's 16th birthday was coming up and we always celebrated that occasion. He gave us all an excuse to enjoy cake and have a great time hanging out with him and our friends. By now it was 2012 and Figaro had been in my life for twelve years. I was just 16 when I found him and bought him. To celebrate his sixteenth birthday, we brought in a carrot cake and of course, Figaro got his can of Guinness. The next day we had fun and played with hula hoops. We rolled them toward him and even tossed them over his back and onto his head. I just could not have had any more fun with Figaro.

When he got a trim not too long after that, he was a gentleman. When Michelle and Ron came up, they generally made us their last client of the day to give us more time to chat. Sometimes they would trim Figaro outside. The one day I had put him in the barn since the sun was a bit strong. I asked Ron if he wanted the light on and he said he was alright. Figaro moved his head over and turned on the light switch. Ron said, "Oh, thank you." I told him to thank Figaro. He thought you needed the light on. Ron thanked Figaro.

Pierre would spoil him after most rides. When we gave him his bath, we would take him out to graze afterwards. It was our thing and it was never going to change. One day Pierre decided to take him to the back half of the property next to the hay fields and go for a walk. Figaro always seemed drawn to the one opening next to the hay field. Even in his paddock, he would sometimes look in that direction. Pierre would say that Figaro had to go to his "romance corner." There were two beautiful white mares, one named Beauty (the other mare's name escapes me). Figaro seemed to be drawn to girls named Beauty. When the mares saw him, they would come to the back corner and rub noses with Figaro. He would even caress their necks. Never acting studdy or rude. When we walked back up, his girls would follow. If I ever won the lottery, I told myself, I would get him those mares. I could always picture him in a field with his two white beauties.

Giving Children A Ride To Remember

Times were good at the farm. However, in July Fig seemed to be dropping weight again. That summer was marked by high temperatures and little rain. Most days I took it easy with him whether we worked or played. I blamed the heat for his weight loss and lack of energy. Like me, Figaro did not enjoy the heat.

We did a lot of liberty work or we would go out for a trail ride with the kids as supervision. This was always fun. Sometimes I would just drop the reins and Figaro would walk behind, quite content being the caboose. This was to show his manners, for he was behind two mares.

One day Morgan had a lesson with two other girls her age. When they were done, they came by the arena to see Figaro playing with Pierre and me. When their mothers arrived and after a brief conversation with them,

281

Pierre asked the girls if they wanted a ride on Figaro. Morgan went first. She had already been on him but she got to show off the bow. Next was a small blonde-haired girl. She had a pony at the farm. She was quite confident as Figaro did the Spanish Walk and the bow. We kept a lead rope on Figaro since these were just short rides. He was a class act the whole time. The parents were not even worried and were all involved with horses in some way. The children sat on him with no saddle or helmets, this was nothing more than a walk and Figaro was beyond trustworthy. On any other horse, I would insist on a helmet even for myself. Also, both Pierre and I were there supervising this impromptu time with Figaro.

The last girl to go up was a very, very shy little brunette. I think the whole time I was at the farm I heard her say two words. When it was Crystal's turn, Pierre asked her if she wanted a ride on Figaro. She nodded her head. She was a bit more nervous so we only did the Spanish Walk. Once we saw her relax in the saddle, we did a bow. Crystal may have not said anything but you could see her smile ear to ear. The next time we saw her, we got a tiny hi out from her. Even in her riding lessons she now seemed to get more confident. Sometimes small things can mean so much. Now she had some bragging rights. In time she would actual say a couple words to us when she saw us. As we chatted, we let Figaro walk around the arena. The girls had fun rolling around on the barrel and they were trying to convince Figaro to roll them on the barrel. He gave it a small push. However, he held back. Even when I got him on the stool, Morgan wanted him to smile but in return Figaro stuck out his tongue as if to say, "I am done for today." The only trick Morgan could get him to do was smile and when someone was around she would show it off to others. Figaro gave her that.

Morgan would lead him in with confidence from the paddock -- with supervision. If this did not give confidence to a child, nothing would. It was a short walk to the barn and Figaro was his big old teddy bear self when she led him in. He would wait for her to put on the shank.

He was very content and he had a small entourage. Even though he seemed to have little energy these days, he still enjoyed a crowd no matter the weather.

Something Is Wrong

In the next couple weeks, Figaro showed subtle signs that something was off. He seemed to put weight back on and he was still stretching before we started work under saddle. He had only started doing this in the last year. Still there was no sign of any muscle strains or his spine being out of alignment.

Then, in the second week of July that year, 2012, Figaro's sheath began to swell up. At first we thought it was just due to lack of exercise. We gave it a week, observing and hoping the swelling would go down. You could touch his sheath, grab it and it seemed to cause him no pain. He was urinating just fine. He had just gotten his second round of regular vaccines and we thought maybe it was a reaction to the shots – though he had had these shots in the past with no problems. We called Rex, our vet. He said it could be a reaction to the shots but in that case the swelling would go down. We had taken his temperature and all was fine. He said if it persisted then he would come out. After a few days Fig's hind legs began to swell as well. To alleviate the swelling, we hosed his sheath and hind legs and Pierre would massage his sheath. This seemed to help and the swelling would go. We started to think this was a circulation issue. He was eating just fine.

I would take him for a walk around the hay field. When we passed the opening to the next field, he seemed to always want to head to that field. I asked him, "Do you want to go there?" Figaro then headed that way before I could give him the slack in the shank. We walked in. Each day that was our routine. I even hand jogged beside him to help the circulation more. Pierre gave me grief for it because he knew of the tendonitis in my knees. My knees would burn. When Pierre watched, I wouldn't jog. When he went into the barn, I would jog Figaro along the back side. I told Figaro, "I don't care buddy, if this is what it takes, I will do it for you. No pain, no gain."

No matter what we did, none of our attempts seemed to help him get better. Just before the fourth day of all this, Leah called and said Figaro did not eat his hay. Now I knew something was not right. We came up as early as we could, took his temperature and still nothing. Now it was time for Rex to come out. Unfortunately his shift was over so the emergency standby came out. He checked him over and could not see anything that stood out. He was baffled himself. They took some blood samples to have them tested to see if anything in his system was out of whack. He said to continue doing what we were doing to try to help the swelling. We also would have to get a urine sample and thanks to the vets at the track, we got a container to collect one. All it took was to sit on Fig's back. Within a moment or two, he urinated. He always had to have a pee before we rode.

Afterwards I sat back and watched him in his paddock. He was grazing so I could not figure out why he would not eat his hay. At this point he was still eating his grain and drinking water. To help with the swelling and to see if an allergic reaction was at work, we gave him an antihistamine to help reduce the swelling; this would rule out allergic reaction. It seemed to help the first few days. But when the antihistamine supply ran out after the seventh day, the swelling came back and even got a little worse. So allergic reaction was now ruled out.

That night when I got home, I usually went on Figaro's Facebook site and posted some photos and videos. This time, I sat down in front of my computer for at least an hour just thinking. I did not know if I should mention what was happening. This had been going on for a week or two already. I figured I should let people know that there would be nothing posted for a while since Figaro was under the weather.

Figaro had about nine hundred Facebook fans at this point. These were Figaro's most loyal fans. I hesitated about mentioning Figaro was not well. I remember my fingers hovering above the keys. Finally something told me to say something. When I mentioned he was not doing well, many inquired. I had no answers to give. When Figaro had injured his leg at least there was some hope. This time we both felt useless. In time, I thought I would have to provide more insight. Only a tiny bit of my usual optimism was hanging on. I had to have faith but it was dwindling. It felt like I was losing my grip. My heart felt sick but I needed to fight to find out what was happening to my buddy. We would not let this bring us down.

Later I would go on his site. I spent as much time researching his symptoms for any hint or clue that came close to explaining what Figaro was experiencing to no avail.

The following day, Leah said he was still not eating his hay. I figured maybe there was something in the hay. We tried another cut. He seemed to take a few bites out of the other hay. The swelling was still there. At least if he would eat then he could keep his strength till we knew what this was. I had another idea. I would get hay cubes. They tend to be a bit more appetizing for some horses. We were lucky, for he seemed to eat the hay cubes. So he would eat more, I got a container and filled it up and he seemed to be eating them. I could not care less how much was in my bank account. This was for him. That day we got a call back from the vet and nothing seemed out of the norm. White blood cells were normal and nothing else indicated an abnormal result. Also a kidney infection was ruled out. What was worse, Figaro was losing weight more and more. By this point he had dropped at least a hundred pounds. I always took a mental note of his condition and it was a good thing we knew his weight. After years of being with horses, I could eyeball a horse and come up with a good estimate about how much weight a horse has lost. In Figaro's case you could tell by his withers and his neck – they had lost their fullness. And now you could see his ribs easily. Even his halter, which used to sit comfortable, was now looking over-sized on his head.

Since he was dropping so much weight, I no longer jogged him. He was just getting tired. Instead I took him for an easy walk around the field and let him graze when he wanted. Afterwards Pierre and I would sit in his paddock and just hang out with him as long as we could. Some nights it was till the sun went down. At this point, when we sat in the paddock, Figaro began to separate himself from Pierre and me. He would go to Pierre more and seemed to be making a point of not hanging out with me as he generally would. When he felt he had enough, he would walk to the back of the paddock and hang out at the end facing toward the second hay field.

After one of our walks, all I could say is, "Figaro, I don't know what is wrong with you. All I want to know is what is wrong with you."

In the past when I had time to think, I could always look forward to the next year. But just as had been the case during the previous summer, I could not seem to see past 2012 -- as if there was a brick wall. I thought maybe it was me being paranoid.

A few days later Figaro went off his feed. He no longer wanted the hay cubes and would only eat Trimax, a high-fat feed, and even then only in small amounts. He seemed to only want sweet things. Rex admitted to being stumped. Nothing was abnormal in Figaro's blood or urine and the kidneys were fine. Rex then suggested that we send him to the veterinary university in the next city for an ultrasound. Maybe there was something internal. He said, "You guys never call. I knew when you called you could not figure this out." He then gave us some Bute (aspirin for horses) to see if this would make him more comfortable. Rex told us two days prior to his appointment to cut him off so that vets at Guelph could see him in full form without medication in his system.

Pierre hated that he could not figure this out. When Figaro walked up to him he said, "I don't know what this is. I don't know if I can fix this, bud." Figaro seemed to want his apples and carrots. At this point I gave him what he wanted.

When nobody was around, I told him what I told him when he had his leg injury. "The day you don't want your apples and carrots, buddy, I will know it is your time. I made this promise to you and I will keep it."

That night I finally filled everybody on his Facebook site that things were not looking good. People asked about his symptoms and some of his fans offered inspirational hope. Others were trying to narrow down what this was, with some even resorting to getting advice from psychics. As hard as it was, I answered all the messages. One person even said she had heard one of her local vets talking about what sounded like Figaro. I thought maybe she had overheard it in Orangeville. When I asked where she heard it, she said in Nova Scotia. I was amazed. Figaro had many fans from across the world. It seemed like everybody was now doing research or trying to give helpful advice. Figaro had his fans. They deserved to be there even in this trying time and I thank them with all my heart. They and their hope kept me strong when deep down I felt like my heart was wrapped in lead.

Figaro's appointment was fast approaching. In the past when horses I knew were sent to this neighbouring town with a veterinary university clinic. They were not too lucky afterwards. I was praying this was not going to be the case. When the day came, we borrowed a trailer from a friend. We got Figaro cleaned up the day before. I had always believed that he needed to look his best.

When we loaded him up, he seemed to know. He was not allowed any hay or feed just in case he needed surgery and so the ultrasound could be read. Figaro in the past would have been annoyed to not be able to eat. This time he did not care. Once we started the ride to Guelph, he only hollered once and remained pretty quiet for most of the ride.

When we finally arrived at the university, we made our way through the various buildings before finally finding the one we were supposed to be in. When we walked through the garage-style door, we came to a rubber-matted aisle with two large stalls to the left and two large stalls in front. On the right wall was a horse-size scale. On the other side, on the left side of the stalls, were many human-sized doorways to the offices. Figaro was placed in the first stall on the left. He announced his arrival as he always did. In a moment or two, an orderly came out and collected his information and took his temperature. In a few minutes he came back out with a tag. The tag had a number and his general information on it and it was placed on his halter.

It seemed like forever till the main vet came out. We explained what had been going on with Figaro. When we told him that we believed he had lost about two hundred pounds, his eyes gave away that he thought we were exaggerating -- even when we told him about seeing Fig's ribs. He looked Fig over and said he looks alright in a somewhat condescending tone. The vet asked us to bring him to the scale. Thankfully Figaro was such a good sport and he went on the scale so agreeably. It was then we saw his actual weight. He was 175 pounds under weight. When the vet asked what his original weight was, we said 1400 pounds. He admitted that he has so many owners come in and exaggerate their horse's weight loss, so he takes their word with a grain of salt.

Now he said ok and seemed to listen to us more carefully. I think he admitted to himself we know what we are talking about after really listening to us. Pierre and I described our work with horses at the track.

The vet said, "So you have seen some stuff." He did not dumb it down or sugar-coat things. We had to wait around a bit longer. I sat down. I could feel my energy just fading. Pierre kept trying to be optimistic. Figaro seemed to be taking in all the noises of the pressure hose cleaning the hallways and the odd horse coming in. He was bombproof to all.

He was bombproof and good thing he was. He just seemed to be accepting what was going on and around him, as if he knew. I sat there looking at him but the hardest thing was acting as if I were strong, when really inside I was crying. I felt it in my bones that this day was not going to end well.

Finally the ultrasound room was ready. We had to walk down the corridor to a small room, passing along the way a horse thrashing around in the wake up or anaesthesia room. Figaro walked with class. Only in the brighter lighting did the vet say he could now see my horse's ribs. Figaro called out once when the door was closed. I guess he knew something was out of the norm. The only time he moved was when they put the gel on for the ultrasound. They tried to warm it up for him but it must have still been cold. Even when the maintenance worker started to pressure hose the door, Figaro did not move. The vet was not happy at all and left the room for a moment. It was then he said, "This horse is pretty bombproof." We told him what he could do and he said we have a possible star in our presence. This time the vet wasn't being sarcastic.

When it came time, he started to scan over his kidney but the ultra sound was blurry. So he then checked his intestines. In his lower intestines, he finally found a spot that was not moving as much as it should. You could tell by the red and blue marks that not much blood was being supplied to that area. I had a bit of hope then. "This is hopeful at least," the vet said. "We found something." The vet wanted to take him to the other, more powerful ultrasound machine. They had to set up everything and in the meantime the vet wanted to get more blood samples and more tests done. So while they did that, we hung out by Figaro's stall. Another horse owner came in and while he waited with his horse, we chatted.

Finally after an hour or so, we lead Figaro down the long aisle. Figaro walked like it was nothing, almost like he had been there so many times before. We finally reached the end of the hallway. We turned to the right and then went through another doorway and into an open space. It was a few doors down and we were in a much larger room, not as bright as the first one. It had an examination stall that Figaro entered even though it was snug. He did not seem bothered. Pierre held on to his head. the head vet asked if it was a problem if some of the students came in. We said no problem. There had to be about twenty students. Figaro did not seem bothered. They brought the more powerful ultrasound over. They decided to check his left side first. They checked the intestines and saw little flow. So they next checked the kidneys since there was suspicion about kidney issues. Once they looked they found a kidney stone the size of a golf ball. The technician admitted kidney stones in horses are rare. This seemed more promising. I looked at Pierre as if we both thought the same thing. Maybe this is all it is. Next it was time to look at his right side.

One student tried shoving him over to move him closer to the bars for the technician. Figaro did not move. I told the student to wait and moved Figaro with one finger. I told him force is not always needed. It was then all the students crammed over to Fig's right side. I did not feel like trying to climb over heads so I took the shank from Pierre and told him to take a look since he knew how to read an ultrasound and x-rays better than I do. They scanned and found his testicle. She said, "Oh, here is his little man."

A moment or two all I could hear was the head vet saying, "Sweet Mother of Jesus!" My stomach turned upside down. After a few minutes of silence, she called in the blood technician. Pierre walked around and he looked at me, his eyes watering a bit. He was trying to hold his composure. He shook his head and I knew.

Then I heard, "Let me see if I can expand the screen to the max." Someone said, "We can't get it all on the screen." Then she moved the ultrasound all over and said she could see them in the intestines, pancreas, liver and lymph nodes -- lumps all over. They expanded the screen to 36 times magnification and still could not get all of the mass on Figaro's kidney. From what they figured the mass was about 36 cm. A horse's kidney is about 23 cm. So you can imagine the size. Now I knew why Fig would adjust himself under saddle. He was moving the mass.

Then the vet decided to do a rectal exam and all he said he could feel was lumps. "This mass," he told the students, "is like a billboard. You should not be able to feel this and in this spot." It was a tumour and all the lumps were tumours. Now to find out if it was cancerous. We would find out in a moment. The vet asked if it was alright to let the some of the students feel. Figaro held his composure. After the second student's exam, you could tell he was not too happy. Then they told us to take him to his stall and wait.

Pierre and I knew this truly was not good. Finally the vet came and we followed him to a small room and sat down at the table. In a moment the head vet came in as well and closed the door. My heart sank. As soon as he put his hands together and clenched, I knew what was coming next. He said they had just got the results of the blood test and with what they saw in the ultrasound, they determined Figaro had lymphatic cancer. Half his body was filled with cancer. The only thing not cancerous was his testicle.

"We feel you will be lucky to have another two weeks," he told us. "It would be better to put him down now." They offered to euthanize him right there, right now and they would provide a free autopsy and could arrange for the body to be picked up or arrange for cremation. He said this is a learning facility and it would be a good learning experience for the students. After they did the autopsy they would put everything back and sew him up.

The shock hit me and the tears could not be held back. He said, "Think about it." I did not need to think about it. He said he would give us a moment to think about it and they both left the room. I did not need to discuss it.

Pierre asked, "What do you want to do?"

I said in as steady voice as I could muster (though the upset and anger filtered through) I said, "No, he will not die here. He will not become another number. I want Figaro to die at home on his own time." Then I said, "I hope Figaro can make it to my birthday," which was then less than two weeks away.

Pierre said, "If needed, can you make the call?"

A bit offended, I said, "I will not let him suffer. He will let me know when it is his time. Regardless I will do what is best for him." Pierre did not argue and went to get the vets. Now I knew what was wrong with him. I hated that there was something and there was nothing I could do about it.

When the vets came back into the room I gave them my answer but they persisted in trying to convince me it would be a learning experience for their students.

I mustered up all my strength and said, "No. He will not die here."

They tried one last time and argued that I would be prolonging my horse's suffering and I told them I would not let him suffer. I would do what was best for him but he was not going to die in that hospital. I have seen the odd autopsy and to lighten the mood sometimes the odd joke comes out. Figaro was not going to have this done and have his organs crammed back in. He did not deserve that. He gave me my answer. He was going to live the rest of his days to the fullest.

That evening as much as I did not want to do it, I gave the verdict on Facebook. All his supporters deserved an answer. I asked Michelle, his blacksmith, to some out and see if she could trim some of his hoof. There is a company that makes a necklace charm out of a piece of hoof. She said no problem. It was then that she suggested we have a party. Not a farewell party but a celebration of Figaro's life. They were going to come out the next day. I invited those who wanted to come up to come and say their goodbyes since we did not know when Fig would die.

That night I just cried myself to sleep. The next few days we were going to spend as much time as we could with him.

On the next day Figaro gave me the final sign. He had eaten very little of his feed. I had placed a large pile of carrots and apples in front of Figaro. Pierre and I satin chairs in his paddock, just watching him. I was praying that the vets would be right and I would have Figaro till my birthday. That was my hope. I knew in my heart that I would be lucky to have even a few more days with him. As much as he did not want his hay, he was still eating his apples and carrots. Now he walked over with his head low, as he did when he wanted to investigate things. He sniffed the apples and carrots and pushed them aside as if searching for the juiciest one. This time, he did not take one bite. He knocked the pile over. He then came over to me and then to Pierre and then he walked slowly to his spot at the back of the paddock and stayed there standing as stoic as he could.

Figaro had stuck to his promise. I got my answer. The next words out of my mouth felt like I had delivered the final blow. I said as I choked on my words, "We will put him down in the next couple days."

Pierre asked, "Are you sure?

I said, "Yes. He gave me the sign. This is what he wants and I have to respect this."

Pierre called the cremation center. Next we would have to call Rex. After much back and forth we decided that Tuesday August 7th at 1 pm was going to be the time. The truck would be there to pick him up at the same time he was put down.

I decided to call everybody and those who wanted to come out would have the next few days to say goodbye. Michelle, Ron and a few others were coming out Sunday and some others on Monday. The next few days I was going to spend each and every minute that I could with him.

Celebration Party

Sunday was just as Michelle called it, a celebration of Figaro's life. We were going to celebrate what he accomplished and all the people he touched along the way. Pierre and I were going to be there early. Rex had told us to give him extra-strength Bute and whatever he wanted to make him comfortable. We tried to make him as pain free as possible. He seemed content, but mostly he seemed to be putting up a front. He was a proud horse and when he did not want to be around us, we let him separate himself from us. We understood that any animal that is ill will separate itself from the others. A part of me felt, though, that he did not want to be weak in front of others.

We headed to the farm. We stopped by a gas station and by a fluke -- because I had not seen it for some time -- I found Vanilla Coke, his favourite.

I picked up the six pack and brought it up. Figaro was going to have whatever he wanted.

When we arrived it was pretty warm. We decided to give him a nice warm bath. By now his coat was oily feeling and his mane was becoming more and more brittle. We just wanted him to feel good. After we bathed him, Pierre took him down to see his white beauties and nuzzle them. They seemed to know something was up and stayed close and grazed awhile as he grazed on the other side.

I wanted Figaro to feel special and I always wanted him dressed up in roses. I even bought him a bouquet of red roses. A Kentucky Derby winner receives roses. In our hearts, he was our champion and he was going to have that honour. He did not need to be the athlete of the year to have won so many hearts. He was the underdog that rose above all obstacles – but not this time. This was something God would not let us overcome. I was given many wonderful moments and a friendship that will stay with me till the day I die.

It was hard enough to look at my buddy who used to be so strong and proud now fading in front of us. His once strong, full neck was now thin. His lush black mane was now brittle and dull. His broad muscles were now sunken in and it took him much strength just to keep himself steady. His ribs used to be barely seen. Now you could count them without even touching them. The worst was to look into his once bright and soft eyes, to now look and see a fading light in them -- and pain.

I put the roses in his mane and took some pictures of him and me.

When Michelle and Ron finally arrived, they came prepared with lawn chairs and drinks. Ron fixed the roses to make them more even. And then we took a few more shots. Michelle trimmed a small piece of hoof off for me. Figaro was a pro and put his foot up.

We then put Figaro in the arena as we sat in our chairs. Figaro hung his head over the board while we chatted. Michelle and Ron took turns giving him a hug. I went in for a bit and sat with him. I was finding every reason to be close to him as much as he was trying to distance himself from me. I remember asking someone why he was doing this. I could not say it any better. "Figaro was always your strength," they said, "and at this time he can't be your strength. That is why he went toward Pierre. When something was bothering him he went to Pierre. Pierre kept telling him, "I can't fix this Fig; I can't fix this, this time."

I zoned in and out of the conversation. I stayed more focused on Figaro. I had his favourite food and drinks right beside me. At one point I was drinking my peach fizz drink. He signalled with his lips that he wanted some. As much as I was thirsty, I gave it to him. He drank it as a baby would drink from a bottle. When he was done he walked away and went wandering around. As he did that I focused back on the conversation. That is when Michelle said something that made me truly feel good.

She said, "In all of the years of being a blacksmith, I see a lot of people say how much they love their horse and yet they will see them once a month." She said to me, "You may have had 12 years with him but you spent the equivalent of 40 years with him."

A part of what she said was right. Only a part of me wishes that it was more. She reminded me of the early years when we first met and she could never understand how I was working with horses all the time yet still want to own one. It was when she fell in love with her own horse that she finally understood. We reminisced and talked about our partnerships with other animals.

Figaro decided to come up to me. The lunge whip had been sitting behind me leaning against the wall. Figaro knocked it down and after sniffing it, picked it up and with the little energy he had was trying to snap it. I took it gently from him and told him you don't have to buddy. You don't need to perform. It was then he picked up his foot and went to bow. I knew what he was doing. Some days when I was stressed or depressed he would sometimes do this to please me. This was breaking my heart. Even with all his pain and through the weakness. He still wanted me to be happy.

I did not want him to continue. So I rewarded him to thank him and moved to the other side of the board. We gave him a Vanilla Coke. Eventually Pierre had a can of Guinness with Figaro and more people came by to pay their respects. Finally Michelle and Ron gave their last hug to Figaro. Michelle told me just before she left that Figaro was the reason Ron wanted a stallion. I think people wanted to say more, but deep down people sometimes don't know what to say and to those who knew me there was nothing they could say.

If I had been told at the university that he needed medication to the end of his days, expensive feed or whatever else, I would have worked two jobs for him. There is no more hopeless feeling than when there is nothing else you can do than watch your friend deteriorate in front of you.

That evening we stayed with Figaro as long as we could and you could tell Figaro was tired. So we left him be till the next day.

Monday we were back up as soon as I was done work. More people came to say their goodbyes. For most of the day we sat in his paddock. Figaro was starting to show more fatigue. He had not eaten any grain now and we knew he was fading. We moved our chairs toward the back of the paddock as Figaro stood by his corner. We let him come to us when he felt it was right. People came into his paddock so he did not have to move. Wendy and her daughter came out and a few others that took lessons came out. Megan and her mother came by and brought some champagne. We had some but Figaro still preferred his Guinness. The champagne was not to his taste but he had a sip or two. He would walk over and say hi and in his own way was saying goodbye as well. He seemed to be distancing himself more and more from me. As much as it pained me, I respected his wishes.

My mom and Granny came by and sat with us in the paddock for some time. We made Figaro a nice warm mash like we used to but this time with some sweet grain. As much as he did not have an appetite he gobbled it all down. My heart almost got excited. I knew he had a good dose of Bute earlier so he would feel nothing at this point. It was just comforting to see him eat.

My Granny and mom were there when I got him. And as my granny said, "I was there in the beginning. I need to be there for him at the end." Thanks to my grandmother. She was going to help pay for his cremation. It was times like this you see who truly steps up to the plate.

Later that evening a close friend, Irene, came out along with a few other friends who used to be with us from Frank's farm. Brenda and Ciara came out. Brenda was a bit unsure since she remembered the really bad days and how Figaro used to be. I reassured her that Figaro was nothing like he used to be. When many had not seen him for awhile they forgot the sheer size of him. Even in his weakened state he was still a big boy. We decided to move Figaro to the small paddock at the end of the arena. It was full of nice tall grass and since the summer was so dry he did not have much to pick at in his paddock so Pierre thought this was a better idea. Figaro picked at the odd piece but seemed more content to roll in the grass with whatever energy he had. Plus Pierre thought his white beauties would be happier to be close to him. They seemed to be like his two beautiful angels. Wherever he was those last few days, they would follow him. At least here they were no more than ten feet away from him.

Luckily Beauty, the one white mare, found a hole big enough to hang her head through and stayed there the entire evening. They kept a close eye on their man. Figaro was content to hang around for awhile as if he knew what was waiting for him the next day. A few times I caught him looking at the opening to the second hay field. I remember walking into the paddock and asking him, "Is that where your spirit needs to go?" We just stood together as if we were having our usual conversation. There were no words but I felt as if I just answered my own question. At a glance in the fields I had noticed the crows were no longer around; the day before there were more than usual. This day, however, as I asked the question to him, he glanced in the other direction. As I looked up I saw it. Not a crow but a hawk hovering and coming closer. It was just gliding on the wind. No sound from it wings just a steady graceful glide. In my hopes this was Figaro's guardian to the next life and not the crows.

I had done my research. I originally thought his little companion was cute and thought nothing more of it. I was even thinking of opening a pub called the Stallion and the Crow. Only after my research did I come to realize why people are so superstitious. In many cultures the crow is the carrier of souls to the next life. If they were seen flying diagonally over a house it meant someone was going to die. In other cultures, when they appear often someone will die. In this case, I guess it was meant to be my sign. I just never looked at it that way. Still I don't look at them as evil but I do wish when I found out he had cancer they were not around. I fought my instinct to throw something at them. All I could say under my breath was, he is not yours yet. If the three-headed hound came from Hades, I would not back down if it meant he would stay. All I could do in this helpless moment was just stay as close to him as possible and try to find comfort in the small things.

As we made our last few rounds, Figaro seemed to get a temporary appetite and was enjoying the two-bite brownies Brenda had brought. Ron, her brother, wanted to come but he was in England at the time. She told me this was killing him since Figaro was the one who introduced him to the Canadian horse. I am glad he didn't see him in this state. This was one reason I did not post pictures of what he looked like on his Facebook page because I didn't want to depress people. I wanted people to remember him strong and proud, like the champion hews... is. I still have stuck to this and will not post a picture of how he ended up. That is why as well we asked Leah and Steven that the day he went down only three people would be there -- Pierre, Rex and the driver of the truck. Pierre was right in telling me not to be there. Not that I did not want to hold my buddy's head. He said it will haunt you. He was right. I have a photographic memory and I would see that the rest of my days. I wanted to remember him strong, that and it seems odd to some but the way Figaro was somewhat pushing me away. I don't think he wanted me to see him go down. A part of me wanted to be there and hold his head.

When the evening got darker it felt like the curtain was going down. Everybody had gone home and given Figaro and us their last hugs. As we led Figaro back to the barn, the white beauties followed along the fence line. Pierre took him into the arena for his final roll and then we took him to his stall. We then braided some mane and tail. We took some from the middle of the mane and from the tail. Our goal was not to make it look like he had lost any mane or tail. I wanted a piece of him but I was not going to disrespect him and make him look bad. He was going to look his best till the end. After we took some mane and tail, Figaro went to the back of his stall. Pierre, Leah and Steven let me have my last quiet moment with him. I stood by the door. Figaro came to me and gave me a little bear hug then went to the back of the stall and did not look back.

However, before I left I whispered in his ear, "If you ever want to get a hold of me through a medium, let's use one of these names and I will know." When Pierre came back in he said, "Do you want to stay longer?" I said, "Figaro said his goodbye. It is time to go home."

Good Bye Fig

Tuesday morning I went to work. We had made arrangements with an acquaintance to take me out for lunch to keep my mind off the time.

Pierre went up early that day and gave Figaro a bath. And put on the new halter I did not have a chance for him to really wear.

Pierre told me they went for a walk and hung out by his white beauties. They stayed by the fence the whole morning. He then took him to see the others horses one last time. When the time came Rex was there and they were waiting for the truck.

Meanwhile I was taken out for lunch. I did not want to eat. We sat in Fortino's and luckily there was no clock for me to see. There was a pact made that I was not allowed to look at a clock. As someone talked, I just sat there knowing the time was coming. Out of nowhere, I felt a warmth pass-through me and my heart sank. I stopped the person mid-sentence and said, "He is gone." They then looked at their watch and I asked the time it is. They said 1:22 p.m.

When I met with Pierre back at the track, he was crying himself and gave me a hug.

I then asked, "What time did he go?" He said all was done by about 1:23 p.m. I knew.

Pierre said when the time came, he let him say goodbye to his girls. He then took him to a spot near his paddock where Rex gave him the first needle. He fought it like he generally did and reared up. Rex apparently said, "That is our boy. A fighter till the end." Within minutes, Figaro was pain free. He started to graze. They he was given a second relaxer shot. They wanted to give Figaro the most peaceful send-off they could. He deserved this. Rex himself had had a bad day and had to put down a few horses that morning. Figaro was going to be his last. He told Pierre he would go home after this one. This one bothered him the most. Now it was time to give the final shot. Pierre said that in all his years of witnessing horses being put down, this was the most graceful. He said Figaro went down as if to lay down, like it was nothing. Pierre said he was so proud right to the end. As he went over Pierre held his head in his lap. Then Rex leaned over Figaro with his stethoscope on his chest to hear his last heartbeat.

After Rex had determined that Figaro was gone, my horse's body was loaded onto the truck -- his own private limo. He had a nice padded cushion so that his beautiful hide would not be harmed and in respect Pierre covered his eyes with a towel. When Figaro was loaded, Pierre went to follow behind. When they were ready to leave, one of his white beauties nickered. Then as he passed the field horses, they were all lined up by the fence line. Most time horses don't stay near when they sense death but they were there. Omer's black Percheron, Beauty, nickered as well as he passed. Pierre followed him as far as the highway. The truck bearing Figaro was going to the right and Pierre had to go left to come get me. It would be a week till I could go pick up his ashes.

Leah and Steven closed the arenas for two weeks out of respect for Figaro. It was really touching.

That summer had been so dry and there was a hay shortage. The next day it rained and it rained heavily all that week. It felt good. As a great comic once said, "I love it when it rains because no one can see me cry." Going to work was so hard. Nobody said much. One friend, Holly asked me how I was and I told her I was doing alright. She pounced on me and gave me a hug. She said, "No, you are not." She was right.

A part of me wanted to go to the farm and hope he was still there. That week when we went to get groceries, I headed for the carrots and apples first. When I picked up the carrots, Pierre said, "You don't need to do that anymore." I broke down. I generally don't break down like that, but this was Fig.

It was a long rainy week. And as we headed down to London to pick up Figaro's ashes, a part of me felt relieved to know that Figaro was going to be near me again. When we were about an hour away, the sun came out. The clouds were still grey in the sky but the rain had stopped. It was as if the whole time we were separated even the angels were crying. It was hard to wrap my mind around my beloved horse being in a pine box. I was just glad he was coming home. As Pierre picked up his ashes he lightened the mood by saying, "You were heavy in life and in death. You are still heavy." It was a long drive. We headed through Fergus towards Erin. Ahead of us the clouds were grey and in the middle the clouds had parted. What happened next strains credulity. I tried to get the camera but it disappeared as fast as it came. One dark cloud looked like a rearing horse, with the knees tucked in like Figaro used to do. I knew my buddy was still there.

Chance, my male cat (aka puma cat), always loved Figaro's smell and would roll in his sweaty saddle pads. When we put Fig's ashes down on the coffee table, he looked and smelled it all over then lay on top of it. No matter where Figaro's ashes are, Chance will go over and lay on them. It was not like him to lie on something like that on a lower level. He likes to be up high. Our other cat would not go near Fig's ashes.

I had never realized until Fig passed the impact he had on people. On his Facebook site alone I received some 1,200 messages and many in my private message board, never mind the countless posts on his wall. He was not just another horse or a page that people liked. He actually touched people, whether it was his photos or our accomplishments or his stories. He was not an athletic champion. He was a jack of all trades, a dream, a reality, an underdog and an inspiration. And that is what made him unique.

Still There

Even in death he seemed to still help me. We never made it to a movie. Two weeks after he died, he was called in for two movies. My first thought: *why could God be this cruel?* After thinking about it some more, I realized he would have made it. This was the cherry on top. We would have made it and in some way we did. I felt much better afterwards.

It has been some years now since he passed. I still can't help but feel he is with me.

About six months after Fig died, I got really sick with a bad case of hives. Then it progressed to my lungs, leading to double lung pneumonia. My lungs were full of fluid. I had kept working, which was clearly a mistake. When I finally went to the hospital I was admitted immediately and spent six days in isolation. After multiple blood tests, an MRI, biopsy and many antibiotics, I was lucky to recover. The doctors said I could have died and a few nights I wanted to. I had much time to think and to take my mind off things, I would think of Fig.

I found lots of comfort there, and something always told me not to give up. I had a hard time even thinking of getting another horse, I was not even sure why I was. What made it hard was Fig. He was my buddy. The next problem was that every time looked at another horse, I was thinking of pursuing the same things I did with Figaro. Then it hit me one day: I was *not* going to do the same thing I did with Figaro. Something said to get a gaited horse, host fund-raiser shows and trail rides to raise money for equine cancer. I felt a new life come back to me. I was not replacing Figaro; I couldn't; I was going to honor him. With this I got new strength. I needed it because once I got out of hospital I had to still sleep upright for two months before I could lie down normally.

By this time I had decided I would be better off on my own. My relationship with Pierre was over, his eyes had wandered and the less said, the better. Figaro's journey to the Rainbow Bridge (the pathway to the afterlife) was leading me down a different path in life. It was a new beginning to fulfill my promise to Fig by telling his story, with a new horse, to make and reach new goals, opportunities to grow, to succeed, gain good health and a chance to be happy again. I will overcome adversity. I am on that road now. Life's lessons are learned and tucked away for reference, good memories are my positive motivation and Figaro is my guiding light.

I have another horse now. My mom encouraged me and advised me not to waste my gift. When I go to see my new little horse, Couper, I still look toward an empty paddock that Figaro has never been in. It is as if he is there. While walking down the aisle of a barn I worked in for the winter months. I felt as if I needed to put my hand out and pat Fig as I used to when bringing him in from the arena.

Why he came into my life, he seemed to be my strength. His death, in part, made me stronger.

I am back on my feet now and I made good on my promise to Figaro that I was not going to let him be forgotten and I was going to write his story. He is always on my mind and always in my heart.

Fare thee well, my faithful friend, and thank you for everything. See you over the Rainbow Bridge one day.

A Message from Figaro with Love

In May of 2014, my mother gave me a gift – a reading with an animal psychic. Many have doubts about psychics, especially animal psychics. However, I have friends who have used this one in particular –the "animal talker," Lauren. She is well known and many owners have solved issues with their horse that others could not figure out. I believe in keeping an open mind and was curious what she would have to say.

Because of the nature of my work, I asked my mother if she could do the reading for me. Later that day she gave me a call. All she could text me was, "Wow."

She told me Lauren was a bit overwhelmed with what Figaro had to say. Figaro had mentioned through Lauren to tell my mom thank you for helping her find him. Apparently he had been searching for me for some time. We had been together in a past life and we got separated. He was so happy to find me again. It was funny since I always felt that in some past life I was in the cavalry. I don't know who or where I was in a past life but it is a comfort to know that Figaro and I were reunited in this lifetime.

Next he wanted total me that he is always looking over me and he is always with me. He must be my guardian angel. In August of 2014 my truck was hit by a transport truck at 80 clicks (kilometres per hour). My truck was wrecked beyond repair and I came out a little sore. That was all.

It was then he brought up the new horse, which he called the baby. He said I am glad she found him. I picked him for her. Lauren said Figaro is with the baby. Which is sort of funny because anyone who has met Couper keeps saying he is an old soul in a young man's body. My mom and have joked many times about the old television series *Married with Children* and how when the old dog Buck died. He was reincarnated into a Cocker Spaniel named Lucky. We thought how funny it would be if that really happened.

Through Lauren, Fig did answer one of my questions. We asked how long he had his cancer and he said two years, which was about right in my own calculations. It was then he said how he always felt hot inside. There was one more thing I was curious about – What did Figaro really think about Pierre? When my mom gave me Fig's answer I was not really surprised. All Figaro said was, "He was just there." Figaro was a true judge of character. He summed it all up in four words—He was just there.

When Lauren continued her reading, when he was put down he was puzzled as to why he was given three needles. I was not aware of this until after the reading. Mom told Lauren that we wanted him to leave this earth in the most humane way. The first needle was given to relax Figaro. The second was to further relax him and bring him closer to almost falling asleep and the final needle was given to send him to the Rainbow Bridge. However, he did thank Pierre for putting a towel over his face and eyes. Even though he was not sure why, he felt this was a very loving gesture. Just before the session was over Mom reminded Lauren about the farms.

At that time Lauren said that the baby was Figaro but he was not whole. His spirit and soul are still at the other farm. I must bring his soul together to make him whole. Lauren said that I had to go to the last farm I was at with Figaro. Was that possible? Mom told her it was possible. Lauren instructed me to go to the last farm we were at and spend some time there. Walk around, then, right afterwards go to the new farm and visit with the baby. This will bring Figaro's soul together with Couper to make it whole. The baby is Figaro so he needs to have his soul taken to Couper to be made whole. (Whether this is true or not, I was not going to leave my buddy in limbo.)

I don't think he will take over Couper's soul, but Figaro will be a part of him and guide him.

Some readers may be rolling their eyes at all this. When asked what warning I should look out for, he asked, "Does she have any food allergies and tell her to take care of her ankle. It will cause her a lot of pain."

Only a few weeks prior to this my ankles were plaguing me. They crack and they pop. I had told no one about this.

To end things he said, "Tell her I do like to stick out my tongue and I liked to dance with my front feet."

The most comforting thing of all was knowing I was not crazy and that he was around me always. This animal communicator answered some questions and brought me a feeling of inner peace.

It is nice to know that I was meant to get another horse and that a part of Figaro is in him. If so, Couper will see the same love and attention as my pal Figaro.

We'll see what the future holds. I may have not gotten a farm while Figaro was alive but I will still pursue that goal and I will call the farm *Figaro's Haven* where I hope to live the dream and build what I wanted for Figaro and me. Just because our story ends does not mean the dream has died.

On May 28th, my mom did the reading with Lauren Bode who had said I needed to go to the farm. My day off was that Friday. Whether I believed it or not, I was going to try.

So I drove out to Erin. I sat by the road and I called his name and whistled the whistle I used to call Figaro. (I couldn't go on the property because the farm had been sold.) I stood outside the gate and I waited for five minutes as I texted my mom. I felt my insides feel different and a bit heavy. I hoped this was the sign. The weather was nice that day, cool but sunny. I drove to the place where Couper, my new little guy, was boarded.

I remember I said, "Figaro, all I can ask is if this is successful please give me a sign." All I could do was try. Couper had just gotten his shots that day so I figured I would just take some photos of him instead of work or play with him.

When I reviewed the photos, I almost fell backwards. I have taken many shots of Couper and in two of them Couper's tongue was hanging out. When I got home I checked Figaro's photos and all I could say was, "Oh my God!" If there were signs, these had to be it. I never felt so light after this. He did not give one sign; he gave me quite a few. I had to show these to my mom and close friends who have seen Couper themselves and they could not deny it. A friend who helped me get a saddle on Couper said the whole time he was around Couper, he never once saw him stick out his tongue. When I showed him the photos, he had to stop and look at them for awhile himself. He then remarked how similar the pictures were; even the way he put his tongue out was the way Fig did it. Best is when people come up and compliment Couper and how he seems like an old soul. If Fig is in there, even just a little, I will take it. Couper is still unique but it is nice to know that Fig is guiding him. There are some things in this world that can't be explained. If our bond is as strong as it is, we will be together till the end of our days and more. We will see where my path leads.

Whatever path I travel, I can't ask for a better guardian angel than Mr. Fig.

Photo by Laura Luszczek

Photo by Laura Luszczek

Photo by Mallory Haigh

Photo by Laura Luszczek

Glossary of Terms

Bit: is a type of horse tack used in equestrian activities, usually made of metal or a synthetic material, and is placed in the mouth of a horse assists a rider in communicating with the animal. It rests on the bars of the mouth in an interdental region where there are no teeth. It is held on a horse's head by means of a bridle and has reins attached for use by a rider.

Bridle: is a piece of equipment used to direct a horse. The "bridle" includes both the headstall that holds a bit that goes in the mouth of a horse, and the reins that are attached to the bit.

Canadian breed: The Canadian horse was first introduced to New France in 1663. The first load of twelve horses was sent via ship by King Louis XIV. There is no record of the breed or region of France from hence they came; some writings mentioned the Royal Stud Farm, and it is believed that most of the horses came from similar ancestries as the Belgian, Percheron, Breton and Dales Pony. What is known for certain is that shipments arrived on a regular basis.

The first ones were given to religious orders and to gentlemen who had an avid interest in agriculture (although they remained the property of the king for three years). A notarized contract obliged the new owners to breed the animals, maintain them, and return a foal after three years to the Attendant. This foal was then entrusted to someone else who was then bound by the same conditions of care and reproduction. In case of breach of contract, there were provisions for fines of one hundred pounds. This much regimented breeding system allowed for their rapid development in the French colony. The horses thrived despite low comfort, hard work, bad roads, and eventually developed the nicknames "the little iron horse" and "the horse of steel".

From 1665 to 1793, the horse population in New France grew from 12 animals to 14,000 animals. To the end of the French regime in 1760, the horses sent from France are the only ones to be developed in the colony. Contact with the English to the South was forbidden because England and France were at war. The topography of the Appalachian Mountains was also a formidable obstacle to outside communication. At that time there were no roads and the only means of long distance travel was by foot or by canoe. For almost one hundred years, these horses multiplied in a closed environment without the benefit of other blood lines. Their common source, lack of cross breeding, and their rapid reproduction created a particular genetic group giving rise to a unique breed: the Canadian horse.

During the 19th century, breeders bred different types of Canadian crosses such as the Canadian Pacer, an amalgamation with the Narragansett Pacer, the "Frencher", a Thoroughbred cross with hotter blood used as saddle horses or roadsters, and the "St. Lawrence", a much heavier draft type, in order to meet a variety of needs. Later, thousands of horses were exported to the United States for both the Civil War and also to use as breeding stock to create roadsters leading to new breeds such as the Saddlebred, Standardbred, Missouri Fox Trotter, and the Morgan. These mass exports lead to a huge drop in the breed population in Canada in the 1870s, and the stud book was opened in 1886 to preserve the breed and prevent possible extinction. In 1895, veterinarian Dr. J.A. Couture set breeding standards for the Canadian Horse and founded the Canadian Horse Breeders Association which still operates today.

In 1913, the Canadian government began a breeding center in Cap Rouge, Quebec. In 1919, this facility was outgrown so the breeding program was transferred to St. Joachim, Quebec, where it was operated jointly by the Canadian and Quebec governments.

In 1940, World War II brought an end to the federal breeding program at St. Joachim. At that time, the Quebec government purchased several of the horses and created their own provincial breeding program at Deschambault. In the 1960s, they worked to breed a taller, more refined horse, which would be suitable for English disciplines. During this time, other private breeders worked to preserve the original type, the Henryville line being an example of this. Eventually the Deschambault herd was sold at auction in 1981. The breed was in danger of disappearing for a second time, with less than 400 horses in the breed register, and fewer than 50 new registrations being recorded per year. However, dedicated breeders rescued the Canadian Horse. New registrations were around 50 per year in 1980 and rose to over 500 new registrations per year in 1999–2000. Since 2000, the new registrations are stable at 450-500 per year. There are now more than 6,000 horses registered.

Today, Canadian Horses can be found in just about every discipline. Be it English, Western, or Driven; Competition, Leisure, or Working; there is a Canadian Horse for everyone.

In addition to the Beaver, the Canadian Horse is commonly seen as an animal symbol representing Canada, especially in connection with images of the Mounties. On April 30, 2002, a bill was passed into law by the Canadian Government making the Canadian Horse an official symbol of Canada. As the Canadian Horse is also "closely associated with the historical origins and the agricultural traditions of Québec", a similar law was passed by the provincial legislature in November 2010, recognizing the breed as a "heritage breed of Quebec".

Why Canadian? Because in 1867, the year of Canada's confederation, the generic term 'Canadien' solely referred to French speaking. At that time, it was natural for the horse, being originally from France and having started its spread through the French colonial area of the St. Lawrence Valley, to be named 'Canadian'.

Capriole: *of a trained horse:* a vertical leap with a backward kick of the hind legs at the height of the leap

Crop: sometimes called a **riding crop** or **hunting crop**, is a short type of whip without a lash, used in horse riding, part of the family of tools known as **horse whips**.

Cryptorchidism/Rig/Cryptorchid: meaning that a testicle had not dropped normally. The horse retains a testicle even though he has been surgically gelded

Dressage: is a competitive equestrian sport, defined by the International Equestrian Federation as "the highest expression of horse training", where "horse and rider are expected to perform from memory a series of predetermined movements."

Foal: A baby horse

Gelding: A male horse that has had his testicles removed. A gelding cannot breed or reproduce

Green broke: the term "**green**" **horses**, it refers to young **horse** that is still in training. Just like in unripe fruit the color is usually **green**.

Ground work: Working with a horse from the ground. Not riding. Lunge lines and surcingles

Halter: a headstall usually with noseband and throatlatch to which a lead may be attached

Hands high: is a non-SI unit of measurement of length standardized to 4 inches (101.6 mm). It is used to measure the height of horses. It was originally based on the breadth of a human hand.

Lead rope: A rope with a snap on one end, that attaches to the halter and used to lead and tie horses or ponies. Leads can be made of leather or synthetic materials and can be flat, woven, twisted or rolled. Lead ropes, or 'leads' as they're sometimes called, come in many different lengths. Most common are lead ropes between seven to ten feet, but they can be longer. Some have a chain between the snap and rope or leather.

Lead shank: or **lead chain** refers to a lead line with a chain attached that is used in a variety of ways to safely control possibly difficult or dangerous horses if they will not respond to a regular lead.

Levade movement in which the horse first lowers its body on increasingly bent hocks, then sits on its hind hooves while keeping its forelegs raised and drawn in.

Lunge line:(longe line: US English, classical spelling) or **lungeing** (UK English, informal USA) is a technique for training horses, where a horse is asked to work at the end of a long line and respond to commands from a handler on the ground who holds the line. It is also a critical component of the sport of equestrian vaulting. Longeing is performed on a large circle with the horse traveling around the outside edge of a real or imaginary ring with the trainer in the middle.

Lunge whip: a **lunge whip** can be used to create stronger driving energy.

Lusitano: is a Portuguese horse breed, closely related to the Spanish Andalusian horse. Both are sometimes called Iberian horses, as the breeds both developed on the Iberian peninsula, and until the 1960s they were considered one breed, under the Andalusian name. Horses were known to be present on the Iberian Peninsula as far back as 20,000 BC, and by 800 BC the region was renowned for its war horses. When the Muslims invaded Iberia in 711 AD, they brought Barb horses with them that were crossed with the native horses, developing a horse that became useful for war, dressage and bull fighting. In 1966, the Portuguese and Spanish stud books split, and the Portuguese strain of the Iberian horse was named the Lusitano, after the word *Lusitania*, the ancient Roman name for Portugal. There are three main breed lineages within the breed today, and characteristics differ slightly between each line.

Mare: A female horse

Passage: is a movement seen in upper-level dressage, in which the horse performs a highly elevated and extremely powerful trot. The horse is very collected and moves with great impulsion.

extended trot

The passage differs from the working, medium, collected, and extended trot in that the horse raises a diagonal pair high off the ground and suspends the leg for a longer period than seen in the other trot types. The hindquarters are very engaged, and the knees and hocks are flexed more than the other trot types. The horse appears to trot in slow motion, making it look as if it is dancing. The passage is first introduced in the dressage intermediaire test II. A horse must be well-confirmed in its training to perform the passage, and must be proficient in collecting while remaining energetic, calm, and supple. The horse must also have built up the correct muscles to do the strenuous movement.

Piaffe: is a dressage movement where the horse is in a highly collected and cadenced trot, in place or nearly in place. The center of gravity of the horse should be more towards the hind end, with the hindquarters slightly lowered and great bending of the joints in the hind legs. The front end of the horse is highly mobile, free, and light, with great flexion in the joints of the front legs, and the horse remains light in the hand. The horse should retain a clear and even rhythm, show great impulsion, and ideally should have a moment of suspension between the foot falls. As in all dressage, the horse should perform in a calm manner and remain on the bit with a round back.

The piaffe was originally used in battle to keep the horse focused, warm, and moving, ready to move forward into battle. In modern times, the piaffe is mostly taught as an upper level movement in Classical dressage.

Prophet's thumb: "The hot desert wind blew against the tent, driving the dust inside. Fatima walked softly in, carrying an earthenware jug full of cold water, and handed it to the Prophet. "Please, stop tormenting yourself, Mohammed," she said, "drink some water!"

"I will drink when the test is over, and the horses can drink, too. I cannot drink knowing they are thirsty," said the Prophet to his daughter.

"I do not understand this test, nor do I like it," said Fatima angrily. "Depriving the horses from drinking for three full days is cruel. I cannot believe you would do it, a man who loves animals better than himself!"

"I must. Allah commanded me -- would you have me disobey God? The spread of Islam depends greatly on the loyalty and strength of our horses. The best of these horses, said Allah, will be honored till the end of time... But it is the evening of the third day now, so let us go to the horses and conduct the test."

He took a horn that hung at the tent's entrance, and walked toward an enclosure where about a hundred horses were confined, a little distance from the water hole of the oasis. The horses looked reproachfully at their beloved master as he quickly opened the gate. Tormented by thirst, the horses galloped to the water hole, but before they could reach it, Mohammed raised the horn to his lips and sounded the call for war.

The horses ignored it. They were so thirsty that perhaps they couldn't even hear it, and went on galloping toward the water. But not all of them. Five mares stopped. Without hesitation, they turned around and returned to Mohammed, ready to do whatever was required of them.

The Prophet stroked their silky manes, tears in his eyes. He led them to the water and envisioned the glorious future as they drank. He knew that these mares would foal the finest of Arab horses, the only horses of pure blood, the horses that would help bring Islam to every corner of the Earth."

The five mares were kept for breeding and it is said that the prophet pressed his thumb in their necks marking them with his thumbprint. A horse with the prophet's thumbprint is said to come from the bloodline of horses that belonged to the prophet Mohammed, it is said that a horse with the prophet's thumbprint should be treasured and treated with great respect, and are thought to be lucky.

Saddle: a supportive structure for a rider or other load, fastened to an animal's back by a girth. The most common type is the equestrian saddle designed for a horse. Single turnout:

Surcingle: a strap made of leather or leather-like synthetic materials such as nylon or neoprene, sometimes with elastic, that fastens around a horse's girth area. A surcingle may be used for ground training, some types of in-hand exhibition, and over a saddle or horse pack to stabilize the load. It also is a primary component of a horse harness.

A basic surcingle is unpadded, attaches around the horse by means of buckles or rings, and has no other hardware. A training surcingle, sometimes called a "roller," has many extra rings attached, running from the ribcage up to the withers area. It usually has padding to relieve pressure on the spine. A variation of this design is used for equestrian vaulting.

Spanish Walk: the horse, in the walk, lifts each foreleg with a pronounced forward and upward thrust

Stallion: A male horse that is fully intact. He has both testicles and he can breed.

Studdy/studdiness: Characteristics, physical and mannerisms of a stallion

Printed in the United States
By Bookmasters